LANGUAGE AND WORLD CREATION IN POEMS AND OTHER TEXTS

Textual Explorations

General editors:
MICK SHORT Lancaster University
ELENA SEMINO Lancaster University

Books published in this series:
Language and World Creation in Poems and other Texts

LANGUAGE AND WORLD CREATION IN POEMS AND OTHER TEXTS

Elena Semino

LONGMAN
London and New York

Addison Wesley Longman Limited
Edinburgh Gate
Harlow, Essex   CM20 2JE
England

and Associated Companies throughout the world

*Published in the United States of America
by Addison Wesley Longman Inc., New York*

First published 1997

ISBN 0 582 303540   Paper
ISBN 0 582 301998   Cased

British Library Cataloguing-in-Publication Data

A catalogue record for this book is available from the British Library

Library of Congress Cataloging-in-Publication Data

Semino, Elena, 1964–
    Language and world creation in poems and other texts / Elena Semino.
        p. cm. — (Textual explorations)
    Includes bibliographical references and index.
    ISBN 0–582–30199–8 (cased). — ISBN 0–582–30354–0 (ppr)
    1. Poetry—History and criticism. 2. Fiction—History and criticism. 3. Schemas (Psychology) 4. Semantics. I. Title.
    II. Series.
    PN1042.S44   1997
    809.1—dc21   96–52564
                                                                        CIP

Set by 35 in 10/12pt Baskerville
Produced by Longman Singapore Publishers (Pte) Ltd
Printed in Singapore

Contents

Preface

This book owes its existence to a number of people who, in different ways, created the conditions in which I could think, write, and re-write. My greatest debt is to Mick Short, who supervised the thesis on which the book is based and always boosted my confidence and sharpened my thinking. The following friends and colleagues gave me the benefit of their advice on drafts of chapters: Caroline Clapham, Geoff Leech, Colin Lyas, Gerard Steen, Katie Wales, and, last but certainly not least, Paul Werth, whose untimely death deprived current text-world theory of its central figure.

The book is dedicated to my mother, Marilena, and to the memory of my father, Gianfranco. They, together with the rest of my family, instilled in me a quiet sense of discipline and self-confidence that is pretty much essential in academic work, and many other things as well. I am also grateful to my daughter, Emily, for waiting to be born until the manuscript had been nearly completed, and to Jonathan for sharing everything with me.

How to use this book

Although one of the main aims of this book lies in bringing together different approaches to the analysis of poetic text worlds, each of the three parts in which the book is divided is self-standing and can be read independently. Each part contains an overview of the literature, a critical discussion of the field, and a number of text analyses. Part I is particularly relevant to readers interested in the traditional stylistic approach to the analysis of poetry. This approach is applied to a range of poems in order to offer new insights into the use and effects of the articles and deictics in poetry. Part II is particularly relevant to readers interested in the application of possible-world theory in literary studies. The most innovative aspect of this part of the book is that it shows how possible-world frameworks, which have been almost exclusively applied to the study of narrative fiction, can be productively extended to the analysis of poetry. Part III is particularly relevant to readers interested in discourse comprehension, psycholinguistics and the use of cognitive theories in text analysis. Different versions of schema theory are compared and contrasted in detail, and reference is made to other influential models of cognition, such as Parallel Distributed Processing and Relevance Theory.

The 'Suggestions for Further Analysis' at the end of each Part are meant for readers who are interested in trying out on other texts the analytical approaches demonstrated in the book. In each case I start by directing readers to further examples from poetry. I then move on to other literary genres (including short stories, novels and plays), and finish with a selection of non-literary texts (notably advertisements and jokes). As a consequence, the sequencing of the suggested analyses does not always follow the sequencing of topics in previous chapters. I do not provide 'answers', but offer guidance in the form of multiple questions, brief comments and references to specific points and concepts in preceding chapters. I also often suggest comparisons between new texts and some of the texts I analyse in the course of the book. Where relevant, I point the reader to published analyses of the texts I refer to and to further readings. I will be grateful to receive any feedback on my 'Suggestions', as well as on the book as a whole, at the following E-mail address: E.Semino@lancaster.ac.uk.

Acknowledgements

We are grateful to the following for permission to reproduce copyright material:

Carcanet Press for the poem 'The Cool Web' and an extract from the poem 'Welsh Incident' by Robert Graves from *COLLECTED POEMS* 1959; Carcanet Press/authors' agents for the poem 'The Absence of a Noble Presence' by John Ashberry from *SELECTED POEMS* 1985; the author, Tony Curtis for his poem 'Sick Child (after munch)' from *THE LAST CANDLES* (Seren, 1989); Faber & Faber Ltd for the poem 'The Jaguar' by Ted Hughes from *NEW SELECTED POEMS 1957–1994* (originally in *THE HAWK IN THE RAIN*); Faber & Faber Ltd/Farrar, Straus & Giroux Inc. for the poem 'A Pillowed Head' by Seamus Heaney from *SEEING THINGS* Copyright © 1991 by Seamus Heaney and the poem 'Talking in Bed' by Philip Larkin from *THE WHITSUN WEDDINGS* Copyright © 1988, 1989 by the Estate of Philip Larkin; Faber & Faber Ltd/ HarperCollins Inc. for part poem 'Wodwo' by Ted Hughes from *NEW SELECTED POEMS 1957–1994* and for the poems 'The Applicant' & 'Morning Song' by Sylvia Plath from *ARIEL*. Copyright © 1961, 1963 by Ted Hughes. Copyright renewed.; Faber & Faber Ltd/Alfred A. Knopf Inc. for poem 'Earthy Anecdotes' from *COLLECTED POEMS* by Wallace Stevens. Copyright 1923 and renewed 1951 by Wallace Stevens; HarperCollins Ltd/authors' agents on behalf of the author for an extract from 'Love in a Colder Climate' by J.G. Ballard from the collection *WAR FEVER* published by HarperCollins, London and Farrar, Straus & Giroux, New York. Copyright © 1990 J.G. Ballard; authors' agents for the poem 'Poem for Roger McGough' by Adrian Henry from *COLLECTED POEMS*. Copyright © 1986 by Adrian Henry; authors' agents for the poem 'Framed' by Roger McGough from *WAVING AT TRAINS* published by Jonathan Cape; authors' agents on behalf of Michael Yeats/ Simon & Schuster Inc. for an extract from the poem 'Long-legged

To my mother, Marilena

and in memory of my father, Gianfranco

Introduction

1.1 The topic of this book

When we read, we actively infer a text world 'behind' the text. By 'text world' I mean the context, scenario or type of reality that is evoked in our minds during reading and that (we conclude) is referred to by the text. This book focuses on the creation of text worlds in poetry. I will explore different ways in which poetic text worlds can be described and classified, and investigate how they are constructed in the processing of texts. In order to do this, I will consider different approaches to the definition of text worlds drawn from theories and methods of analysis developed in text linguistics, literary semantics and cognitive psychology. Although my main focus throughout is a detailed analysis of the language of texts, I will gradually build up an interdisciplinary approach to the study of poetry, in which linguistic analysis is complemented by concepts and theories developed outside language studies. A wide range of British and American poems in English are analysed, dating mostly, although not exclusively, from the twentieth century. In addition, I will provide examples of how the same type of analysis can be applied to the study of other text-types, both literary and non-literary.

The process of constructing worlds from texts is often described as central to comprehension. Enkvist, in particular, has argued that the interpretability of texts cannot be explained simply in terms of grammatical correctness and of explicit links between sentences, but ultimately depends on the readers' ability to imagine meaningful worlds in their interaction with the language of texts:

> ...a text is interpretable to those who can build around that text a scenario, a text world, a state of affairs, in which that text makes sense.
> (Enkvist 1991: 7; see also Enkvist 1989;
> Enkvist and Leppiniemi 1989)

The following is one of Enkvist's examples:

> The ball rolled slowly across the line. The goal-keeper was writhing in pain. The fans shouted. The dance of triumph was interrupted by a whistle. The referee declared the kick offside. (Enkvist 1991: 6)

In spite of the absence of overt links between sentences (such as conjunctions, cross-reference, etc.), Enkvist argues, this text is easily interpretable for people who have some knowledge, however limited, about football: the text world involves a football match where one of the teams has a goal disallowed by the referee. The process of interpretation can be described as an interaction between the text and the reader's background knowledge, which results in the construction of a text world characterized by a set of specific states of affairs (Enkvist 1989: 166 and throughout).

When we read poetry, the process of constructing meaningful worlds around texts may not be as straightforward as in the case of Enkvist's example, but the results can be considerably more challenging and rewarding. Talking about the interpretative difficulties posed by modern poetry, Enkvist makes the following remark:

> Perhaps the reason why many people dislike modern poetry is that they lack the imaginative ability of surrounding their texts with a meaningful scenario; to others, such exercises of the imagination may be a source of pleasure.
>
> (Enkvist 1991: 9; see also Enkvist 1989: 183)

While exploring different approaches to the study of poetic text worlds in the course of this book, I will touch on some of the potential difficulties that Enkvist hints at in his comment. As a preliminary example, I will begin to discuss the poem that will be analysed in detail in the final chapter of the book, 'The Applicant' by Sylvia Plath:

THE APPLICANT

First, are you our sort of a person?
Do you wear
A glass eye, false teeth or a crutch,
A brace or a hook,
Rubber breasts or a rubber crotch,   5

Stitches to show something's missing? No, no? Then
How can we give you a thing?
Stop crying.
Open your hand.
Empty? Empty. Here is a hand   10

To fill it and willing
To bring teacups and roll away headaches
And do whatever you tell it.
Will you marry it?
It is guaranteed   15

To thumb shut your eyes at the end
And dissolve of sorrow.
We make new stock from the salt.
I notice you are stark naked.
How about this suit—   20

Black and stiff, but not a bad fit.
Will you marry it?
It is waterproof, shatterproof, proof
Against fire and bombs through the roof.
Believe me, they'll bury you in it.   25

Now your head, excuse me, is empty.
I have the ticket for that.
Come here, sweetie, out of the closet.
Well, what do you think of that?
Naked as paper to start   30

But in twenty-five years she'll be silver,
In fifty gold.
A living doll, everywhere you look.
It can sew, it can cook,
It can talk, talk, talk.   35

It works, there is nothing wrong with it.
You have a hole, it's a poultice.
You have an eye, it's an image.
My boy, it's your last resort.
Will you marry it, marry it, marry it.   40

This is not an easily interpretable poem, particularly at a first reading. Its difficulty does not result from lexical or grammatical complexity, but from the fact that the construction of a text world involves a number of problems: (i) the identity of the speaker is rather hard to pin down (an interviewer? a seller? a father?); (ii) apparently contradictory information is given about the gender of the addressee (*Do you wear . . . rubber breasts* in line 5, but *My boy* in line 39); (iii) some of the objects referred to by the speaker are likely to be perceived as impossible, since they do not exist in the actual world (*a rubber crotch* in line 5, a suit that is *shatterproof, proof / Against fire and bombs through the roof* in lines 23–4); (iv) the speaker's words are reminiscent of several types of situations that readers are likely to be familiar with (interviews, sales pitches, marriage arrangements), but the world of the poem is not fully consistent with the reader's knowledge and expectations about any of them.

These problems will be discussed in depth in Chapter 9. What begins to emerge from my list of interpretative difficulties, however, is the possibility of describing the poem's text world in at least three different ways, namely as:

(a) a situation of discourse involving a speaker, a hearer, and a number of third-person referents within a particular communicative context;
(b) a set of states of affairs that are partly impossible if compared with the 'real' world;
(c) a cognitive construct that arises in the interaction between the text and the reader's previous knowledge.

These descriptions correspond to the three approaches to the analysis of text worlds that I will discuss in the course of the book. The first of these approaches is commonly adopted in the study of poetry. The second has been developed in literary studies for the analysis of narrative fiction, but has seldom been applied to poetic texts. The third is more innovative, since it involves the application to poetic text analysis of theories and concepts that originated in artificial intelligence and cognitive psychology. In order to introduce and contextualize these approaches in more detail, I will now consider some general issues on the role of text-world construction in the interpretation of literary texts.

1.2 Literature, text worlds and contexts

The process whereby a context or world is built around a particular text has often been presented as a peculiarity of literary communication, resulting, it is argued, from the fact that literary texts, unlike other texts, exist in a contextual vacuum. The following claims have been made in relation to poetry in particular:

> The poet is both free of context and bound to create it: free of any binding real context, he is bound to supply verbally the context that gives objects attributes, scale, setting and significance.
>
> (Nowottny 1965: 43)

> Poetry is virtually free from the contextual constraints which determine other uses of language, and so the poet is able – in fact compelled – to *create* situations within his poems.
>
> (Leech 1969: 187; author's italics)

> [Poetry] is essentially dislocated from context, set aside: it presupposes no previous or existing situation outside that created by itself. . . . It exists apart, complete in itself, self-contained in its own pattern.
>
> (Widdowson 1984: 146)

The big variable in the significance and implications of these statements is, of course, the meaning of the word 'context'. In this section I will discuss the relationship between literary communication and different types of contexts, and reflect on the resulting consequences for the study of literary text worlds (see Fowler 1986: 86–90 for a similar discussion).

One fairly obvious sense in which literary communication may be said to be context-free is the fact that it does not take place in a situational context shared by addresser and addressee. Rather, the producer and the receiver of the message (the author and the reader), are typically dislocated both across space and time. As a consequence, the subject-matter of the text is independent from any specific extra-linguistic context of communication. This contrasts, for example, with classroom teaching or party chit-chat, where communication may rely upon, and is often directly influenced by, the immediate setting of the interaction.

The existence of a split between the context of production and the context of reception of the text, however, is a common feature of a wide range of discourse types, including the vast majority of writing (e.g. letters, newspaper articles, the book you are reading now) as well as some spoken forms of communication (e.g. leaving messages on telephone-answering machines). More importantly, face-to-face communication does not necessarily revolve around the shared communicative situation, but is often characterized by a displacement between the topic of talk and the setting in which talk takes place: a conversation at a party, for example, may involve both comments on the furniture in the room and jokes, anecdotes or stories where the immediate situation is largely irrelevant. Smith (1982) captures this opposition by drawing a distinction between 'situation-dependent' language, i.e. language whose interpretation is directly dependent on the situation in which it is uttered, and 'context-dependent' language, i.e. language whose interpretation depends solely on the interplay between the words of the text and the interpreter's previous knowledge (in Smith's description, 'context' corresponds to the linguist's 'co-text' (e.g. Brown and Yule 1983)).

If a dislocation between addresser and addressee and a displacement between subject-matter and situational context are common features of human communication, why is it that these aspects are often singled out in discussions of literary discourse in general and poetry in particular?

As for the dislocation between addresser and addressee, it may be argued that literary communication is often associated with larger historical, geographical and cultural 'gaps' than many other discourse types: while today's editorial in *The Times* is unlikely to be widely read after tomorrow, Wordsworth's poems are still read today and will probably be read for hundreds of years to come, in Britain and elsewhere, and both in English and in translation. The main answer to the question in the previous paragraph, however, is to do with the tendency, or possibility, for literature to be fictional: while we expect the world of *The Times* editorials to be related and faithful to specific states of affairs in the real world, we do not make similar demands of poetry. As Leech puts it, poems are not necessarily fictitious, but 'they leave the choice between fact and fiction open' (Leech 1969: 196). In this sense, the relationship between the worlds of literary texts and 'real' contexts in Nowottny's sense, can be somewhat looser and freer than in other types of discourse. Moreover, the worlds of poems may involve fictional speakers and fictional addressees interacting in fictional contexts of utterance: the relationship between the first-person speaker in Plath's 'The Applicant' and the poet herself, for example, is not the same as the one we expect between the first-person speaker in a personal letter and the person who wrote it (see Widdowson 1975: 53). This explains a fairly general tendency to treat poetic text worlds primarily as fictional contexts of discourse (e.g. Fowler 1986; Leech 1969; Widdowson 1975), which corresponds to approach (a) in the previous section.

What is obscured in the quotations given at the opening of this section is the fact that, in spite of the dislocation between authors and readers, literary communication does take place in a context. In this case, by 'context' I mean the broad complex of institutions, activities, roles, functions and conventions that each culture associates with the production, distribution and interpretation of texts that are regarded as literary (see, for example, Pratt 1977; Schmidt 1982). In contemporary Western cultures for example, literary communication involves certain text-types (primarily poems, novels and plays), a variety of participant roles (e.g. writer, reader, literary editor, literary critic), specific institutions (e.g. publishers, literary societies, literary publications, academic journals), a wide variety of social settings and activities (e.g. specific sections in libraries, bookshops, newspapers and magazines; literary competitions; literary readings; performances of plays; teaching of literature in schools and universities), a range of possible functions (e.g. aesthetic, moral, subversive, educational), a wide intertextual context, and possibly a set of specific interpretative conventions (such as those suggested by Culler 1975; Fairley 1988; Schmidt 1982). All this obviously has an influence over what is written, what is read, and what is generally regarded as literary. In this sense, I agree with Pratt that 'literature is a context too, not the absence of one' (Pratt 1977: 99).

This leads me to consider an even wider notion of context, namely that of context of culture (originally coined by Malinowski 1935), which can be defined very generally as:

> . . . the whole network of social and economic conventions and institutions constituting the culture at large, especially in so far as these bear on particular utterance contexts and influence the structure of discourse occurring within them. (Fowler 1986: 88)

Clearly, all texts and text-types – be they literary or non-literary – are influenced by the context of culture in which they are produced. Indeed, it could be argued that the strongest unifying factor in current work in the linguistic study of literature is an increasing tendency to relate the production and reception of literary texts to their social, cultural and ideological background (e.g. Fowler 1986; Carter and Simpson 1989; Sell 1991; Toolan 1992; see Widdowson 1992 for a dissenting voice). It is also true, however, that some types of texts – including literary texts – may project realities that are somehow at odds with the context of culture in which they originate, or, more specifically, with what is regarded as 'real' or 'possible' by a particular culture or society. As Fowler points out, this phenomenon is typically associated with fictional genres:

> Non-fictional discourse refers to any individual entities and activities which are both familiar and known to exist within the society referred to by the text. Fictional discourse may refer to such entities, but also adds references to imaginary individuals and events which have not existed (or it is immaterial whether or not they existed). Now these

fictional creations may be more or less compatible with the norms of the context of culture. (Fowler 1986: 89)

Fowler goes on to provide examples of different degrees of 'compatibility' between the worlds of literary works and their contexts of culture, from nineteenth-century realistic novels such as Balzac's at one extreme, to fantasies such as *Animal Farm, The Faerie Queen* and *Gulliver's Travels* at the other (Fowler 1986: 89–90).

The ability to project worlds that are somehow alternative to the 'real' world is often presented as a crucial property of literary texts:

> The most comprehensive definition of 'literary text' might be: a text whose world stands in a principled *alternativity* relationship to the accepted version of the 'real' world.
>
> (de Beaugrande and Dressler 1981: 185; authors' italics)

> New, strange, forgotten or dreamed-of situations and contexts can be experienced, so that the receiver can enter new social roles, new models of reality, new systems of norms. (Schmidt 1982: 63)

> Poems . . . express, therefore, what no other use of language is capable of expressing: a kind of converse reality, a different existential order in another dimension of experience. (Widdowson 1984: 149)

In order to exemplify such claims, reference is usually made to texts similar to the ones at the 'incompatible' extreme of Fowler's scale, i.e. texts whose worlds contain obviously impossible and counterfactual elements, such as the giants of *Gulliver's Travels* or the articulate animals of *Animal Farm*. When it comes to poetry in particular, the emphasis tends to be on the presence of 'impossible' speaking voices, such as those of Tennyson's 'The Brook' (Leech 1969: 198) or of Shelley's 'The Cloud' (Widdowson 1975: 48). From this point of view, text worlds can be described on the basis of the kinds of impossible elements they contain. As I will show, this method of analysis is well established in fictional and literary semantics, and corresponds to the second of the three approaches to the study of text worlds that I outlined earlier.

I will also argue, however, that the notions of impossibility and counterfactuality do not exhaust the ways in which a text world may be perceived to be alternative in relation to what a particular culture regards as the 'real' world. Alternativity may arise from the projection of unconventional perspectives on the world of reality, and from the breaking of expectations that do not depend on general notions of possibility but on our knowledge of social and cultural conventions. I will argue, for example, that the main reason why the world of Sylvia Plath's 'The Applicant' has a disturbing and defamiliarizing effect is because it incorporates elements that, on the basis of our background knowledge, we tend to associate with very different types of situations. In order to deal with this wider notion of alternativity, I will propose a third approach to the analysis of text worlds, one that focuses on how text worlds result from the interaction between the language of texts and the knowledge that readers apply to them (see approach (c) at the end of the previous section). Within this perspective, the relevant notion of context is a *cognitive* one: it has to do with the assumptions and expectations that the reader brings to bear in the interpretation of a text (see Sperber and Wilson (1986, 1995) for a cognitive definition of 'context'). Unlike the first two approaches, this kind of method does not rely on techniques of analysis developed specifically for the study of literary texts, but draws on general models of comprehension developed within cognitive psychology and artificial intelligence.

1.3 The structure of this book

This book is divided into three parts, each corresponding to one of the approaches to the study of text worlds that I briefly introduced in the previous two sections.

Part I ('Poetic Text Worlds as Discourse Situations') consists of Chapters 2 and 3. Here I approach poetic text worlds as discourse situations characterized by different types of voices and different types of relationships between speakers, hearers and settings. The emphasis is on those features of language that, as Leech (1969: 183) argues, 'are especially important for the "reconstruction" of situations', namely definite articles and deictics. The method of analysis is one that is common in linguistic studies of literary texts: I describe the ways in which definite articles and deictics are used in a particular text and consider their implications for the situation of discourse that readers are likely to imagine. The discussion draws from influential accounts of the use of definite reference and deixis in ordinary language (especially Lyons 1977; Levinson 1983; Quirk *et al.* 1985), and aims to build on the work that stylisticians have done on the poetic use of definite articles and deictic expressions (e.g. Leech 1969; Fowler 1986). In particular, I question the validity of the claim that the occurrence of definite articles and deictics in poetry constitutes a deviation from ordinary language use (e.g. van Dijk 1976; Dillon 1978; Fowler 1986), and I make a number of suggestions concerning the function of these linguistic features in the construction of contexts from texts. In Chapter 2 ('Definiteness, Indefiniteness and Context Creation') I consider the effects of the use of the definite article to introduce referents that have not been previously mentioned, and I propose an account of the contrast between definite and indefinite reference in the projection of text worlds. My argument is exemplified in a detailed discussion of the use and effects of definite and indefinite articles in Ted Hughes's 'The Jaguar' and Robert Browning's 'Meeting at Night'. In Chapter 3 ('Deixis and Context Creation') I highlight the range of situational contexts of discourse that may be projected by different poetic texts, and I focus in some detail on examples where deictic shifts and inconsistencies lead to changes in the role or identity of the speaking voice. The chapter makes reference to a wide range of poems (from John Donne's 'The Flea' to Wilfred Owen's 'Anthem for Doomed Youth'), and includes detailed analyses of Philip Larkin's 'Talking in Bed' and Elizabeth Bartlett's 'Charlotte, Her Book'.

Part II ('Poetic Text Worlds as Possible Worlds') consists of Chapters 4 and 5. Its focus is on the approaches developed in logical and literary semantics under the general heading of 'possible-world theories', which have dominated the study of fictional worlds for the last couple of decades (e.g. Eco 1979, 1990; Doležel 1976a, 1988; Wolterstoff 1980; Maitre 1983; Pavel 1986; Allén 1989; Ryan 1991a). In Chapter 4 ('Possible-World Theory, Fiction and Literature') I trace the development of the notion of 'possible worlds' from logic to the semantics of fiction and literature. In particular, I show how possible-world models have been used in order to:

(a) describe text worlds as complex structures made up of a central domain counting as actual and a number of alternative domains counting as non-actual (such as characters' belief worlds, wish worlds, fantasy worlds, etc.) (e.g. Eco 1979, 1990; Ryan 1991a; Werth forthcoming);

(b) classify text worlds on the basis of the accessibility relations (Kripke 1971) that link them to the actual world, i.e. on the basis of criteria such as logical possibility, physical possibility, taxonomic possibility, and so on (e.g. Maitre 1983; Ryan 1991a).

In Chapter 5 ('Possible-World Theory and the Analysis of Poetic Text Worlds') I show how possible-world models can be applied in practice to the analysis of individual poems and to the characterization of different poetic genres. The chapter includes an analysis of the modal structure of Marvell's 'To His Coy Mistress', a possible-world approach to the description of deviant discourse situations, and a discussion of the differences between the worlds of realistic poetry (e.g. Eliot's 'Journey of the Magi'), nonsense verse (e.g. Lear's 'The Jumblies') and postmodernist poetry (e.g. Ashbery's 'The Absence of a Noble Presence').

Part III ('Poetic Text Worlds as Cognitive Constructs') consists of Chapters 6, 7 and 8, and proposes a method for the analysis of text worlds that combines linguistic analysis with the cognitive theory of knowledge and comprehension commonly known as 'schema theory'. The central claim of schema theory is that our background knowledge is organized in chunks (schemata) containing generic information about the different types of objects, people, situations and events that we have encountered in our past experience (e.g. Eysenck and Keane 1990). Comprehension, within this framework, crucially depends on the activation of a set of schemata that successfully accounts for a particular input. Although modern schema theory is usually traced back to the work of the psychologist Bartlett (1932), its development into an influential model of human knowledge started in the 1970s, as a result of the mutual influence between artificial intelligence and cognitive psychology (e.g. Schank and Abelson 1977). The bulk of Chapter 6 ('Schema Theory and Literature') consists of an overview of the development of schema theory, focusing in some detail on three particularly influential versions (Rumelhart 1980; Schank and Abelson 1977; and Schank 1982). The central concepts of the theory are exemplified with reference to some of the poems introduced in the previous chapters and to Ballard's story 'Love in a Colder Climate'. In the final part of the chapter I introduce a number of studies that have taken a schema-theory approach to the study of literature and I discuss the recent tendency to define literariness as the property of texts that challenge and/or alter the reader's existing schemata (e.g. Cook 1994; Weber 1992). In Chapter 7 ('Schema Theory and the Analysis of Poetic Text Worlds') I demonstrate an approach to the analysis of poetry based on the notion that, in cognitive terms, a text world can be said to result from the set of schemata that a reader applies to the interpretation of a particular text. Two poems are analysed in detail: Seamus Heaney's 'A Pillowed Head' and Sylvia Plath's 'Morning Song'. Linguistic analysis and schema theory are combined in order to show how the worlds projected by the two poems are likely to have different effects on readers. I argue that while Heaney's poem projects a world that is likely to reinforce the reader's existing schemata, Plath's poem evokes a set of partially clashing schemata, and therefore projects a more challenging and problematic world. In Chapter 8 ('Metaphor, Schema Refreshment and Text Worlds') I explore the implications of a method of analysis based on schema theory for the role of figurative language, and of metaphor in particular, in the construction of poetic text worlds. This narrowing of focus on non-literal language is motivated by the inadequate treatment that figurative expressions receive in possible-world theory, where they are dismissed as irrelevant to the issue of world creation. The chapter provides an overview of major trends in the study of metaphor and proposes a cognitive account of the effects of similarity across domains in metaphorical connections. The chapter includes detailed analyses of Tony Curtis's 'Sick Child *(After Munch)*' and of Robert Graves's 'The Cool Web', showing how the interaction between schemata triggered by metaphorical expressions affects the world-views that readers construct in the processing of texts.

Finally, Chapter 9 ('Conclusion: The World of Sylvia Plath's "The Applicant"') brings together the three approaches to the study of text worlds discussed in the course of the book in the analysis of a single poem, namely Sylvia Plath's 'The Applicant'. This chapter has two main aims: (i) to demonstrate that linguistic analysis, possible-world theory and schema theory can usefully complement one another in the study of texts, and (ii) to provide a final discussion of the strengths and weaknesses of the different approaches, particularly in the light of their applicability to text analysis. Indeed, the book as a whole demonstrates how the detailed analysis of a range of texts provides an ideal testing ground for the power and scope of different theories.

While poetry is my main focus throughout, I also aim to show how the same methods of analysis can be applied to texts from other genres, both literary and non-literary. Thus, most chapters include brief analyses of non-poetic texts. In addition, each part of the book ends with a section entitled 'Suggestions for Further Analysis', where you will find examples drawn not just from poetry but also prose fiction, drama, jokes and advertising.

Part I

POETIC TEXT WORLDS AS DISCOURSE SITUATIONS

Definiteness, indefiniteness and context creation

2.1 Introduction

In the opening stanza of Robert Frost's 'Stopping by Woods on a Snowy Evening' a traveller begins a series of reflections as he[1] stops to enjoy the sight of the snow falling upon the nearby woods:

> Whose woods these are I think I know.
> His house is in the village though;
> He will not see me stopping here
> To watch his woods fill up with snow.

The first four lines of the poem create the impression that we have direct access to an individual mind musing about his immediate surroundings, and signal the existence of a wider setting with which the unknown traveller is somehow familiar. These effects, I will argue, are triggered respectively by the choice of deictic terms (*these, I, here*) and by the occurrence of the definite article in the noun phrase *the village*.

Definite articles and deictics share the semantic property of definiteness: they introduce referents that hearers or readers are usually expected to be able to identify uniquely on the basis of the co-textual, contextual or world knowledge that they share with the producer of the message. Definite expressions are therefore normally used to indicate the existence of a precise and recoverable match between the words of a text and some aspect of the relevant textual, situational, societal or cultural context, or, ultimately, of the world at large (Leech 1969: 193; Quirk *et al.* 1985: 265, 362). For example, if I ask one of my students 'How did the exam go?', my use of the definite noun phrase *the exam* indicates that I have a specific examination in mind and that I am confident that my addressee will have no difficulty understanding which particular exam I am talking about. The context within which I expect the relevant referent to be uniquely identifiable may vary in nature and size: the examination I am referring to may be the only one the student is taking that year, the one that relates to the course I teach, the one that the student has just taken, and so on. If my assumption about the unique identifiability of the referent is mistaken, a communicative hiccup will occur: my addressee may look puzzled, ask for clarification, or start talking about a different examination from the one I had in mind.

Strictly speaking, such an explanation of the use of definite reference does not apply to cases such as *the village* in Frost's poem, where readers cannot uniquely identify the referent of the noun phrase within the previous text or some extra-linguistic context. This 'unanchored' use of definite expressions, which is conventional in literary texts, is therefore often treated as deviant, and is usually associated with two major (and opposite) effects: the involvement of the readers within the evoked situation on the one hand, or their exclusion from the position of addressees of the poetic speaker's message on the other. More importantly, it is often pointed out that such definite expressions play a crucial role in the construction, or rather implication, of contexts from texts: when we come across *the village* in 'Stopping by Woods on a Snowy Evening' we do not grind to a halt and conclude that the poem is a failed attempt at communication. Rather, we include within the world that we are constructing around the text a village that is uniquely identifiable for the poem's first-person speaker. In this sense, unanchored definite expressions are important sources of inferences in text-world creation.

2.2 Definite articles: basic meaning and uses

The basic function of the definite article *the* is to indicate that the referent of the noun phrase in which it is included is uniquely identifiable within the contextual or general knowledge shared by addresser and addressee (Givón 1978: 296; Leech 1981: 157; Quirk *et al.* 1985: 265). The definite article does not, however, contain in itself any indication as to how the relevant context or entity can be recovered: it signals identifiability without providing any guidance towards identification (Halliday and Hasan 1976: 72; Halliday 1985: 161). The knowledge which is required in order to successfully identify the reference can be of many different kinds, as shown by the examples below[2] (phrases to be discussed are highlighted for ease of reference):

(1) Can you pass me *the hammer* please?

(2) Have you taken *the dog* out for a walk yet?

(3) *The Vice-Chancellor* is having a reception for all new members of staff next week.

(4) *The Prime Minister* will be giving a speech in Parliament tomorrow.

(5) According to medical evidence, excessive exposure to *the sun* has potentially harmful effects for people's skins.

(6) I wish I had never gone to Jill's party last week-end. *The party* was O.K., but when I left to go home I found that my car had been stolen.

(7) Have you heard about Peter and Susan's wedding? Well, apparently *the minister* was late, *the best man* lost *the rings* and *the cake* tasted pretty awful. A complete disaster!

(8) John and I haven't been to *the cinema* for ages.

(9) *The man* who crashed into our new car is our next-door neighbour.

(10) Do you know what time *the first post* is? I need to send this letter as soon as possible.

In examples (1) to (5) the referents of the definite expressions are uniquely identifiable on the basis of shared knowledge about different portions of extra-linguistic reality: the immediate visible situation in (1), the family or domestic set-up in (2), a specific institution in (3), a certain country or political system in (4) and the general 'planetary' environment in (5). Most accounts of the definite article draw a distinction between **immediate situation** uses, which include (1) and (2), and **larger situation** uses, which include (3), (4) and (5) (Hawkins 1978: 110–20; Quirk *et al.* 1985: 266–7; Gallaway 1987: 61–2). As far as (5) is concerned, the definite reference to *the sun* can also be explained on the basis of the uniqueness of the referent, which also applies, for example, to cases like *the Pope, the earth, the universe,* and so on (Quirk *et al.* 1985: 266–7; Halliday 1985: 293; Gallaway 1987: 61).

Examples (6) and (7) are instances of the **anaphoric use** of the definite article, which accounts for those cases where the definite referent has become part of shared knowledge as a result of some element of the previous text (Halliday and Hasan 1976: 72; Hawkins 1978: 107–10; Halliday 1985: 293; Quirk *et al.* 1985: 267; Gallaway 1987: 59–61). In cases like (6), where the head of the definite noun phrase (*party*) is identical to its antecedent, the notion of anaphoric reference is relatively straightforward: *the party* refers back to *Jill's party* in the previous sentence and is therefore uniquely identifiable within the current discourse. Example (7) is more problematic. On the one hand it is intuitively obvious to readers familiar with British-style church weddings that the referents of the noun phrases *the minister, the best man, the rings* and *the cake* can be treated as part of shared knowledge on the basis of the previous mention of a specific wedding. On the other hand, however, the notion of anaphoric reference is not sufficient in itself to account for the appropriateness of the use of definite reference; rather, it needs to be combined with an appeal to the addressee's general knowledge of the world, including the probable, or even necessary, presence of ministers, best men, rings and cakes within the relevant type of wedding celebrations. This particular use of definite reference, which is known as **indirect** or **associative anaphora**, is therefore usually explained by saying that the referents of the definite expressions have been indirectly introduced by means of a previous reference to some entity with which they are associated (Hawkins 1978: 123–30; Quirk *et al.* 1985: 267–8; Gallaway 1987: 60).

A similar argument can be expressed more precisely, and possibly more elegantly, in terms of schema theory, which will be introduced in detail in Chapter 6. In brief, a schema is a portion of background knowledge that contains generic information about different types of events, situations, people or objects (see Eysenck and Keane 1990: 275). In discourse comprehension, schemata are important sources of inferences and expectations. Once a schema has been activated by means of one or more linguistic triggers (e.g. *Peter and Susan's wedding*), the participants, entities and relationships which are normally included in it (e.g. minister, best man, rings and cake) can be considered as having been implicitly introduced, and can therefore be preceded by the definite article when they are mentioned for the first time (see Schank and Abelson 1977: 41; Cook 1994: 13). In fact, an indefinite first mention of the central elements of a currently active schema could be a source of misunderstanding, as is the case with the following revised version of (7) above:

> (7a) Have you heard about Peter and Susan's wedding? Well, apparently *a minister* was late, *a best man* lost *some rings* and *a cake* tasted pretty awful. A complete disaster!

Here the use of indefinite determiners to introduce some of the predictable components of weddings has a rather puzzling effect:

firstly, it seems to undermine the assumption that church weddings typically involve only one minister, and only one best man; secondly, it does not make clear whether the rings and cake in question are the ones we expect to be among the essential and uniquely identifiable components of a traditional British wedding.[3] I will return to the relationship between definite reference and schemata later in this chapter and in Part III.

Let me now turn to the remaining examples of the uses of the definite article. Sentence (8) is an instance of what has been defined as the **sporadic** use of the definite article, where the following noun indicates some institution of human society which is instantiated by separate objects and events at different places and times. Other examples include references to *the theatre, the radio, the paper,* and so on (Quirk *et al.* 1985: 269–70). Finally, in (9) and (10) the heads of the definite noun phrases (*man* and *post*) can be identified uniquely on the basis of information provided within the noun phrases themselves, namely by means of postmodification in (9) (*the man who crashed into our new car*) and of the logical meaning of the premodifier in (10) (*the first post*). Such instances are in some cases treated as separate uses of definite reference, i.e. the **cataphoric** use in (9) and the **logical** use in (10) (Quirk *et al.* 1985: 268–70). In other cases they are classified under the same heading, such as **unfamiliar** uses (Hawkins 1978: 130ff.) or **noun modification** (Gallaway 1987: 63ff.).

2.3 Definite articles in poetry

If we reconsider the opening stanza of Frost's 'Stopping by Woods on a Snowy Evening' in the light of my brief overview of the meaning and uses of the definite article, it will become clear why some literary uses of definite reference have been described as deviant, or at least as different from ordinary language use (e.g. van Dijk 1976: 38; Dillon 1978: 65). As I pointed out earlier, the noun phrase *the village* in 'Stopping by Woods on a Snowy Evening' does not seem to comply with the fundamental requirement that definite referents should be uniquely identifiable within the contextual or general knowledge shared by addresser and addressee, but rather seems to assume some kind of previous knowledge that readers do not possess.

Such instances of definite first mention of unintroduced and unrecoverable referents are quite common in literature in general and poetry in particular, as shown by the opening stanzas of the two poems quoted below.

> Yes, I remember Adlestrop—
> The name, because one afternoon
> Of heat the express-train drew up there
> Unwontedly. It was late June. (Edward Thomas, 'Adlestrop')

> At night, by the fire,
> The colours of the bushes
> And of the fallen leaves,
> Repeating themselves,
> Turned in the room,
> Like the leaves themselves
> Turning in the wind. (Wallace Stevens, 'Domination of Black')

Some of the definite references contained in the two extracts are justified by the presence of postmodification (e.g. *the colours of the bushes*); others can be explained anaphorically (e.g. *Adlestrop— The name*) or on the basis of the assumed uniqueness of the particular referent (*the wind*). In cases like *the express-train* and *the room*, however, the use of the definite article seems to attribute an unwarranted familiarity and contextual identifiability to referents that do not qualify for any of the uses of definiteness introduced above.

This kind of mismatch between the actual and the implied communicative contexts appears to give rise to what Leech has called a 'situational incongruity', namely:

> a special kind of violation, . . . which arises when a piece of language is somehow at odds with the immediate situation in which it occurs.
> (Leech 1969: 183)

In other words, unanchored definite references are situationally incongruous insofar as they occur in a context that does not meet the normal requirements for the use of definiteness. More specifically, Leech argues that, because literary communication does not rely on a given situational context shared by writer and readers, poets are compelled to create one by means of 'implications of context', i.e. of various linguistic devices (including definite articles and deictics) which indicate what kind of situation each instance of language use is likely to occur in (Leech 1969: 183–9). Similarly, van Dijk points out that the peculiar character of literary communication allows the use of deictics and determiners not in reference to any actual extra-linguistic context, but to various aspects of 'a semantically constructed non-factual possible world' (van Dijk 1976: 40).

2.3.1 The presuppositional value of definite reference

The definite article can in fact be used in ordinary language to introduce referents that are not necessarily already part of the addressee's contextual knowledge. Consider the following examples:

(11) Beware of *the dog*. (from Hawkins 1978: 112; Leech 1983: 92)

(12) My daughter kicked *the child-minder*. (from Gallaway 1987: 51)

In cases such as these, it is the occurrence of a definite expression that informs the addressee of the existence and uniqueness of the entity in question within the relevant context of reference. Definite expressions, in other words, do not necessarily *rely upon* shared knowledge, but can *produce* shared knowledge. This is because definite articles carry in themselves a **presupposition** of the unique existence of the referents of the noun phrases they introduce[4] (Hawkins 1978: 114, 189–91; Leech 1981: 289; Gallaway 1987: 45–7). The poetic instances of unanchored definite references introduced in the previous section can therefore be explained in relation to the presuppositional value of definiteness, whereby, in the absence of any prior identification, definite expressions lead the addressee to assume the existence and uniqueness of their referents within the relevant context.

The difference between the literary and the non-literary examples lies in the way in which definite referents can be identified uniquely on the part of the addressee. In (11) and (12), the presupposition of existence concerns the addressee's knowledge of the extra-linguistic world, in which the relevant referents can be uniquely identified. In the literary examples, on the other hand, existence and unique identifiability are usually limited to the world that readers mentally construct on the basis of the text. In fact, even in ordinary discourse the assumption that the referents of definite expressions can be uniquely identified by the addressees within extra-linguistic reality only applies to a limited range of uses, such as 1 above (*Can you pass me the hammer?*). In cases like (7) and (12), to quote only the most obvious examples, it is unlikely, and ultimately irrelevant, that the addressee is in a position to identify uniquely the referents of *the minister* and *the child-minder* among all real-world instances of ministers and child-minders. What matters is that a uniquely identifiable referent is assumed to exist within the world that the addressee constructs for the particular discourse. The presupposition of existence and unique identifiability carried by definite reference, in other words, primarily applies to what has been called the 'universe of discourse' that is relevant to the particular communication (Givón 1978: 293; Johnson-Laird and Garnham 1979: 377; Brown and Yule 1983: 252).

The extent to which definite referents can be uniquely identified *outside* the specific universe of discourse is not determined by the use of definite reference in itself, but rather depends on the nature and purpose of the communication (Du Bois 1980: 233; Gallaway 1987: 53). In the case of *Can you pass me the hammer?*, for example, the discourse is directly concerned with the observable extra-linguistic situation and the addressee is requested to locate and act upon the referent of the definite expression. In order for the definite reference to be successful, therefore, the addressee needs to be able to identify uniquely the referent of *the hammer* in the immediate situational context. In literature, on the other hand, the degree of overlap between the universe of discourse and extra-linguistic reality is often irrelevant. This results in a greater freedom in the attribution of definiteness to unrecoverable referents, and explains the greater role played by definite reference in the production of shared knowledge and in the construction of contexts from texts. Similar considerations apply to other discourse types, such as jokes and anecdotes, where the addressee is not required to locate and interact with the referents of definite expressions, but rather to imagine a world in which such referents can be treated as definite. Advertisers also often exploit the presuppositional value of definite reference to evoke specific contexts with which the target audience is supposed to identify (see 'Part I: Suggestions for Further Analysis', Section 3).

The use of unanchored definite expressions in the poetic examples quoted above can therefore be explained within a comprehensive notion of definite reference, which takes into account the presuppositional implications of definiteness on the one hand and the flexible nature of the notion of unique identifiability on the other. Within this wider perspective, the poetic use of definite reference does not need to be described in terms of deviation from ordinary language use.

2.3.2 The effects of unanchored definite references in poetry

The definite first mention of unfamiliar and non-identifiable referents in literature has been associated with different kinds of effects. The most conventional claim concerns the production of an *in medias res* effect, whereby readers have the impression of being plunged into the middle of a situation or of entering a story in mid-telling (e.g. Leech and Short 1981: 96–7, 181; Wales 1989: 111). As for the position of the reader with respect to the text world, there seem to be two main lines of argument. Because the use of definite reference seems to assume the existence of an addressee who already knows and/or can uniquely identify the relevant referents, it has been argued that texts like the ones quoted above ignore or negate the presence of the reader, who seems to be overhearing a conversation between other people or to intrude upon somebody's private reflections (van Dijk 1976: 54; Dillon 1978: 66–7; Wales 1989: 111). Conversely, it has also been claimed that such poems establish a relationship of solidarity and intimacy between writers or fictional speakers on the one hand, and readers on the other (Halliday 1985: 228; Wales 1989: 228; Cook 1994: 13).

The two arguments are in fact the opposite sides of the same coin. Definite reference is usually assumed to be addressee-orientated, i.e. it is expected to reflect the speaker's judgement of the addressee's present situation and state of knowledge (Hawkins 1978: 97). In those cases where the attribution of definiteness does not seem to take into account the reader's actual familiarity with the referents, definite reference can be interpreted as either addresser-orientated or addressee-orientated. If it is interpreted as addresser-orientated, the resulting impression is that of overhearing the poet (or a fictional character) talking to him/herself; if it is interpreted as addressee-orientated, the addressee could be either an implicit, fictional interlocutor, or the reader. In the latter case, readers will feel that they are treated as insiders or intimates because of the assumption, carried by definite reference, that they share in the speaking voice's situation or experience. The effect or impression that will prevail in each case will presumably depend on a variety of factors, such as the subject-matter of the text (e.g. personal vs public), the presence of any references to a fictional interlocutor or to a fictional communicative situation (e.g. the opening *Yes* in 'Adlestrop'), and ultimately on the attitudes and subjective reactions of individual readers. It should not be forgotten, however, that literary texts are, by and large, *meant for* an audience of readers who are unfamiliar with at least some of the referents that are introduced as definite. The various *in medias res*, 'overhearing' or 'intimacy' effects are therefore all part of the world that readers construct while reading, which may include, among other things, a communicative situation with respect to which the readers may position themselves in various ways.

To sum up, the primary and more basic function of unanchored definite references is to do with the 'furnishing' of the evoked text world itself. This results from the presuppositional value of definite reference: when the referent of a definite expression cannot be retrieved on the basis of the co-text or from general world knowledge, readers will simply have to assume its existence within the fictional situation. The definiteness of expressions like *the village*, *the express-train* and *the room* in the poetic extracts quoted above does not require that readers should try to uniquely identify their referents within a shared, pre-existing context, but rather that they construct a context in which such referents can be uniquely identified, and therefore legitimately treated as definite.

2.3.3 The contrast between definiteness and indefiniteness in the construction of text worlds

In the previous discussion I have suggested that the presuppositional value of definiteness leads readers to assume the existence of definite referents within the world they construct during the reading of a text, and to regard them as uniquely identifiable within that world. In the poetic examples quoted so far, this leads to the conclusion that definite noun phrases like *the village*, *the express-train* and *the room* indicate aspects of the relevant text worlds that are familiar to the *persona* whose voice is presented in the poem, and, possibly, also to some addressee whose existence and identity are not explicitly revealed. Conversely, if it is assumed that it is the reader who is being addressed by the voice speaking in the text, the occurrence of unanchored definite references can be interpreted as an indication of the involvement of the reader in a relationship of solidarity and intimacy with the fictional speaker and/or with the poet.

In this section I will discuss some more complex examples, where the alternation between definite and indefinite articles can be related to the status of referents within the text worlds.

'The Jaguar' by Ted Hughes

The contrast between definiteness and indefiniteness plays a crucial role in determining the status of referents within the zoo scene
presented in Hughes's poem below.

THE JAGUAR

The apes yawn and adore their fleas in the sun
The parrots shriek as if they were on fire, or strut
Like cheap tarts to attract the stroller with the nut.
Fatigued with indolence, tiger and lion

Lie still as the sun. The boa-constrictor's coil   5
Is a fossil. Cage after cage seems empty, or
Stinks of sleepers from the breathing straw.
It might be painted on a nursery wall.

But who runs like the rest past these arrives
At a cage where the crowd stands, stares, mesmerized,   10
As a child at a dream, at a jaguar hurrying enraged
Through prison darkness after the drills of his eyes

On a short fierce fuse. Not in boredom—
The eye satisfied to be blind in fire,
By the bang of blood in the brain deaf the ear—   15
He spins from the bars, but there's no cage to him

More that to the visionary his cell:
His stride is wilderness of freedom:
The world rolls under the long thrust of his heel.
Over the cage floor the horizons come.   20

Apart from the noun phrase *tiger and lion* (line 4), where the co-
ordinating structure allows the omission of the article (Quirk *et al.*
1985: 255n.), in the first two stanzas all the animals, people and
objects composing the zoo setting are introduced as definite: *The
apes* (line 1), *The parrots* (line 2), *the stroller with the nut* (line 3),
The boa-constrictor's coil (line 5). In the third stanza, however, the
indefinite article is used in reference to the element of the scene
that provides the topic of the poem, *a jaguar* (line 11), and its
habitation, *a cage* (line 10), while other participants are still treated
as definite, e.g. *the crowd* in line 10.

The function of the indefinite article is usually defined by linguists in negative terms: referents are introduced as indefinite if
they are not uniquely identifiable within the contextual knowledge

shared by addresser and addressee (Quirk *et al.* 1985: 272). This is the case with the cottage mentioned in the example below:

> (13) On my way to town, I stopped to look at *a very nice Georgian cottage.*

The presupposition of existence and unique identifiability in context which is inbuilt in definite meaning does not therefore apply to indefinite reference, which is used to *assert* rather than presuppose the existence of referents within the relevant universe of discourse. This is the case, for example, with the setting and the main character of the scene evoked by the following poem:

> A nun in a supermarket
> Standing in the queue
> Wondering what it's like
> To buy groceries for two.
>
> (Adrian Henry, 'Poem for Roger McGough')

Here the indefinite introduction of *a nun* and *a supermarket* indicates that the relevant referents are not assumed to be uniquely identifiable by the reader or by an implicit addressee, nor that they need to be constructed as familiar to the speaking *persona*.

In 'The Jaguar', however, the contrast between definite and indefinite referents does not seem to be satisfactorily captured by the notions of unique identifiability in context and of assumed familiarity to the poem's speaker. Rather, the distribution of definite and indefinite articles seems to establish a difference in the *status* of referents within the evoked text world, which can be expressed in terms of the visual notions of foreground and background. Definite reference is used to introduce unmarked and relatively unimportant entities, forming the background of the scene. The indefinite article, on the other hand, is reserved for the main topic of the poem and the focus of the metaphoric profusion of the final stanzas (see Eco 1990: 274ff.).

This contrast can be attributed to the fact that the use of the indefinite article in the third stanza deviates from the pattern established in the first part of the poem, where all participants in the zoo scene were referred to by means of definite noun phrases. This results in the foregrounding of the jaguar among the other elements of the scene. However, it is also possible to account for this effect on the basis of the difference between definite and indefinite reference in relation to background knowledge. I mentioned earlier that referents that have not been previously mentioned are normally introduced as definite if they are predictable or 'default' elements of a currently active schema (Schank and Abelson 1977: 41). This implies that the definite first mention of a series of entities belonging to the same schema can function as a signal that the producer of the message has activated such a schema and that the addressee needs to do the same in order to interpret the text. Once a certain schema has been activated, indefinite reference is reserved for optional elements of that schema, or for entities that are not regarded as normally included in it (Du Bois 1980: 238–9).

In 'The Jaguar' the definite introduction of *The apes, The parrots, the stroller with the nut,* and so on induces the reader to activate a ZOO schema[5] and to interpret the definite expressions as indicating some of its default elements. The use of indefinite reference, however, seems to ignore the status of the jaguar and its cage as predictable elements of the schema, and indicates that they are somehow perceived as surprising or novel by the fictional observer. The jaguar, in other words, is not presented as a predictable component of the evoked scene, but as the element that characterizes this particular realization of the ZOO schema and that makes it interesting and memorable (Eysenck and Keane 1990: 280). The surprisingness of the jaguar's behaviour is conveyed by the long series of metaphors contained in the second half of the text: the jaguar of the poem does not behave like a tired and unnaturally quiet zoo animal, but has all the fierceness and power of a beast in the wild.

Finally, it may seem paradoxical that indefinite status should be attributed to the only referent of whose existence in the fictional situation readers are aware before the reading of the text, given that 'The Jaguar' is the title of the poem. In fact the definite article is often used in titles to make a cataphoric reference to a central element of the text, where the same referent may, as is the case here, then be re-introduced as indefinite. It has been argued that this use of definiteness in titles is meant to provoke the readers' curiosity and to encourage them to read the text, in which the knowledge deficit that the definite reference has created will be satisfied (Weinreich 1971; Hoek 1981). I have suggested elsewhere that definite reference in titles can also be explained in terms of the postulation of referents, as is the case with the use of the definite article in general (Semino 1990a: 13–16). Definite titles, in other words, establish the existence and unique identifiability of their referents as a consequence of the presuppositional value of definiteness, and place such referents at the centre of attention because of their role as titles. In 'The Jaguar', therefore, the definite introduction of the jaguar in the title and its indefinite status in the text both help to produce the same effect, i.e. placing their referent in a foregrounded position within the poem's text world.

'Meeting at Night' by Robert Browning

The following poem by Browning provides another example of how the alternation between definite and indefinite reference can be used to signal the speaking voice's attitude towards the various elements of the text world, rather than simply to differentiate between uniquely identifiable and non-uniquely identifiable entities.

MEETING AT NIGHT

The grey sea and the long black land;
And the yellow half-moon large and low;
And the startled little waves that leap
In fiery ringlets from their sleep,
As I gain the cove with pushing prow,   5
And quench its speed i' the slushy sand.

Then a mile of warm sea-scented beach;
Three fields to cross till a farm appears;
A tap at the pane, the quick sharp scratch
And blue spurt of a lighted match,   10
And a voice less loud, through its joys and fears,
Than the two hearts beating each to each!

In the first stanza of the poem the majority of the noun phrases are definite. In the second stanza the opposite is true. This contrast can partly be explained on the basis of various factors determining the definite status of referents. *The grey sea* (line 1), *the long black land* (line 1), *the yellow half-moon large and low* (line 2) owe their definiteness to the conventional uniqueness of their referents in general world knowledge, while *the startled little waves* (line 3) and *the slushy sand* (line 6) refer to entities that can be regarded as default elements of a VOYAGE AT SEA schema, which has been activated by the previous references the sea, the land, and so on. The definiteness of *the cove* (line 5), on the other hand, does not seem to be completely justified within this schema, but rather suggests that the various elements of the scene are familiar and uniquely identifiable for the fictional speaker.

It does not, however, seem to be satisfactory to explain the contrast between a definite expression like *the cove* in the first stanza
and an indefinite expression like *a farm* in the second stanza
simply on the basis of their familiarity and unique identifiability
for the fictional speaker. It is difficult and ultimately not very
enlightening to conclude that the cove can be uniquely identified
by the fictional speaker within the evoked text world while the
farm cannot, especially considering that the character/narrator is
looking for a specific farm, and seems to know exactly where it is
(*three fields to cross till a farm appears*).

As with 'The Jaguar', the opposition between definiteness and
indefiniteness can be more satisfactorily interpreted as expressing
the fictional speaker's perception of different referents and, consequently, as indicating their relative status within the text world.
In 'Meeting at Night', the fact that the existence of the various
elements of the seascape in the first stanza is treated as presupposed can be seen as reflecting the attitude of the main character,
for whom the sea trip is simply a means to an end, a relatively
unexciting sequence of scenes and actions which enable him to
reach his loved one.

The beginning of the second stanza, which opens with the
marker of temporal transition *then* (line 7), coincides with the
final part of the journey, which rapidly takes the fictional speaker
within sight of his destination and, finally, to his beloved. Here
the use of indefinite reference appears to reflect the excitement
and anticipation of the narrator, who no longer presupposes, but
rather explicitly states, the existence of entities and the occurrence of events, as if they were in some way not totally familiar or
predictable: *a farm* (line 8), *a tap* (line 9), *a lighted match* (line 10),
a voice (line 11). If these indefinite references were made definite,
the result would be to turn what is presented as a unique and
fateful occurrence into a regular, almost routine event.

As with 'The Jaguar', the alternation between definiteness and
indefiniteness in 'Meeting at Night' seems to indicate the degree
of 'taken-for-grantedness' or 'newsworthiness' that the speaking
voice attributes to the various referents, and therefore results in
a distinction between backgrounded and foregrounded elements
within the world of the poem. In other words, the opposition between definite and indefinite reference does not simply affect the
identifiability of referents, but has wider implications for the way
in which they are positioned within the worlds that readers construct around texts. My analyses also highlight the fact that texts

do not simply project contexts or worlds in a neutral way, but inevitably describe these contexts or worlds from a particular perspective. In both poems the perspectives of the particular poetic speakers lead to the attribution of different amounts of importance to the elements included in the worlds of the texts.

NOTES

[1] For the sake of simplicity, I will attribute to each poetic *persona* the same gender as that of the poem's author, unless the text appears to suggest otherwise.

[2] My discussion focuses on the specific use of the definite article (e.g. Are you taking *the car* today?), as opposed to its generic use (e.g. *The car* is a major source of pollution) (see Quirk *et al.* 1985: 265).

[3] By referring to the notion of schema it is also possible to highlight the cultural dimension of the use and interpretation of indirect anaphora. Schemata vary from culture to culture: a British person's schema for weddings, for example, is liable to be quite different from that of a Chinese person. As a consequence, the use of indirect anaphora will often assume the possession of culturally specific knowledge on the part of the addressee. While most British readers will find example (7) totally straightforward, readers from other cultures may have a different response: they may find the definite references to *the minister, the best man*, etc., rather puzzling, but they are likely to conclude that the referents of the various definite expressions must be predictable components of the WEDDING schema of the culture in which the text was produced. Definite reference, in other words, does not necessarily rely on shared schemata, but may also enable interpreters to infer the content of (variants of) schemata with which they are not familiar.

[4] Presupposition is a complex and much studied phenomenon whereby some linguistic expressions indicate that a particular fact or set of facts is taken for granted as being true by the texts in which these expressions occur. So, for example, the sentence 'Mary stopped having piano lessons' presupposes that Mary did at some point have piano lessons, while the sentence 'Mary welcomed the new headteacher' presupposes the unique existence of a new headteacher in the relevant context. These presuppositions result respectively from the use of the verb *to stop* and of the definite article in the noun phrase *the headteacher*. The most common litmus test for presupposition is negation: presupposed items are usually unaffected by turning the sentences in which they occur into negatives. So the sentences 'Mary didn't stop having piano lessons' and 'Mary didn't welcome the new headteacher' still carry the presuppositions that I spelt out earlier. For an overview of issues to do with presupposition, see Levinson (1983, chapter 4).

[5] Capitals will be used throughout to 'name' schemata.

3

Deixis and context creation

3.1 Introduction

Let me begin by quoting again the opening of Frost's 'Stopping by Woods on a Snowy Evening' with which I started the previous chapter:

Whose woods these are I think I know.
His house is in the village though;
He will not see me stopping here
To watch his woods fill up with snow.

The first stanza of the poem establishes a fictional context of utterance – an imaginary discourse situation in which a traveller articulates his thoughts about the current setting and the imminent progress of his journey. The first-person pronouns *I* and *me* explicitly signal the presence of a speaking *persona*, whose location in space and time functions as the anchorage point for the interpretation of the demonstratives *these* and *here* and of the various present tense verbs in the stanza. Personal pronouns, demonstratives and tensed verbs are prototypical members of the category of **deixis**, which includes all the linguistic means by which reference is made to the component elements and dimensions of the situational context in which communication takes place. All deictic expressions are inherently definite in meaning, but, unlike the definite article, they provide some guidance towards the identification of the relevant referents, normally by relating them to the current location of the speaker (Lyons 1977: 647; Halliday 1985: 292).

The nature of deictic expressions is often described in relation to the theory of signs proposed by Peirce (Peirce 1932; see also Wales 1989). Peirce argued that signs can be divided into three categories, depending on the relationship between the sign (which may be a word, a gesture, a picture, and so on) and the entity or

entities it refers to. **Icons** are signs that resemble the form of their referents. So, for example, the picture above can be described as a sign that iconically represents the object car. **Symbols** are signs that stand in an arbitrary relationship with their referents – a relationship that is determined by cultural conventions. The word 'car', for example, has a symbolic relationship with the four-wheeled machine that I use to go to work. The relationship between 'car' and this object is arbitrary (other languages use different letters and sounds for the same object), and needs to be learnt as part of the conventions that make up the English language. Finally, **indexes** are signs that stand in a relationship of proximity or causality with their referents. So, for example, thunder and lightning indicate a storm, while a particular noise may indicate cars or traffic.

The term 'deixis' derives from the Greek word for 'pointing with the finger', and deictic expressions may therefore be seen as linguistic 'pointers', guiding the addressee's attention to the relevant referent from the speaker's position within the context of utterance. Following Peirce's triadic classification of signs, therefore, philosophers have often regarded deictics as purely **indexical** expressions, which do not possess a full lexical value, but rather signal a direct relationship between sign and referent (Bar-Hillel 1954). The meaning and function of deictic elements is however more adequately captured by the term **indexical symbols** (Burks 1948), which implies that deictics do not simply 'point' at a referent in an arrow-like fashion, but also carry an invariant symbolic meaning. This symbolic meaning is represented by the nature of the relationship that deictic expressions signal or establish between their referents and the centre of orientation of the deictic context (i.e. normally the speaker/writer). So, for example, both *this* and *that* can be used to point at something in the situational context, but they differ in that *this* signals a close or **proximal** spatial relationship between the speaker and the referent, whereas *that* indicates a remote or **distal** relationship between them. In the extract from 'Stopping by Woods on a Snowy Evening' readers are able to reconstruct the speaker's position in relation to his situational context thanks to the symbolic meaning of the deictic expressions contained in the text.

3.2 Deixis: main uses and categories

Although deictic expressions can occur in a wide variety of discourse types regardless of the simultaneous presence of referents, addressers and addressees, their basic use is linked to spoken face-to-face communication, where the above conditions actually hold (Lyons 1977: 637–8; Levinson 1983: 63; Rauh 1983: 12–13). In Lyons's terms, this type of interactional context represents the **canonical situation of utterance**, which involves:

> ... one–one, or one–many, signalling in the phonic medium along the vocal-auditory channel, with all the participants present in the same actual situation able to see one another and to perceive the associated non-vocal paralinguistic features of their utterances, and each assuming the role of sender and receiver in turn ... There is much in the structure of languages that can only be explained on the assumption that they have developed for communication in face-to-face interaction. This is clearly so as far as deixis is concerned.
>
> (Lyons 1977: 637–8)

Within this context, the selection and interpretation of deictic expressions will be closely dependent on who is speaking at each particular moment in time. Deixis is, in other words, fundamentally egocentric, i.e. it normally takes the speaker's or writer's spatio-temporal location as the basic zero-point or unmarked **deictic centre**, in relation to which all other elements are positioned (Lyons 1977: 638; Levinson 1983: 63–4; Rauh 1983: 12; but see Jones 1995 for a thought-provoking critique of the egocentricity of deixis). In Bühler's terms, the first-person speaker's here-and-now represents the **origo**, i.e. the point of origin of the deictic field (Bühler 1982: 13). Deixis is therefore organized along three primary dimensions, namely **person**, **place** and **time**, with the speaker functioning as the centre of orientation for the positioning of other elements along each dimension.

Person deixis is to do with the expression of participant roles for each individual utterance within a communicative event. The first-person pronoun refers to the producer of the utterance, the second-person pronoun to the addressee, and the third-person pronoun to any other person or entity, whether or not they are potential candidates for the other two roles. First- and second-person pronouns are therefore intrinsically deictic, since their reference is inextricably linked to each individual utterance or instance of discourse: every time the speaker changes, for example, the reference of the pronoun *I* varies accordingly (Benveniste 1971: 217). Third-person pronouns, on the other hand, do not encode a specific participant role, and may therefore be used non-deictically (Benveniste 1971: 217–21; Lyons 1977: 638–9).

Place deixis is to do with the expression of spatial locations with respect to the position of the speaker. This is typically achieved by means of the demonstratives *this* and *that* and of the deictic adverbs *here* and *there*. In both cases the distinction between the two members of the pair encodes the opposition between locations that are perceived as close to the speaker (*this/here*) and locations that are perceived as distant (*that/there*). Other kinds of expressions can function as place deictics, such as the verbs *come* and *go* (Levinson 1983: 83) and the adverbs *away* and *opposite* as used in the examples below:

(1) Preston is only about 20 miles *away*.
(2) Barbara lives in the house *opposite*.

Deictics can also express *psychological* or *emotional* distance, in which case they reflect the speaker's attitude towards entities or people, rather than signalling purely spatial relationships. This use is known as **empathetic deixis** (Lyons 1977: 677; Levinson 1983: 81; Quirk *et al.* 1985: 374). Consider the two examples below:

(3) I would be really pleased to meet *this* new friend of yours some time.
(4) I don't want *that* new friend of yours to come anywhere near this house!

Here the difference between *this* and *that* is not to do with physical distance, but with the speaker's attitude to the addressee's new friend: in (3) the speaker expresses the wish to have a close relationship with the friend, while in (4) the relationship is constructed as deliberately distant.

Time deixis is to do with the expression of temporal points or periods in relation to the time when the utterance is produced. Such temporal relationships are primarily expressed by means of tense distinctions (Lyons 1977: 677–90; Levinson 1983: 76–9) and of deictic adverbs of time (*now, then, soon, lately*), as well as by a variety of temporal expressions involving a deictic dimension, such as *yesterday, last month, next Thursday*, and so on. In the canonical situation of utterance, where addresser and addressees are simultaneously present, the time of production of the utterance (**coding time**) coincides with the time of reception of the utterance (**receiving time**), so that the temporal deictic centre includes the hearer as well as the speaker (see Levinson 1983: 62).

Besides the basic categories of person, place and time, a number of other dimensions have been considered as falling within the scope of deictic reference. The participants' social roles and mutual social relationships, for example, can be encoded by means of a variety of linguistic devices such as address forms, modals, or the grammatical person of the verb in languages which have a *T/V* distinction.[1] So, for example, the same person may be addressed as *Katie* or as *Professor Wales*. Those who use *Katie* assume a close, possibly familiar relationship with the addressee, whereas those who use *Professor Wales* assume a more distant, formal relationship with the same person. This phenomenon is known as **social deixis** (Levinson 1983: 89–94; Rauh 1983: 38–9). It is also possible to make deictic references to portions of the ongoing discourse, which is itself a component of the situation of utterance. Expressions like *in the next chapter, in the previous discussions*, etc., are all examples of **discourse deixis** (Levinson 1983: 85–9; Rauh 1983: 41–2). The other linguistic phenomena that have been claimed to fall within the domain of deixis, such as anaphora (Lyons 1977: 670ff.), modality, case and intonation (Rauh 1983: 32–40), are not directly relevant to the purposes of this book, and will not therefore be included in the discussion.

In all the examples introduced so far, deictic expressions are anchored relative to the speaker's spatio-temporal location, although the hearer may in some cases be included within the deictic centre. Speakers also have the option of anchoring deictic expressions to a different centre of orientation, as shown in the examples below:

(5) When I move to London, you can *come* to stay with me any time.
(6) I'll *come* to see you in your office tomorrow at 4.00.
(7) I *was* on my way to work yesterday, when all of a sudden *this* guy *walks* up to me and *says*. . . .

The anchorage point for the deictic verb *come*, which in unmarked cases indicates movement towards the speaker's location at the moment of utterance, is shifted to the speaker's future home-base in (5) (Levinson 1983: 83–4) and to the addressee's position at a specific future moment in time in (6). In (7) the switch from the past tense (*was*) to the present tense (*walks, says*) marks a shift in the temporal deictic centre from the time of utterance to the time of the recounted event (**reference** or **content time**) (see Levinson 1983: 84). Similarly, the use of the demonstrative of proximity *this* can be seen as reflecting the speaker's perception at the time of the narrated event, in which case the spatial deictic centre is temporarily shifted from the location of the *I* as speaker to that of the *I* as character in the story. In all these examples, which are instances of what is known as **deictic projection** (Levinson 1983: 64), the context in which deictic expressions are disambiguated is not directly available to the addressee but needs to be reconstructed on the basis of the deictic references themselves.

3.3 Deixis in poetry

The use of deixis in poetry introduces a dimension of dialogue or 'address' within the text, which is presented as the utterance of an individual speaking *persona* in an imaginary communicative context. In Todorov's terms, deictic expressions function as markers of a fictional 'enunciation' (i.e. speech event) within the 'enounced' (i.e. narrated event) of the poem (Todorov 1981: 324). As I said earlier, readers have to imagine a fictional discourse situation on the basis of the symbolic meanings of the deictic elements in the text (Culler 1975: 166; Fowler 1986: 90; Austin 1994: 37–8).

As in the case of the definite article, the poetic use of deixis is often described as deviant or, to use Fowler's term, 'unnatural' with respect to ordinary language (Fowler 1986: 90), due to the absence of a shared communicative context in which the reference of deictic expressions can be disambiguated (see also Leech 1969; Culler 1975). In fact, the use of deixis in poetry can be seen as an extension of its more basic use in face-to-face communication, or, to follow Lyons, in the canonical situation of utterance. In his classic theory of deixis, Bühler claims that many deictic expressions can be used both in what he calls **demonstratio ad oculos**, where addresser and addressee share the same perceptual space, and in **deixis am phantasma**, where neither the addresser nor the indicated object is part of the situational context in which the addressee is located (Bühler 1982). In particular, he argues that, in the latter case:

> ... the narrator takes the listener into the realm of the memorable absent, or fully into the realm of constructive imagination, treating

him there to the same deictic words that he may see and hear what is there to be seen and heard . . . not with the outward eye, ear, etc., but with what, in contrast, is called the 'inner' or the 'mind's' eye or ear. . . . (Bühler 1982: 22)

Following Bühler, Rauh (1983) accounts for different types of deictic uses in terms of a continuum, from reference within the canonical situation of utterance to the projection of absent, imaginary spaces (as in Bühler's *deixis am phantasma*). In the latter cases, the addressee will not be able to assign indexical meanings to deictic elements but rather:

> has to create a cognitive space in which he locates the centre of orientation via the symbolic meaning of the deictic expressions.
>
> (Rauh 1983: 47)

Building on Rauh's notion of a cline of deictic uses, Green (1992) has proposed that the use of deixis in poetry should not be treated as a deviation from a non-literary 'norm', but simply as the occurrence of a particular linguistic phenomenon within a particular type of discourse. The construction of a fictional-speaking subject whose existence is limited to the world projected by the text can therefore be seen as one of the features that characterize the poetic use of deixis (alongside other fictional genres) in relation to its use in other written discourse types, such as letters or travel reports.

The absence of a clear-cut discontinuity between the use of deixis in poetry and in ordinary face-to-face communication can be appreciated more fully if we consider that the latter also involves active context creation on the part of the addressee. Consider the following utterances:

(8) If you *come* and stand *here* you will be able to see the top of the tower.

(9) Don't forget that people drive on the left *here.*

(10) You may go *now.*

(11) I am *now* working on a UN project.

In (8) it is the speaker's current physical location within a restricted spatial setting (e.g. a room, a square, etc.) that is relevant to the disambiguation of the place deictic *here*, whereas in (9) the reference of the same adverb falls within a much wider context (a whole country), and the spatial deictic centre includes the hearer as well as the speaker. Similarly, in (10) the time span which is indicated by the time deictic *now* is limited to the few seconds immediately following the actual uttering of the word, whereas in (11) the reference of *now* extends well before *and* after the time of utterance.

Even in such rather trivial examples the context that is relevant to the disambiguation of deictic expressions is not fixed once and for all prior to the communicative interaction, but needs to be adequately identified by the addressees on the basis of the content of the utterance and of their general knowledge of the world (see Brown and Yule 1983: 52). The process whereby readers of poetry actively construct fictional discourse situations from the deictic references in the texts can therefore be seen as an extension of the interpretative strategies that underlie the smooth running of everyday communication.

3.3.1 Poetic voices, contexts and readers

As a result of the egocentric nature of deictic reference, the interpretation of deixis in poetry requires that readers construct an image of a speaking subject functioning as deictic centre, whether or not this presence is made explicit by the occurrence of first-person pronouns inside the text. Such poetic *personae* cannot be straightforwardly conflated with real-life authors, but are to be regarded as poetic constructs, that result from the readers' interpretative engagement with the language of texts (see Culler 1975; Widdowson 1975; Easthope 1983; Herman 1989; Pallotti 1990; Austin 1994).

The perceived distance between the imagined poetic *persona* and the poem's author, however, varies from text to text, and actually constitutes one of the crucial distinguishing factors between different poetic subgenres, such as, for example, the lyric poem and the dramatic monologue.[2] The extent to which readers identify the poetic speaker with the poet in each individual case depends on a combination of textual evidence and extra-textual information.[3] In the case of Wordsworth's 'I Wandered Lonely as a Cloud', for example, a strong identification between poet and *persona* is encouraged by factors such as the evidence of Dorothy Wordsworth's diaries, the readers' generic expectations about Romantic poetry and the fact that the *persona* is referred to as *a poet* within the text itself (see also Austin 1994: 1–2 and throughout). In Browning's dramatic monologues, on the other hand, a clear discontinuity is established between the author and the various figures who act as first-person speakers, such as the monk of

'Soliloquy of the Spanish Cloister' and the sixteenth-century Italian duke of 'My Last Duchess'. Such discontinuity is likely to be even greater when poets choose as first-person speakers entities that do not, in the actual world, possess the power of speech, such as dead people (as in Emily Dickinson's 'I Heard a Fly Buzz when I Died'), inanimate beings (as in Sylvia Plath's 'Elm'), or imaginary creatures (as in Ted Hughes's 'Wodwo') (see also Leech 1969: 197–8; Widdowson 1975: 47ff.). In section 5.3 I will propose a possible-world approach to the description and classification of deviant speakers such as these.

More generally, the communicative situations evoked by different poems may vary considerably, not only with respect to the identity of the poetic *persona*, but also with respect to the scope of the deictic field, the presence and status of the addressee, the position reserved for the reader, and the mode of discourse in which the *persona* is imagined to be engaged – such as, for example, interactive speaker, solitary narrator, impersonal observer, and so on (cf. Fowler 1986: 96; Verdonk 1993: 116). In the rest of this section I will illustrate such variability with reference to specific examples.

Let me begin by taking a closer look at the opening of the Wordsworth poem mentioned above:

> I wandered lonely as a cloud
> That floats on high o'er vales and hills,
> When all at once I saw a crowd,
> A host, of golden daffodils;
> Beside the lake, beneath the trees,
> Fluttering and dancing in the breeze.

The use of the first-person pronoun *I* explicitly signals the presence of a speaking voice, while the use of the simple past tense (*wandered, saw*) establishes a clear separation between the time of the recounted event, or content time, and the time of the fictional speech event, or coding time (see Green 1992: 132). The *persona* is therefore constructed as a personal narrating voice located in an unspecified context of utterance, with no explicit addressee other than the narrator himself.

In Frost's 'Stopping by Woods on a Snowy Evening' (see 2.1 and 3.1), the situation in which the *persona*'s act of discourse takes place is also the scene that is described in the poem. The fictional context of utterance, in other words, coincides with the context of reference, i.e. the situation that constitutes the subject-matter of

the text (Fowler 1986: 89). The poem's explicit first-person speaker
refers deictically to his immediate surroundings, and functions as
the deictic centre of a specific spatio-temporal setting. The place
deictics of proximity *these* and *here* signal that the speaker is positioned *within* the situation that he is talking about, while the use
of present tenses (*think, know, is*) indicate the simultaneity of content and coding time. As in Wordsworth's poem, no reference is
made to an audience or to a specific addressee. The lack of any
explicit dialogic elements, together with the use of proximal deixis
of both place and time, lead the reader to construct the poem's
persona as a solitary muser, thinking or talking to himself about his
current situation. Rather than listening to a narrative voice, the
reader experiences the discourse of an immediate participant in
the fictional world.

A similar situation is projected by John Donne's 'The Flea', the
main difference lying in the dialogic nature of the first-person
speaker's utterance. 'The Flea' dramatizes a conventional poetic
situation, in which an eager (male) lover tries to dissuade a reluctant (female) partner from her coy attitude to sexual behaviour.
The well-known argument is that the woman's refusal to agree to
sexual intercourse is unjustified, since the two bodies have in fact
already been made one by a flea, who has been sucking blood
from them both:

> Marke but this flea, and marke in this,
> How little that which thou deny'st me is:
> It suck'd me first, and now sucks thee,
> And in this flea, our two bloods mingled bee;

As in Frost's poem, content and coding time are marked as simultaneous by the occurrence of present tenses, while the proximal
time deictic *now* also seems to signal that the sucking of the addressee's blood on the part of the flea takes place during the
unfolding of the speaker's utterance. The use of the proximal place
deictic *this* for the flea indicates that the context of reference and
the context of utterance coincide in terms of both space and time.
In this case, however, the deictics are used by the speaker to point
out aspects of a shared situational context to a specific addressee,
explicitly referred to by means of the second-person pronouns
thou and *thee*. The opening imperatives (*Marke . . . and marke*) can
also be read deictically as signals of the existence of another participant to whom the commands are addressed (Green (1995:
22) has suggested the category of 'syntactic' deixis to capture the

potential deictic value of grammatical forms such as imperatives and interrogatives).

The scene evoked by 'The Flea' is a (fictional) canonical situation of utterance, within which the two participants, a mutually visible object and the time of utterance are referred to deictically. The discourse role of the poetic *persona*, therefore, is that of participant in what we imagine to be a dialogic exchange with another member of the fictional world. The fact that a spoken context of utterance is constructed from a written text emphasizes the separation between the real and the fictional enunciations: the referents of the personal pronouns in the text are likely to be perceived as fictive *personae*, while author and reader are not directly present or involved within the constructed text world. This is the kind of situation where readers seem to be relegated to the role of invisible eavesdroppers on a conversation between others.

The poems discussed so far contain explicit references to a speaking voice in the form of first-person singular pronouns. Let me now turn to some examples of less clearly individualized voices. In the poem 'Anthem for Doomed Youth' by Wilfred Owen, the proximal demonstrative *these* highlights the spatial dimension of an implied situation of utterance, and therefore mobilizes a poetic *persona* functioning as deictic centre, even if no explicit reference is made to a first-person speaker. Here, however, the discourse situation lends itself to more than one possible reading, depending on the way in which the deictic expression in the first line is interpreted.

> What passing-bells for these who die as cattle?
>   Only the monstrous anger of the guns.
> Only the stuttering rifles' rapid rattle
>   Can patter out their hasty orisons.

If *these* is taken as an indicator of physical distance, the resulting context of utterance is a war scene, with the speaking *persona* acting as an observer/commentator on the inhumanity of the soldiers' deaths. Such a reading may be triggered by extra-textual knowledge about Owen's life, who fought and was eventually killed in World War I. It is also possible, however, to interpret *these* as being used not to indicate spatial proximity, but rather to highlight the speaker's empathy with the unfortunate referents of the noun phrase *these who die as cattle*, and, possibly, to elicit a similar attitude in the reader. The relevant situation of utterance can then be identified more generally as the historical period of the

Great War, in which the poem was actually composed and first received by its contemporary readers. Any reader can, in any case, place himself or herself within the deictic centre by adopting an appropriate psychological distance towards those who lose their lives at war.

Owen's poem, in other words, allows both a specific and a universal reading. Within a specific reading, the discourse situation of the poem corresponds to a particular war period, or even a particular time and place in that war. Within a universal reading, the poem applies to all wars in general, and its discourse situation includes the readers as well. This is a common ambiguity in poetry, where we often expect specific personal experiences to have a wider universal validity for humanity as a whole. What interpretation is favoured in each individual reading of a poem will depend on variables such as the readers' knowledge of the context in which the text was written, their cultural and historical distance from the author, and their preferences in the attribution of specific or general significance to poetry.

In Philip Larkin's 'Days', the choice of first-person deixis contributes to the construction of a rather generic type of voice. This is the opening of the poem:

> What are days for?
> Days are where we live.

Here the first-person pronoun *we* is used in its most inclusive sense, to refer not only to an implicit speaker and his addressees (presumably the readers), but to a wider set of people, including, if not the whole human race, at least the members of the culture to which the author belongs.[4] The opening question can also be attributed a deictic function, insofar as it sets up a potential position for another participant in the discourse (see Green 1995). Here, however, the interrogative is largely self-addressed, since question and answer seem to belong to the same voice. No other deictics occur in the text, and noun phrases tend to be used to make generic references, as in the case of the indefinite noun phrase *days* in the quotation above. The individuality of the speaker is therefore somewhat backgrounded: the poem's *persona* is presented as a generic and impersonal commentator on a universal aspect of the human condition.

These brief analyses have shown how the nature and scope of the context that is constructed for each individual poem crucially depends on the choice of deictic expressions in the text, but is also affected by the combined effect of a range of variables, including the content of the text as a whole and the reader's attitudes and background knowledge. It has also become clear that the degree of overlap that readers are likely to perceive between speaking *persona* and author is partly determined by the mode of discourse in which the fictional voice is engaged. Impersonal and abstract poetic voices, such as that of Larkin's poem, tend to be regarded as vehicles of the authors' own views and feelings; on the other hand, with interactive speakers such as the one in Donne's poem, readers are much more likely to establish a boundary between author and *dramatis persona*.

3.3.2 Deixis and voice shifts in two twentieth-century poems

Most discussions of deixis in poetry tend to overlook the fact that poems do not necessarily project unique and stable voices located within fixed deictic contexts, but may involve variations in deictic centre, which may in turn signal a change in the projected context of utterance and in the discoursal role or identity of the speaking *persona* (cf. Herman 1989; Wales 1993; Tate 1995). Such neglect for the potential complexities of poetic voice reflects the controversial Bakhtinian view that poetry, unlike fictional prose, is essentially monologic (Bakhtin 1981) and the related assumption that poems, unlike novels, project single-layered discourse situations, i.e. tend to involve one level of communication between one addresser and one (set of) addressee(s) (see Leech and Short 1981: 257ff.).

The poems that I will analyse in this section contain examples of various kinds of deictic shifts and inconsistencies, which undermine the possibility of constructing a single and fixed discourse situation that can apply to the whole text. The first poem ('Talking in Bed' by Philip Larkin), although deceptively uncomplicated at a first reading, involves subtle changes in the speaking *persona*'s position and mode of discourse as a result of a shift in deictic centre. This text suggests that variations in poetic voice can be found well beyond the literary trends with which they are commonly associated, such as modernist poetry (Easthope 1983: 147) and postmodernist poetry (McHale 1992).[5] The second poem ('Charlotte, Her Book' by Elizabeth Bartlett) provides a poetic example of a complex discourse situation (Leech and Short 1981: 257ff.), with one voice embedded inside another.

'Talking in Bed' by Philip Larkin

In 'Talking in Bed', changes in the use of deixis mark shifts in the projected situation of utterance and in the *persona*'s mode of discourse. More specifically, the spatial deictic centre shifts from outside to within the context of reference, with a consequent change in the speaker's position relative to the situation he is talking about: the exacerbation of communication problems between partners sharing the same bed.

TALKING IN BED

Talking in bed ought to be easiest,
Lying together there goes back so far,
An emblem of two people being honest.

Yet more and more time passes silently.
Outside, the wind's incomplete unrest   5
Builds and disperses clouds about the sky.

And dark towns heap up on the horizon.
None of this cares for us. Nothing shows why
At this unique distance from isolation

It becomes still more difficult to find   10
Words at once true and kind,
Or not untrue and not unkind.

Commenting on the status of the poem's speaking *persona*, Verdonk (1991) has touched upon the difficulties posed by the text's deictic choices to the construction of a stable context of utterance:

> If we do try to anchor the speaker to a particular situation, he turns out to be quite elusive. This is evidenced by the poem's topography, marked by a sequence of lexical deictics, 'in bed', 'there', 'outside', 'about the sky', 'on the horizon', and 'at this unique distance from isolation', which, as anchors for the speaker's physical or mental presence, are hardly specific. Indeed, the diffuseness of location justifies that the persona is both a participant in the poem's discourse situation and an external onlooker commenting on it.[6] (Verdonk 1991: 102)

More precisely, the poem starts off as a general reflection on a universal situation and then develops into a more personal evocation of a specific experience, with a corresponding shift in the position and discourse role of the poetic speaker.

In line 2 the setting evoked by the title and the first line of the poem (*Talking in bed*) is referred to again by means of the adverb *there.* As Lyons (1977: 676) and Levinson (1983: 67) have argued, the use of *there* in this context is simultaneously anaphoric and deictic:

> it is perfectly possible, as Lyons (1977a: 676) points out, for a deictic term to be used *both* anaphorically and deictically. For example in:
>
> (40) I was born in *London* and have lived *there* ever since
>
> *there* refers back to whatever place *London* refers to, but simultaneously contrasts with *here* on the deictic dimension of space, locating the utterance outside London. (Levinson 1983: 67, author's italics)

The choice of the distal adverb *there* in Larkin's poem, therefore, does not simply make an anaphoric reference to a location that has been previously mentioned in the text, but also positions the speaker *away from* that location. The *persona*'s lack of immediate involvement in the situation he describes is confirmed by the fact that in line 3 the two bed partners are introduced as third-person referents by means of the noun phrase *two people.* The first stanza, in other words, sets up the projected context of utterance as separate from the context of reference. The speaker observes the situation from outside, and therefore acts as a generic and impersonal commentator on a particular aspect of human relationships.

The landscape description (lines 5–7) is interestingly ambivalent in its status as to specificity or generality. The definite references to the wind, the sky and the horizon can be interpreted deictically as specific situational references, or non-deictically as references to elements of a universally shared environment (Quirk *et al.* 1985: 266–7; Green 1992: 122–3). Similarly, the adverb *outside* may function both deictically (in relation to a deictic centre located <u>inside</u> a house/bedroom) and anaphorically (i.e. in relation to the previous reference to talking *in bed*). As a result, the represented scene may be constructed either as a specific situational setting, or as a generic, symbolic landscape mirroring the gloominess of the described human experience (see Verdonk 1991: 105).

Little ambivalence remains after line 8, however: the shift to proximal space deixis (*none of this* in line 8, *at this unique distance from isolation* in line 9) and the use of the first-person pronoun *us* (line 8) in reference to the two lovers mark a change in perspective. The spatial deictic centre is now located within the context of reference, and the speaker is an immediate participant talking about himself and his partner. The impersonal and relatively detached observer of the first stanza has changed to an explicit *dramatis persona* who is directly involved in the represented situation. The ambivalence of the landscape description of lines 5–7 can therefore be explained in terms of a transition between two different discourse situations.

As in the case of the ambiguity in 'Anthem for Doomed Youth' (see 3.3.1), it can be argued that the two discourse situations of Larkin's poem correspond to two distinct ways in which poems may achieve their significance: by dealing with themes of universal relevance on the one hand, and by portraying individual experiences of intense personal resonance on the other. As a result of the described shifts in deixis, both strategies are represented in Larkin's approach to the difficulties of communication within couples.

'Charlotte, Her Book' by Elizabeth Bartlett

Bartlett's 'Charlotte, Her Book' revolves around a dead four-year-old girl, who was fostered out before she died and who appears to be talking in the first person throughout most of the poem. In fact, I will argue that the text projects a complex discourse situation involving two voices: that of the dead Charlotte, and that of an unidentified and probably adult person who has come across Charlotte's drawing book. The presence of two voices and the particular nature of the girl's predicament (both in life and in death) are reflected in the choice of personal, temporal, spatial and social deixis. My analysis of deictic choices, and of wider stylistic choices throughout the poem, will lead to the conclusion that Charlotte's voice is mediated through the other speaker's discourse. In other words, I will argue that Charlotte's first-person speech takes place within the memory and imagination of an adult *persona* (another possible interpretation of the poem will be discussed in note 8 at the end of the chapter).

CHARLOTTE, HER BOOK

I am Charlotte. I don't say hello
to people and sometimes I bite.
Although I am dead I still jump
out of bed and wake them up at night.

This is my mother. Her hair is blue   5
and I have drawn her with no eyes
and arms like twigs. I don't do
what I'm told and I tell lies.

This is my father. He has a mouth
under his left ear. I'm fed up   10
with drawing people, so I scribble
smoke and cover his head right up.

I am a brat kid, fostered out because
my mother is sick in the head,
and I would eat her if I could,   15
and make her good and dead.

Although I am only four I went away
so soon they hardly knew me,
and stars sprang out of my eyes,
and cold winds blew me.   20

My mother always says she loves me.
My father says he loves me too.
I love Charlotte. A car ran
over Charlotte. This is her book.

The most noticeable sign of the potential presence of two voices
and discourse situations is the fact that Charlotte occurs both as
first- and third-person referent. More precisely, what sounds like
a long monologue in which Charlotte talks about herself in the
first person (lines 1–22) is framed within a discourse situation
where another first-person speaker refers to the girl in the third
person. This other voice emerges in the title ('Charlotte, Her
Book') and in the last two lines of the poem:

I love Charlotte. A car ran
over Charlotte. This is her book.

The two *personae* and discourse situations are of course rather
different. Because she is presented as being dead, Charlotte is a
representative of those deviant voices that are made possible by a
conventional poetic licence (see 3.3.1). The other speaker appears
to possess the default features of being adult and being alive. More
importantly, the construction of a context of utterance for Charlotte's discourse – which obtains for ninety-five per cent of the
poem – is rather problematic, particularly as far as spatial and
temporal deixis are concerned.

The simple past tense is used by both speakers to refer to
Charlotte's death: *I went away* (line 17), *A car ran/ over Charlotte*
(lines 23–4). Both discourse situations are therefore placed at a
time following that event. Some occurrences of the present tense
in Charlotte's discourse, however, are inconsistent with such a conclusion. Charlotte uses the present tense in reference to:

- her state of being dead: *Although I am dead* (line 3)
- her persistent interferences with the world of the living in spite of being dead: *I still jump/ out of bed and wake them up at night* (lines 3–4)
- her general situation and habits during her lifetime: *I am a brat kid* (line 13), *I am only four* (line 17), *My mother always says she loves me* (line 21), *I don't say hello/ to people and sometimes I bite* (lines 1–2), etc.
- her activity of drawing pictures of her parents and her description of those pictures: *This is my mother. Her hair is blue/ and I have drawn her* (lines 5–6), *This is my father. He has a mouth/ under his left ear* (lines 8–9), *I'm fed up/ with drawing people, so I scribble/ smoke* (lines 10–12), etc.

In other words, coding time is constructed both as following the girl's death and as simultaneous with activities and states of affairs that, strictly speaking, are only compatible with her being alive.

As for place deixis, the use of *this* in lines 5 and 9 (*This is my father, This is my mother*) reinforces the effect of the present tenses by indicating that the context of utterance in which Charlotte is positioned coincides with the context of reference that includes the girl's drawing book. In line 24, the same place deictic is used by the other speaker in relation to what we have to conclude must be the same referent: *This is her book.* The same object is therefore deictically presented as spatially proximal by two different voices within two different contexts of utterance. The two references to Charlotte's book on the part of the second speaking *persona* also occur in foregrounded positions: one in the title, the other in the final line of the poem.

The foregrounding of Charlotte's book both within the text and within the two projected discourse situations contributes to the construction of a coherent interpretation for the deictic choices described so far. The sight of Charlotte's drawing book has triggered memories of the girl in an anonymous adult *persona* (possibly her foster mother), who imagines her come alive again and speak about herself. The discourse situation revolving around Charlotte is therefore embedded within the other speaker's words. This explains the contradictions in the temporal deictic context implied by Charlotte's words and the use of the demonstrative *this* throughout the poem: they reflect a situation where the dead Charlotte returns to her lifetime environment and activities in the imagination of a living person who used to be close to her.

The presence of a different, adult voice behind the words

attributed to Charlotte is revealed by other linguistic choices in the poem, notably the occurrence of expressions that are rather improbable for a four-year-old, such as *brat kid, fostered out* (line 13), and *stars sprang out of my eyes/ and cold winds blew me* (lines 19–20).[7] A more detailed analysis of the lexis of the poem would reveal the kind of mixture of styles and registers that Bakhtin regarded as characteristic of the novel (see 9.2.3 for a further discussion of the poetic use of style variation). Other features of the speech attributed to Charlotte seem to reflect someone else's point of view, particularly that of her foster parents. Charlotte's claim that *Although I am dead I still jump/ out of bed and wake them up at night* (lines 3–4) can be interpreted as an indirect reference to her parents' disturbed sleep after the child's death. Similarly, in *Although I am only four I went away/ so soon they hardly knew me* (lines 17–18), the focus is on the effect that Charlotte's premature death had on her parents (the use of the verb of cognition *know* with *they* as subject can be read as a signal that we are being presented with the point of view of someone other than Charlotte (see Short 1994)).

A final problem with the deixis of the poem arises in the attribution of reference to the noun phrase *my mother*, which occurs three times in the poem (lines 5, 14 and 21). While there is no doubt that in line 14 the referent is Charlotte's natural mother (*fostered out because/ my mother is sick in the head*), the other two occurrences of the noun phrase are ambiguous. The presence in both cases of a parallel reference to *my father* (lines 9 and 22) seems to indicate that Charlotte is here referring to her foster family (significantly, no father is mentioned in the fourth stanza in connection with Charlotte's natural mother, which suggests a one-parent family background). In other words, Charlotte's predicament as a foster child allows for the possibility that the social deictic centre in which she is positioned may shift from her foster family to her natural family and back again.

To conclude, the deixis used in the poem contributes to project a complex discourse situation, in which a rather problematic context of utterance revolving around a deviant voice is embedded within the discourse of a more conventional (but largely backgrounded) speaking *persona*.[8]

NOTES

[1] *T/V* Languages have a distinction in second-person address between a polite, distant form, such as *vous* in French or *Sie* in German, and a familiar, informal form such as *tu* or *du*.

2 See, for example, Rader (1984; 1989) for a classification of Victorian *I*-poems according to the relationship between first-person speakers and real authors.

3 Some literary theories, notably Anglo-American New Criticism, deny the legitimacy of any link between *persona* and author (cf. Jefferson and Robey 1982; Hawthorn 1987). While I consider poetic speakers as separate entities from real-life writers, I do not wish to ignore the varying degree of distance that may exist between them. Many readers tend to assume a default identity between *persona* and author, and only revise this assumption if faced with strong evidence to the contrary (as in the case of non-human or inanimate speakers). It is also important to bear in mind that, as suggested by Austin (1994: 96 *et passim*), readers may in some cases identify the author with a voice or character *other than* the main first-person speaker in a text.

4 It is ultimately up to individual readers to decide whether they feel they are included in the reference of *we*. On the whole, Larkin's poem seems more likely to be read on a universal scale than Owen's: the daily cycle affects all human beings, but not everyone has direct experience of war and its consequences.

5 In Semino (1995) I have discussed Larkin's poem alongside Ted Hughes's 'Wind', where changes in time deixis mark shifts in the speaking voice's mode of discourse.

6 Verdonk's list of what he calls 'lexical deictics' seems rather problematic. *In bed* does not appear to be deictic. The prepositional phrases *about the sky, on the horizon* and *at this unique distance of isolation* are not deictic because of lexical choices but as a result of the definiteness of the noun phrases they contain. The reference to *the sky* can be interpreted as non-deictic, since the sky belongs to the class of 'unique' referents which are normally presented as definite regardless of context (Quirk *et al.* 1985: 266–7).

7 Line 19 (*and stars sprang out of my eyes*) can be read as a reference to the description of the Virgin in the book of Revelation (12, 1), and to other poems which have alluded to it in the history of English poetry, such as Dante Gabriel Rossetti's 'The Blessed Damozel' and Christina Rossetti's 'In Progress'.

8 The interpretation that I have offered is only one of the possible readings of the poem. A number of alternatives have been suggested to me in the course of seminars and workshops involving this poem. One in particular poses a valid objection to my own proposal. Some readers have argued that only Charlotte speaks in the poem, partly using the first person and partly referring to herself in the third person, as children often do. This explains the simplicity and relative clumsiness of the syntax of the last two lines of the poem (which my interpretation attributes to an adult voice):

    I love Charlotte. A car ran
    over Charlotte. This is her book.

All three sentences are short and have very simple structures: respectively, Subject–Verb–Object: Subject–Verb–Object; Subject–Verb–Complement. Moreover, in the second sentence Charlotte's name is repeated rather than being replaced by a pronoun (i.e. *A car ran over her*), and an active structure is used where a passive structure would have made more sense, since Charlotte has just been mentioned and can be treated as given information (i.e. *She was run over by a car*). The interpretation I have proposed does not account for these features of the text. On the other hand, the alternative reading fails to explain the presence of 'adult' language in the poem, the prominent position reserved to Charlotte's book, and the fact that some parts of the poem reflect the point of view of someone other than Charlotte. A reading that could successfully account for all of these different aspects would, of course, be more satisfactory than both my own interpretation and the alternative outlined above.

Part I: Suggestions for further analysis

1. Definiteness, indefiniteness and context creation in poetry

The opening of Edward Thomas's poem 'Adlestrop' was briefly mentioned in 2.3 in order to introduce the notion of unanchored definite references in poetry. The poem describes an unexpected stop during a train journey and the opportunity it offered to the speaker for experiencing the beauty of the surrounding countryside. Examine the use of definite and indefinite reference in the text as a whole. To what extent can each choice be explained in the light of the definitions and uses of the articles discussed in 2.2 and 2.3.3? Is there an opposition between the references to the 'station' scene and the description of the surrounding countryside? Consider this opposition in the light of my analyses of 'The Jaguar' and 'Meeting at Night' in 2.3.3. Can it be argued that in 'Adlestrop', too, the contrast between definiteness and indefiniteness is partly used to express the speaker's attitude to different types of elements of the context in which he finds himself? Do any other linguistic features of the text contribute to create an opposition between the first and the second half of the poem (e.g. lexis, sentence structure, enjambment)? For a detailed stylistic analysis of this poem see Short (1996: 94–6).

2. Deixis and discourse situations in poetry

Wilfred Owen's poem 'Dulce et Decorum Est' gives a vivid portrayal of the horrors of war and challenges the traditional idealistic view that dying for one's country is a heroic and honourable choice. To what extent and on what basis can the first-person speaker in the poem be identified with the author? Consider the use of deixis in the poem, focusing particularly on person and time deictics. How do choices of personal pronouns and tense signal changes in the poetic speaker's mode of discourse (i.e. from narration of past events, to report of current experiences, to direct appeal to an addressee)? How do other aspects of the language of the poem highlight the shifts in the speaker's discourse roles? Consider, for example, verse organization and verb phrases. What kind of addressee is implied in the final stanza of the poem? What possible positions are available for individual readers depending on their background, experiences and attitudes to war?

3. Definiteness, deixis and discourse situations in advertising

The method of analysis demonstrated in Part I of this book is particularly relevant to the study of advertisements, since advertising is a genre where the setting up of vivid contexts and discourse situations is often crucial to the achievement of the text producers' goals. Many advertisements aim to evoke particular situations that the target audience will identify with, in order to persuade them that they need to buy the advertised product. Definite articles can be used to achieve an effect of immediacy and involvement by creating a shared background. A further effect of involvement can be created by setting up discourse situations in which the consumer is addressed directly by a personal voice. The use of deixis is crucial here in evoking voices and establishing relationships between addressers and addressees. In studying advertisements, you may want to focus on the kind of issues that I have considered in relation to poetry in Chapters 2 and 3. For example:

- To what extent can the use of definite and indefinite articles in a particular advertisement be explained in terms of notions such as anaphoric reference and the lack/availability of shared knowledge?
- To what extent is the presuppositional value of definiteness exploited to establish referents and contexts whose existence serves the advertisers' goals?
- Is the opposition between definiteness and indefiniteness used to distinguish between foreground and background in a particular context and with what effects?
- Is there an explicit speaking voice and/or a specific addressee?
- What mode of discourse does the speaker engage in?
- Are there any shifts or inconsistencies in the evoked discourse situation?

- What kind of addressee is implied by the language of the advertisement?
- What positions are available to individual interpreters?
- How do choices of articles and deixis interact with choices in other areas of language (and visuals) in order to evoke particular contexts and discourse situations?
- What kind of attitudes and background knowledge does the advertisement rely on?

An excellent and accessible discussion of pronouns in advertising can be found in Myers (1994, chapter 6). See also Cook (1992, chapter 8) for a discussion of voices in advertisements, and Fairclough (1992: 113–17) for an analysis of an advertisement that focuses on contradictions in the setting up of positions for addressers and addressees.

Part II

POETIC TEXT WORLDS AS POSSIBLE WORLDS

Possible-world theory, fiction and literature

4.1 Introduction

Consider the opening of the poem 'Elm' by Sylvia Plath:

I know the bottom, she says. I know it with my great tap root:
It is what you fear.
I do not fear it: I have been there.

Constructing the discourse situation of this poem requires some suspension of disbelief, since we have to accept the fact that the projected text world includes a speaking tree. Imagining worlds that are impossible by the standards of what we call the 'real' world is an activity that we engage in (and enjoy) from childhood onwards. In this and the next chapter I will look at how such fantasy text worlds can be described and classified by drawing on possible-world theory, which, over the last couple of decades, has triggered considerable advances in the study of literary text worlds.

The notion of possible worlds, which was devised by philosophers and logicians to solve a number of problems in logical theory, has been increasingly extended to provide a theoretical base for fundamental issues within the study of fiction. These include the logical properties of sentences of, and about, works of fiction, the ontological status of fictional entities, the definition of fiction, and the nature of the worlds projected by different types of fictional and/or literary texts. In this chapter I will trace the development of possible-world frameworks from philosophical logic through the semantics of fictionality to the description and classification of fictional worlds in general and literary worlds in particular. Following the prevailing trend within literary semantics, I will draw my examples from narrative prose and drama. In the next chapter I will demonstrate how the possible-world framework can be applied to the analysis of poetry, and I will discuss its validity in the light of both theoretical and practical considerations.

4.2 Possible worlds in logic

The idea that the actual world is only one of an infinity of possible worlds was initially adopted by logicians between the late 1950s and the early 1960s, and has since become one of the central tenets of modal logic. The popularity of this notion is due to the fact that it provides a framework within which it is possible to determine the truth-values of propositions beyond the constraints of the actual world, and particularly to define the concepts of possibility and necessity (Loux 1979; Doležel 1979: 194). Within a one-world model, where the actual world represents the only frame of reference, propositions can be classified as true or false, but no satisfactory definition can be given of the modal properties of possible truth, possible falsity, necessary truth and necessary falsity (Bradley and Swartz 1979: 13). Let us consider the following sentences:

(1) Iraq invaded Kuwait in 1990.
(2) Iraq invaded Kuwait in 1989.
(3) Iraq invaded Kuwait in 1990 or it is not the case that Iraq invaded Kuwait in 1990.
(4) Iraq invaded Kuwait in 1990 and it is not the case that Iraq invaded Kuwait in 1990.

The propositions expressed by (1) and (2) can be classified as, respectively, true and false in relation to the actual world.[1] The same can also be said to apply to (3) and (4) respectively, but here the attribution of truth and falsity is not determined by what happens to be the case in the actual world: our intuitions and the laws of logic tell us that (3) is always *necessarily* true and (4) *necessarily* false regardless of the sets of states of affairs they are applied to. By referring to *sets of states of affairs*, however, I have already implicitly moved away from the one-world model with which I had started. Clearly, in order to distinguish between possible and necessary truth, and possible and necessary falsity, we need to refer not just to the actual world but also to sets of hypothetical alternatives to the actual world. Logicians call these alternative sets of states of affairs 'possible worlds'.

It was Leibniz who originally suggested that our actual world is only one of an infinity of possible worlds, and that necessary truth is truth across all possible worlds (Leibniz 1969: 333–4 and throughout; Bradley and Swartz 1979: XV). Although modern logicians do not necessarily share Leibniz's optimistic view that the actual world was chosen as the best of all the possible worlds existing in God's mind, they have developed his basic intuition that modal notions need to be considered within a multiple-world perspective. More precisely, they have adopted as the frame of reference of logical discourse an infinite number of possible alternatives to the actual world, defined as abstract sets of states of affairs where every proposition is either true or false. The modal properties of propositions can therefore be defined as a function of the distribution of their truth-values across the set of all possible worlds: possible truth applies to propositions that are true in at least one possible world, possible falsity to propositions that are false in at least one possible world, necessary truth to propositions that are true in all possible worlds, and necessary falsity to propositions that are false in all possible worlds (Bradley and Swartz 1979: 13–18).

I am now in a position to be more precise about the truth-values of the sentences introduced above. The proposition expressed by (1) is possibly true, since it is true in our actual world, but may be false in some other possible world. Conversely, the proposition expressed by (2) is possibly false, since it is false in our actual world, but may be true in some other possible world. As a disjunction of two logical contradictories, the proposition expressed by (3) is necessarily true, since one of the two disjuncts has to be true in each individual possible world (Bradley and Swartz 1979: 17). As a logical contradiction, the proposition expressed by (4) is necessarily false, since, in order for a world to be regarded as possible, individual propositions cannot be simultaneously true and false (Bradley and Swartz 1979: 4).

The most influential formulation of the possible-world approach to logic is Kripke's 'model structure', which he describes as consisting of a set of objects K, a specific object G belonging to K and a relationship R between the members of K. According to Kripke, the set K can be taken as the set of possible worlds, the privileged member G as the actual world, and R as the relationship of relative possibility or accessibility between the worlds included in the set. The model assigns to each individual proposition a separate truth-value for each possible world, which leads to the kind of approach to the description of modal properties that I introduced above (Kripke 1971: 63–72). The definition that is adopted for the relationship R within each application of the model amounts to a criterion for deciding what types of worlds belong to K, or, in other words, for distinguishing between worlds that count as possible alternatives to G and worlds that do not. Different values of

R will result in different definitions of what is a possible world and what is an impossible one (Pavel 1975, 1986: 44–5; McCawley 1981: 275). Later in this chapter I will show how literary scholars need to consider a very wide range of definitions of 'possibility' in order to account for the many different ways in which fictional worlds may depart from the actual world.

For the purposes of logic, the label 'possible' applies to all those sets of states of affairs which do not break the logical laws of non-contradiction and of the excluded middle (Ronen 1994: 54; Ryan 1991a: 31). The law of non-contradiction states that, given a proposition p (e.g. *Shakespeare was born in 1564*), it is not possible that both p and its opposite *not-p* (e.g. *It is not the case that Shakespeare was born in 1564*) are true in a given world. The law of the excluded middle states that, given a proposition p, either p or its opposite *not-p* must apply in a given world: in other words, the 'middle' option whereby neither p nor *not-p* is true is ruled out. The possible worlds of logic may therefore have a larger or smaller inventory of objects than the actual world (e.g. they may include two moons rotating around the earth, or no moon at all), or they may have the same inventory of objects but different sets of attributes or properties (e.g. they may include a purple Eiffel Tower). Examples of impossible worlds are worlds where the number nine has an even square root, where the circle can be squared (mathematical truths are logically necessary truths), where it is both true and false that the earth has a moon, and so on (Bradley and Swartz 1979: 3–8, 21). The set of logically possible worlds, therefore, embraces worlds that are impossible according to different criteria, such as physical, technological or psychological possibility. A world where animals can talk and people can undertake intergalactic travel is physically and technologically impossible, but still within the boundaries of logical possibility (Bradley and Swartz 1979: 6–7; Maitre 1983: 15).

The attractiveness of the concept of possible worlds for philosophers and logicians goes beyond its applicability to the modal properties of propositions. The possible-world approach has been successfully extended to a wide variety of areas, such as the modal relations between propositions, the working of truth-functional and modal operators, the notions of implications and validity, the truth-values of counterfactuals, and so on (Bradley and Swartz 1979; McCawley 1981: 311ff.; Ryan 1991a: 48ff.). It is claimed, however, that possible worlds are more than a convenient abstraction invented for the benefit of a restricted community of scholars. As

Loux puts it, 'possible worlds are anchored in prephilosophical thinking' (Loux 1979: 62). Imagining unrealized possibilities, considering alternative ways in which things might have been, are common human activities. By developing a theory of possible worlds, therefore, logicians and philosophers have simply formalized for their own purposes notions that are part of the cognitive experiences of all human beings (Bradley and Swartz 1979: 1–2; Loux 1979: 62–3; Rescher 1979: 166).

4.3 Possible worlds and the semantics of fictionality

Fiction-making can be regarded as a prime piece of evidence for the philosopher's claim concerning the wide relevance of possible-world theories. The construction of alternative realities by verbal or visual means is a universal cultural phenomenon, and ordinary people have no difficulties in extending their everyday notions of truth and falsity to the products of such activity. Anybody familiar with Shakespeare's *Othello*, for example, would attribute different truth values to the sentences *Othello killed Desdemona* and *Othello did not kill Desdemona*. Similarly, it is a question of common sense to perceive a difference in the modes of existence of Othello and Desdemona on the one hand, and of the even square root of the number nine on the other. By applying to fiction a rigid one-world frame, traditional logic was unable to accommodate such distinctions. In this section I will show how the notion of possible world has been borrowed by theories of fiction, as Eco puts it, 'in order to reconcile common sense with the rights of alethic logic' (Eco 1990: 64).

4.3.1 Fictional entities and fictional discourse

Early attempts to consider fiction in logical terms resulted in the relegation of discourse about fictional entities to the realm of falsity or to the limbo of neither-truth-nor-falsity. Starting from the assumption that actual existence is the only form of existence and that the actual world provides the only valid 'universe of discourse' (Pavel 1986: 13; Doležel 1989: 222), philosophers treated references to Othello and Emma Bovary in the same way as they treated references to *the King of France* within a twentieth-century context (Levinson 1983: 169ff.). Let us consider the sentences mentioned above:

(5) Othello killed Desdemona.
(6) Othello did not kill Desdemona.

Within traditional logical semantics, both sentences were treated either as false (since they erroneously assume the existence of non-existent individuals), or as neither true nor false (since they refer to imaginary entities with no referents in the actual world) (see Ronen 1994: 35). Such counter-intuitive conclusions result from what Pavel has called a 'segregationist' ontology, which draws a sharp distinction between the domain of the actual on the one hand, and the domain of the non-actual on the other, with no attempt to discriminate between different types of non-actuality (Pavel 1986; Ryan 1991a: 15–16). Within this view, fictional objects lie outside the domain of true discourse, since they belong to the same undifferentiated set of non-actual entities that includes impossible objects such as the square circle and hypothetical individuals such as the present King of France (Doležel 1989: 222; Pavel 1986: 43).

The possible-world model frame, on the other hand, legitimizes the existence of non-actualized possible sets of states of affairs, and extends the application of truth-values to non-actual entities and situations (Pavel 1986: 43–4; Doležel 1988: 482, 1989: 230). Othello can therefore be described as a non-actual individual who inhabits a fictional possible world where he possesses certain specific properties, including that of being the killer of his wife Desdemona. The proposition expressed by the sentence *Othello killed Desdemona* is therefore true in the possible world projected by Shakespeare's play, and possibly true according to the modal system outlined above. The proposition expressed by the sentence *Othello did not kill Desdemona*, on the other hand, is false in the world of Shakespeare's play, and possibly false overall, since it may be true in a different possible world where Iago's plot does not succeed.

A possible-world semantics of fictionality accommodates the existence of fictional entities, and accounts for our intuitive attributions of truth and falsity to sentences about fictional objects and situations. The move away from a one-world segregationist ontology corresponds to a shift in priorities and objectives: the traditional approach was mostly concerned with the logic of non-fictional discourse, and therefore tended to regard fiction as an anomalous and marginal domain; on the other hand, the possible-world approach reflects the need for a framework where fiction can be explored as a central and pervasive cultural phenomenon. As Pavel puts it:

> ... while in dealing with scientific concepts one may feel justified in eliminating nonexistent entities, the poetics of fiction needs a technique for *introducing* such entities. The purpose of the poetics of fiction cannot consist of the purification of language and ontology: on the contrary, poetics must account for unregimented linguistic practices and construct appropriate descriptive models to help us understand what happens when we use fictional statements.
>
> (Pavel 1986: 16, author's italics)

4.3.2 Possible worlds in fiction

The logical notion of possible worlds cannot be mechanically transferred to the semantics of fictionality. In modal logic, possible worlds are abstract alternatives to the actual world postulated for the purposes of performing logical operations. They are complete, insofar as, for every proposition p, either p or *not-p* is true in each individual world (e.g. the proposition expressed by the sentence *Iraq invaded Kuwait in 1990* is either true or false in every possible world); they are comprehensive, insofar as they include all necessarily true propositions (e.g. the proposition expressed by the sentence *There is no even square root of the number nine*); and they are consistent, insofar as they do not contain logical contradictions (Heydrich 1989: 192). These properties do not apply equally to fictional worlds.

The worlds of fiction are the products of the individual or collective imagination, and can be projected by means of a variety of media (verbal, visual, gestural, etc.). In other words, they are cultural and artistic constructs, whose existence depends on the production and interpretation of communicative objects, such as spoken or written texts, pictures, dances, and so on. As a consequence, they differ from the worlds of logic in a number of respects: (i) they are concrete or 'furnished' worlds, in the sense that they deal with specific entities and situations (Doležel 1976a: 12n; Eco 1989: 346–8, 1990: 65–7); (ii) they are 'parasitical' (Eco 1989: 352), i.e. they rely on the receivers' knowledge of the actual world for their interpretation; (iii) they are incomplete, since they do not assign truth-values to all conceivable propositions; (iv) they are not always consistent, i.e. they may include logical contradictions and defy necessary truths. I will now discuss the last three properties in more detail.

Fictional worlds are only partially described in the text or other object by which they are projected. For example, nowhere does Shakespeare's play tell us that Othello possesses two legs; yet, we are likely to agree that the sentence *Othello has only one leg* expresses a false proposition in relation to the world of Shakespeare's play, and that a dramatic production featuring a one-legged Othello is taking liberties with the text (cf. Ryan 1991a: 51). Similarly, we are likely to assume that the London inhabited by Sherlock Holmes is the capital of the United Kingdom whether or not Conan Doyle explicitly tells us that this is the case. In other words, we use our knowledge of reality to fill any relevant gaps in the content of fictional worlds. It is in this sense that fictional worlds are parasitical on the actual world (Eco 1989: 352, 1990: 75; Teleman 1989: 200). In reconstructing the content of fictional worlds, we operate with an underlying assumption that they share the same properties as the actual world unless we are explicitly told otherwise. When we do have to make some adjustments, we still assume that everything else matches the world of our experience (Pavel 1986: 104–5): while allowing for supernatural intervention in the Odyssey, we still expect Ulysses's ship to be subject to the same natural and physical laws as real ships. This phenomenon – which, on careful consideration, can be recognized as a component of interpretative processes in general – has been described by Teleman as the **Principle of Isomorphism** (Teleman 1989: 200) and by Ryan as the **Principle of Minimal Departure** (Ryan 1980: 406, 1991a: 48ff.).

The fact that we can be fairly confident about Othello possessing two legs does not mean that we can assign truth or falsity to *any* proposition in relation to the world of Shakespeare's play. The truth-value of the statement *Othello had nightmares the night before he killed Desdemona*, for example, is destined to remain indeterminate, in the same way as it is impossible to answer the famous question about the number of Lady Macbeth's children (Wolterstoff 1980: 131–4; Pavel 1986: 75, 107). Unlike the worlds of logic, fictional worlds are widely acknowledged to be inherently incomplete (Doležel 1988: 486–7, 1989: 233–4; Eco 1990: 64–82; Maitre 1983: 38; Ronen 1994: 114ff.).[2] As one of the few advocates of the maximal completeness of fictional worlds, Ryan significantly runs into problems when she tries to prevent her Principle of Minimal Departure from introducing computers into the world of 'Jabberwocky', or the writing of Thomas Aquinas into the world of *Little Red Riding Hood* (1991a: 53–4). The parasitical nature of fictional worlds needs to be acknowledged in order to account for the way in which fictional scenarios are constructed in the process of interpretation, but it cannot be stretched to make them into maximal states of affairs where every proposition is either true or false. Completeness is a crucial prerequisite of the possible worlds that are postulated for the purposes of logical calculus, but it is irrelevant and ultimately counterproductive when extended to the culturally determined products of fiction-making.[3]

Finally, the class of fictional worlds is wider than that of the possible worlds of logic, since it includes worlds that are inconsistent, and therefore logically impossible (Wolterstoff 1980: 155–7; Doležel 1989: 238–40; Eco 1990: 75–9; Pavel 1989: 259). Doležel mentions the novel *La Maison de Rendez-vous* by Robbe-Grillet as an example of a world made impossible by a number of internal contradictions: the same place is and is not the setting of the novel, the same event is claimed to have occurred in several different ways, and so on (Doležel 1988: 492–3, 1989: 239–40).[4] A visual counterpart of this type of world is provided by paintings such as Magritte's *Le Blanc-seign*, where a horse-rider is portrayed as simultaneously occupying different positions (or no position at all) in relation to a group of trees in a wood (cf. Eco 1989: 353). In these cases, incoherence performs an aesthetic function, by providing, as Pavel put it, 'a space of dizziness and playful transgression' (Pavel 1989: 259). Clearly, the notion of logical possibility is at the same time too wide and too narrow to account for fictional worlds. It is by exploring and redefining this notion that different classifications of literary text worlds have been proposed. I will therefore return to this topic in 4.6 below.

To conclude, the adoption of a possible-world framework opens up a variety of stimulating possibilities in the semantics of fictionality, but also requires significant readjustments as far as the central concepts are concerned. As I have shown, fictional worlds are quite different from the possible worlds of logic. In the next section I will consider the implications of the possible-world model for the definition of fictionality.

4.3.3 Possible worlds and the definition of fictionality

The notion of possible world has been invoked to remedy some of the shortcomings of the approach to the definition of fictionality proposed, among others, by Searle (1975). Searle points out that the utterances that make up fictional discourses share the same formal properties as non-fictional utterances, but lack the corresponding illocutionary force.[5] Assertions about fictional entities and situations, in particular, do not satisfy the relevant felicity conditions, whereby speakers must sincerely believe in and commit themselves to the truth of their statements in order for the speech act of asserting to be successfully performed (Searle 1969: 66). The essence of fiction, therefore, lies in the suspension of the normal conventions for the performance of illocutionary acts, which results in the production of *pretended* speech acts on the part of fictional authors (Searle 1975; see Ohmann 1971 for a similar argument). A major problem with Searle's proposal lies in his claim that, in practice, works of fiction are made up of a mixture of serious and pretended illocutions, depending on whether or not the author believes them to be true and intends them to be taken as such. This leads to two major difficulties. First of all, authors do not necessarily express their own beliefs in easily identifiable narratorial statements, but may do so in a variety of ways, such as through the voices of characters (Pavel 1986: 25). Secondly, even accepting its practical viability, Searle's suggestion would result in the logical fragmentation of the discourse of novels and in the ontological fragmentation of fictional worlds, whereby some parts of a text world would be fictional and others would not (Ryan 1991a: 65). Fictionality is best regarded as a property of whole texts and worlds, rather than as a feature of individual sentences or entities (Pavel 1986: 42).

In recent years the illocutionary approach to fictionality has been reformulated within a possible-world framework. Wolterstoff (1980) defines fictionality as a particular stance in the action of world-projection that is carried out in communication. Taking inspiration from Sidney's claim that the poet 'nothing affirmeth, and therefore never lieth' (Wolterstoff 1980: 106), Wolterstoff argues that the essence of fiction does not reside in the nature of the projected states of affairs, but in the way in which they are projected. Historians – as well as liars – project worlds in an affirmative mode: they *assert* that certain states of affairs are the case in the actual world. On the other hand,

> . . . the stance characteristic of the fictioneer is that of *presenting*. The fictive stance consists of *presenting or offering for consideration*, certain states of affairs – for us to reflect on, to ponder over, to explore the implications of. . . . It is not necessary to a work of fiction that the states of affairs indicated be false, nor that the author believes them to be false. He may in fact believe them all to be true, and that they may all *be* true. What makes him a fictioneer is that he nothing affirmeth but something presenteth. (Wolterstoff 1980: 233–4)

Ryan (1980, 1984, 1991a, 1991b) provides a more cogent and comprehensive version of this kind of approach. She also argues that fiction is better described as a mode of speaking rather than a mode of being, and proposes to 'characterize the fictional gesture in the framework of modal logic and the semantics of possible worlds' (Ryan 1991a: 16). Ryan starts from the premise that reality has a modal structure, i.e. it consists of a world that is regarded as actual and an infinity of alternate possible worlds. Similarly, she regards fictional worlds as systems of reality where a domain counting as actual is surrounded by a variety of domains that count as non-actual, such as wishes, dreams, fantasies, and so on (see 4.5.1 below). The essence of fiction-making, according to Ryan, lies in an act of 'recentering', whereby the frame of reference for the notions of possibility and actuality is shifted from the actual world to an alternate possible world (Ryan 1984, 1991a/b: 21ff. and throughout). As a consequence,

> ... nonfictional texts describe a system of reality whose center is occupied by the actually actual world; fictional ones refer to a system whose actual world is from an absolute point of view an APW [i.e. alternate possible world]. (Ryan 1991a: 24)

The alternate possible world that acts as the actual world of the fictional universe may of course overlap to different extents with the interpreter's actual world (Ryan 1980: 414ff.).

Fictional recentring, according to Ryan, also involves an act of impersonation on the part of the author, who takes on the identity of a substitute speaker, a *persona*, addressing a substitute hearer within an alternate possible world (Ryan 1980, 1991a: 61–79). This clearly ties in with the idea, discussed in the previous chapter, that in the interpretation of literary texts one cannot, by and large, assume a strict relationship of identity between first-person speakers inside texts and real-life authors. The fictional gesture does not, within this framework, constitute an illocutionary category such as requesting or asserting, but rather 'a meta-speech act, an illocutionary modality, ranging over speech acts' (Ryan 1991a: 67). Although the rules that Ryan specifies in order to determine the range of applicability of the notion of fictionality are not without problems (see Semino 1993), it is undeniable that the idea of recentring captures a prototypical component of the notion of fictionality.

To conclude this section, I would like to consider the question of the attribution of fictionality to texts and worlds from the interpreters' rather than the producers' end. All approaches to the definition of fiction which include an illocutionary element tend to privilege the author's intention in decisions about fictionality. Ryan explicitly claims that fictionality is determined once and for all by the author's intent, which cannot be overruled, as it were, by the way in which individual readers or cultures decide to view a particular text. More specifically, she argues that those who accept the possibility that texts may move in and out of the fictional realm (notably Pavel 1983a, 1986: 79ff.) confuse fictionality with pleasure-orientated reading (Ryan 1991a: 76–8). Although Ryan does acknowledge that fictionality depends in part on the relationship between the readers' actual world and the world presented as actual in the fictional universe, she supports what may be called a top-down approach to the attribution of fictionality (see 6.2 for a detailed discussion of top-down and bottom-up processing in comprehension):

> The question of fictionality is decided neither by the semantic properties of the textual universe nor by the stylistic properties of the text, but is settled a priori as part of our generic expectations. We regard a text as fiction when we know its genre, and we know that its genre is governed by the rules of the fictional game. (Ryan 1991a: 46–7)

In contrast, a bottom-up approach maintains that readers decide that a text projects a fictional world when they come across features that contrast with their own conceptions of actuality (Eco 1979: 20–37; Maitre 1983: 79). I would argue, that, as with comprehension in general, top-down and bottom-up processing are bound to interact with one another. We always approach texts with expectations about their fictional or non-fictional nature, due to our knowledge of different genres, authors, and so on. Such expectations, however, may be reconsidered and revised in the light of the perceived degree of overlap between the world projected by the text and our model of the actual world (see Schmidt 1980).

4.4 Fictionality and literature

Although the preceding section was ostensibly concerned with fictional worlds in general, many of my examples were drawn from works of literature. This is also true of the vast majority of possible-world studies, which tend to focus on literary texts, and particularly on literary narratives (e.g. Doležel 1976a, 1976b, 1979, 1980;

Maitre 1983; Ryan 1991a). The relationship between literature and fiction, however, is seldom considered as an issue in its own right. In some of his recent work, for example, Doležel seems to use the term 'fiction' and 'literature' almost interchangeably:

> The primary purpose of this paper is to incorporate the problem of truth into the framework of *literary* semantics [author's italics], i.e. into an empirical theory of meaning production in *fictional* texts [my italics]. (Doležel 1980: 23)

> In the reception of *fictional* worlds, access is provided through *literary* texts which are read and interpreted by actual readers.
> (Doležel 1988: 485; my italics)

Others explicitly declare that fictionality is an inherent and essential property of literary discourse (Martínez-Bonati 1981: 15, 77 and throughout; Meneses 1991: 291).

This reflects a wider tendency within literary studies, whereby literature is defined in terms of fictionality (see, for example, the quotations in 1.2 above). Widdowson claims that an essential property of literary texts is the projection of alternative realities beyond social and cultural norms (e.g. Widdowson 1975: 47, 1984: 149, 1987, 1992: 24). Schmidt identifies the essence of literariness with two conventions of text production and reception, the Polyvalence Convention and the Aesthetic Convention (Schmidt 1982). The Aesthetic Convention states that in literary communication the accepted model of reality loses its position as the main frame of reference, so that texts are not evaluated on the basis of their practical usefulness or their faithfulness to the actual world, but in terms of other criteria, such as interestingness, originality, novelty, and so on. This results in the construction, through literature, of alternative models of reality (Schmidt 1982: 50–7, 75–80 and throughout, 1984). Schmidt does recognize the need not to confuse literariness and fictionality (Schmidt 1980, 1982: 81 and throughout), but crucially relies on the latter for the definition of the former. Both Widdowson and Schmidt stress that the projection of alternative worlds is ultimately aimed at conveying messages that bear upon what is regarded as the actual world. In particular, both claim that the projection of a different reality plays a crucial role in raising awareness of the fundamental relativity of the norms and conventions that determine people's lives and world-views (Schmidt 1982: 265; Widdowson 1992: 77ff. and throughout).

Although I accept the validity of such claims, I believe that fictionality and literariness need to be considered as separate properties, which, however, show considerable overlap in their specific instantiations. In spite of the fact that literature is not always fictional and fictions are not always literary, it can be argued that fictionality and literariness tend to co-occur in their prototypical realizations. As Ryan puts it:

> it is in conjunction with each other that the properties of 'literariness' and 'fictionality' reach their purest manifestation. A culture with no fiction but a literature appears as unlikely as a culture with fiction but no literature – no texts consumed for the sake of pleasure.
>
> (Ryan 1984: 121)

The literary canon includes, for example, Mary Wollstonecraft's non-fictional essays on women's rights alongside Marlowe's *Doctor Faustus* and Virginia Woolf's *Orlando*. The former, however, are likely to be regarded as less prototypically literary than the latter. Indeed, they originated as part of a non-literary genre and were then incorporated within the body of English literature (see, for example, *The Norton Anthology of English Literature*, Vol. II). On the other hand, the domain of fiction includes a range of non-literary genres, such as jokes and advertisements.

I would therefore argue that a central property of literature is a potential for what Ryan calls 'fictional recentering', and that this potential is often, but not necessarily, realized by individual genres and texts. As a consequence, the notion of possible world as developed within the semantics of fictionality is relevant to the study of literary text worlds, even if some of these worlds are intended as factual representations of the actual world and need to be treated as such. The main contribution of possible-world theory to literary semantics has been to provide a framework for the description of the worlds projected by different types of literary texts and genres, particularly on the basis of their relationship with what is taken to be the world of empirical reality. The literary bias of the models that have been proposed for the description and classification of fictional worlds can in fact be explained in the light of the wide variety of worlds that can be projected by texts included within the boundaries of literature. It is to an overview of such models that I will devote the rest of this chapter. Although I will continue to use primarily the general term 'fictional' worlds, I will focus more specifically on issues that are relevant to the study of literary text worlds.

4.5 Possible-world approaches to the description of fictional worlds

Possible-world models can account not only for the relationship of fictional worlds to the actual world, but also for the internal structure of the worlds of fiction. In this section I will firstly consider a possible-world approach to the description of fictional worlds, and then refine the notion of impossibility in relation to fiction and literature.

4.5.1 The internal structure of fictional worlds

Fictional worlds may consist of a single ontological domain governed by a single set of laws, or may be divided into several domains, governed by separate sets of laws (Pavel 1980, 1986: 54–64; Doležel 1988, 1989; Ryan 1985, 1991a: 40–3, 1991b). The first group includes homogeneous worlds such as those of realistic novels and traditional fairy tales. In realistic novels, the domain that is taken as actual is governed by the same laws that apply to the world of reality. In fairy tales, the actual domain includes entities and phenomena that break the laws of nature (such as fairies, articulate animals, and magical transformations), but there is no separation between the natural and the supernatural spheres: Cinderella inhabits the same sphere as her fairy godmother and is a direct witness to the transformation of the pumpkin into a coach (Ryan 1985: 721–2). The second group includes heterogeneous world structures, such as those of myth and medieval mystery plays, where the domain of the actual consists of two separate spheres, namely the supernatural or sacred sphere on the one hand, and the natural or profane sphere on the other. Although contact between the two spheres is possible, they are separated by relatively well-defined boundaries: Ulysses cannot converse with Neptune in the same way that Cinderella can converse with the fairy (Doležel 1989: 234–5; Ryan 1991a: 40–1).

Pavel refers to such divided ontologies as 'salient' structures, and points out that this notion is particularly relevant to the study of literary text worlds (Pavel 1986: 58, 61). A contemporary example is provided by the play *Top Girls* by Caryl Churchill. The play opens with a group of women having a meal in a restaurant. The group includes the nineteenth-century traveller Isabella Bird, the thirteenth-century Japanese courtesan Lady Nijo, the ninth-century woman Pope Joan, and two guests from other fictional worlds, namely Chaucer's Griselda and Griet, who appears in the painting *Dulle Griet* by Brueghel. The meal takes place in the twentieth-century and is organized by Marlene, a twentieth-century career woman. Marlene is the link between the chronologically and ontologically impossible world of the first scene, and the realistic world of the second part of the play, which is concerned with the lives of a group of contemporary women. Apart from Marlene's presence in both, however, the two domains are totally separate for the purposes of the plot, although the audience is, of course, invited to draw parallels between the two sets of characters (who were played by the same actresses in the first performance of the play; see Churchill (1982)).

Fictional worlds are therefore better seen as universes made up of one or more worlds, or subworlds. This is not only relevant to split ontologies like the ones discussed so far, but applies much more generally. Most fictional worlds, and especially the ones that are projected by narrative texts, can be described as possessing a modal structure, with one world functioning as actual, and a variety of possible worlds functioning as non-actualized alternatives of the actual domain (Pavel 1986: 64; Ryan 1985: 719, 1991a: 109). Such non-actualized alternatives are represented by the beliefs, wishes, intentions and fantasies of the characters that populate the actual domain.[6] Ryan (1985, 1991a: 109ff.) provides the following catalogue of types of alternative possible worlds that may be included within a fictional universe (besides the domain that is taken as actual):

(a) **Epistemic** or **Knowledge Worlds**, represented by what characters know or believe to be the case in the actual domain;
(b) **Hypothetical Extensions of Knowledge Worlds**, represented by the characters' hypotheses about future developments in the actual domain;
(c) **Intention Worlds**, represented by the characters' plans to cause changes in the actual domain;
(d) **Wish Worlds**, represented by alternative states of the actual domain that are desirable or undesirable for a particular character or group;
(e) **Obligation Worlds**, represented by alternative states of the actual domain that are good or bad according to the moral principles of a certain character or group;
(f) **Alternate** or **Fantasy Universes**, represented by the characters'

dreams, fantasies, hallucinations, or by the fictions composed by the characters themselves.

The alternative worlds that are included in a fictional universe may stand in a variety of relationships with each other and with the domain functioning as actual. When there is a perfect corres- pondence between the actual domain and all subworlds within the fictional universe, the situation may be described as one of equilibrium: everybody has complete knowledge of the actual domain, everybody's wishes are realized, all moral obligations are fulfilled, and so on (Ryan 1985: 733, 1991a: 120). When the cor- respondence is less than perfect, the situation is one of conflict, which is likely to lead to some action being taken on the part of one or more characters. Ryan identifies different types of conflict that may arise within a fictional universe (Ryan 1985: 732–6, 1991a: 119–23). There may be conflict between the actual domain and the private worlds of characters. In *Moby Dick*, for example, there is a conflict between the actual domain, where Moby Dick is alive, and Captain Ahab's wish world, where Moby Dick is dead and Ahab has had his revenge against the whale who has devoured his leg. At the end of *Romeo and Juliet*, Romeo kills himself as a result of a mismatch between his knowledge world, where Juliet is dead, and the actual domain, where Juliet is in a state of deep sleep. There may be conflict between the private worlds of an individual character: in *Crime and Punishment* the satisfaction of Raskolnikov's wishes conflicts with the rules imposed by his obligation world. There may even be conflict inside a character's private world, when characters have, for example, inconsistent desires or contra- dictory moral laws: Hamlet's indecision can be seen as the result of his inability to define the boundaries of his obligation world (i.e. what he is morally obliged to do) in the light of what he has discovered about the actual domain (i.e. that his father has been murdered). Finally, there may be conflict between the private worlds of different characters: in the novel *I Promessi Sposi* (*The Betrothed*), by the nineteenth-century Italian author Alessandro Manzoni, there is a contrast between the joint wish worlds of the two main characters, Renzo and Lucia, who want to get married, and the wish world of a local nobleman, who wants Lucia for himself and consequently tries to prevent the marriage.

My discussion so far has been based on a tacit assumption that it is possible to distinguish between what counts as 'actual' within a fictional universe and what counts as 'non-actual'. This is the case where there is an authoritative voice (e.g. a third-person narrator) who describes the actual domain, and less authoritative voices (e.g. characters), who describe the content of their own private worlds. Doležel argues that, depending on the source of the relevant narrative statements, different states of affairs may carry different degrees of 'authentication' within a fictional universe, i.e. they may be regarded as more or less true of the actual domain (Doležel 1980).[7] In third-person omniscient narration, such as in Cervantes's *Don Quixote*, it is possible to distinguish between authenticated and non-authenticated states of affairs: the existence of wind-mills is authentic in the actual domain, whereas the giants only exist in Don Quixote's imagination (Doležel 1980: 11–15). Conversely, in non-omniscient third-person narration or, even more, in first-person narration it is not always possible to determine what belongs to the actual domain and what to the private worlds of the characters (Doležel 1980: 17–20). The first-person narrator in Ken Kesey's *One Flew Over the Cuckoo's Nest*, for example, is not totally reliable (he is a patient in a lunatic asylum), so that readers cannot always decide what is and is not the case in the actual domain of the story.

Literature provides more extreme examples of problematic authentication in the construction of fictional universes. In William Faulkner's *As I Lay Dying*, the role of narrator is occupied alternatively by several different characters in the story. Readers therefore have no privileged access to the actual domain, but can only partially reconstruct it by combining the knowledge worlds of the characters/narrators. A similar situation occurs in Julian Barnes's *Talking it Over*, where the participants in a love triangle take turns in giving their version of events to an anonymous interviewer. In cases such as these, although authentication is partially impeded, it is not totally blocked. The blocking of authentication results in the creation of indeterminate worlds.

4.5.2 Authentication, indeterminacy and impossibility

According to Doležel, fictional existence depends on authentication: a non-actualized possible entity becomes a fictional existent when its membership in a particular fictional universe is established by a reliable voice. Different modes of fictional existence result from different degrees of authoritativeness of the authenticating source (Doležel 1989: 237). As Ronen puts it:

Variations of authority produce a fictional world whose structure is fundamentally modal, containing sets of fictional facts alongside sets of relativized elements attributed to the characters' knowledge, beliefs, thoughts, predictions. (Ronen 1994: 176)

Doležel points out, however, that some developments in contemporary literature have radically questioned the authenticating norm and have produced fictional worlds without authentication (Doležel 1980: 20–4, 1988: 491–3, 1989: 238–40). How can this be achieved, and what is the nature of these worlds?

Authentication can be blocked, first of all, by means of what Doležel describes as a kind of pragmatic failure. This occurs when the act of authentication is 'self-voiding', i.e. it is not performed seriously. Doležel borrows this notion from Austin's theory of speech acts, where:

> ... a performative utterance is said to be self-voiding if it is 'abused', if, for example, it is issued 'insincerely' (Austin 1971: 14f.). Just as the breach of felicity conditions does, self-voiding deprives the speech act of its performative force. (Doležel 1989: 238)

Examples of self-voiding texts are provided by Russian *skaz* narratives, where narrators take an ironic attitude towards their own authenticating authority, and tend to shift from first- to third-person narration and from omniscient narration to explicit declarations of their own lack of omniscience (Doležel 1980: 22, 1989: 238). Postmodernist authors such as John Fowles also produce self-voiding texts: the disclosure of the fictitious nature of literary and narrative conventions in novels such as *The French Lieutenant's Woman* undermines the narrator's authenticating authority (Doležel 1988: 491, 1989: 238). The worlds projected by self-voiding texts are indeterminate, insofar as:

> On the one hand, possible entities seem to be brought into fictional existence since conventional authentication procedures are applied; on the other hand, the status of this existence is made dubious because the very foundation of the authenticating mechanism is undermined. Ultimately, it is impossible to decide what exists and what does not exist in the fictional worlds constructed by self-voiding narratives.
> (Doležel 1989: 238)

Authentication can also be blocked by means of what Doležel describes as a semantic strategy. This occurs when an apparently reliable and 'serious' narrator gives contradictory accounts of what is the case in the fictional world. As an example, Doležel mentions the story 'Roads of Destiny' by O. Henry, where three different and equally 'authentic' versions are given of the protagonist's death. In this case, the fictional world violates the law of non-contradiction by including all three versions, and is therefore logically imposs- ible. Such impossible worlds prevent the authentication of fictional existence because of their own logico-semantic structure. As a consequence, Doležel argues, logically impossible worlds cannot be made fictionally authentic (Doležel 1988: 492, 1989: 238–9; see also McHale 1987: 33–4).

A similar strategy in the creation of an impossible world is dis- cussed by Eco in reference to the story *Un Drame Bien Parisien* by Alfonse Allais. Eco shows how, as the story unfolds, the reader is led to imagine a fictional world that is then proved to be inaccess- ible from the domain that is presented as actual. At the same time, however, this world is reintroduced within the actual domain by having the two main characters behave as if they too had shared the readers' erroneous expectations. The world projected by the story is therefore revealed as logically impossible (Eco 1979: 240ff.). Drawing on Doležel's claim that impossible worlds cannot be made authentic, Eco argues that such worlds can be *mentioned* but can- not be *constructed* (Eco 1990: 76). In other words, we can say that a certain fictional world contains a long-haired bald man or a square circle, but we cannot actually conceive of such a world (in the same way as we cannot conceive, for example, of the worlds of Escher's drawings). Such violations of the laws of logic have been particularly associated with postmodernist writing, where 'imposs- ibilities, in the logical sense, have become a central poetic device' (Ronen 1994: 55). I will return to the difficulties posed by post- modernist poetry in the next chapter.

What is required of the interpreters of impossible worlds is, to borrow Eco's wording, 'flexibility and superficiality' (Eco 1990: 76). This applies not just to the interpretation of logically imposs- ible worlds, but of worlds displaying other types of impossibility, such as worlds that break natural laws. When we read *Little Red Riding Hood*, for example, we accept the existence of a talking wolf without attempting to rewrite the course of evolution or to con- sider the brain structure of that particular animal (Eco 1990: 76). Our enjoyment of worlds that contain impossible elements is de- pendent, as Maitre puts it, on a tendency to focus on intelligible features and to ignore unintelligible ones (Maitre 1983: 17, 72–3). The reason why that comes so naturally probably lies in the fact that we adopt a similar attitude to many phenomena in the actual world. In the same way as I can interact with a computer on a daily basis without really understanding (or asking myself) how it works, so I can follow Orlando's sex changes and survival across the centuries in Virginia Woolf's novel without considering the implications for the character's biology.

4.6 Possible-world approaches to the classification of fictional worlds: an overview of typologies

A number of typologies of fictional worlds have been developed within the framework of possible worlds. In this section I will introduce three of these classifications, which are at the same time representative of the work that has been done in this area and relevant to the purposes of this book. They were proposed respectively by Doležel (1976a, 1976b), Maitre (1983) and Ryan (1991a, 1991b).

4.6.1 Doležel's typology of narrative fictional worlds

At the end of the 1970s, Doležel developed a theory of narrative semantics based on the idea that it is possible to isolate a limited set of basic macro-constraints that underlie the formation of stories. He identified such global story-forming constraints as the four modal systems of deontic, axiological, epistemic and alethic modality (Doležel 1976a, 1976b). The deontic system consists of the concepts of permission, obligation and necessity; the axiological system consists of the concepts of goodness, badness and indifference; the epistemic system consists of the concepts of knowledge, ignorance and belief; the alethic system consists of the concepts of possibility, impossibility and necessity (Doležel 1976a: 7). Doležel coined the term 'atomic' stories for those stories that are formed under the constraints of a single modal system. Atomic stories can be regarded as the basic structures of narrative. 'Molecular' stories, on the other hand, consist of more complex sequences made up of more than one atomic story, and are therefore based on more than one modal system (Doležel 1976a: 7, 1976b: 144).

Atomic stories are classified on the basis of the modal system by which they are governed. Doležel therefore distinguishes between deontic, axiological, epistemic and alethic stories. Deontic stories project worlds governed by rules of prohibition and obligation.

This leads to two basic narrative sequences: prohibition–violation–punishment, when somebody carries out a prohibited action; obligation–fulfilment–reward, when somebody performs a task that has been required of them. Axiological stories project worlds characterized by the degree of desirability that different narrative agents attribute to entities and states of affairs. The prototypical structure of an axiological story is lack–acquisition–possession. This amounts to the classical 'quest' narrative, where a character (the hero) pursues a desired object. The sequence is often complicated by a conflict of interests with another character (the villain) who has to be defeated in order for the quest to be successful. Epistemic stories project worlds that are built around some knowledge gap that needs to be filled. Prototypical epistemic stories are 'mystery' or detective stories involving a transition from ignorance or erroneous belief into knowledge. Finally, alethic stories project worlds that are governed by different laws of possibility from the actual world, i.e. alternative possible worlds. This category includes, for example, fantastic stories, where the laws of physical possibility are broken, and science-fiction stories, which feature objects and activities that are technologically impossible relative to the stage of development of the world in which they are produced. Doležel points out that this classification of narrative worlds is in fact open-ended, since further modalities can be added to the system (Doležel 1976a: 8–12; Weber 1992: 15–17).

Doležel's aim in constructing this typology was to arrive at a model that could account for existing stories and also be used as an algorithm to generate new ones (Doležel 1976a: 9, 1976b: 145ff.). Although nowadays such an enterprise is not as fashionable as it was a few decades ago, Doležel's system has often been applied to the description of the internal structure of fictional universes. Ryan's notions of knowledge worlds, wish worlds, obligation worlds and fantasy worlds introduced earlier draw on Doležel's suggestion that the systems of epistemic, axiological, deontic and alethic modality can act as basic world-building constraints (Ryan 1991a: 111). Weber (1992) uses the notions of deontic, axiological and epistemic modality to describe the ideological distance between the world-views of different characters in novels. Dickens's *Hard Times*, for example, can be interpreted as a conflict between the deontic world of obligation championed by Gradgrind, and the axiological world of Sissy, Stephen and Rachel, which is based on the values of goodness and badness in relation to the individual and the community (Weber 1992: 107–19).

4.6.2 Maitre's typology of fictional worlds in novelistic literature

Maitre's main aim in her book *Literature and Possible Worlds* is to 'allow a place for "possible-world analysis" alongside more established approaches' to the study of literature (Maitre 1983: 9). For reasons of space, the book excludes poetry and drama, and focuses exclusively on novels (Maitre 1983: 10–11). Maitre provides two separate but partially overlapping categorizations of fictional worlds. She starts from a typology of the 'possible worlds of fantasy' (Maitre 1983: 65), and then moves on to a wider categorization of fictional worlds in general. In giving an overview of Maitre's framework, I will follow the same order.

Under the label 'fantasy', Maitre subsumes two types of possible non-actual worlds: those that could never be actual on the one hand, and those which are highly unlikely ever to be actual on the other. The first category prototypically includes the worlds of Fairy Stories and Ghost Stories, which feature physically impossible phenomena such as articulate animals, magical metamorphoses and supernatural interventions.[8] The second category includes Science Fiction and Escapist Fiction, which feature situations and events that are not straightforwardly impossible, but rather highly improbable. The presence of intergalactic travel and of highly intelligent robots in science-fiction novels results in the projection of worlds that are impossible in the present state of technological development, but not in an absolute sense. In the same way, Maitre argues, escapist novels include occurrences that '*strain* but do not *break* the physical laws of the actual world' (Maitre 1983: 69). She refers, in particular, to the far-fetched enterprises carried out in James Bond novels, and to the improbable love stories narrated in romantic fiction (Maitre 1983: 68–72).

As far as fictional worlds in general are concerned, Maitre's typology involves:

> . . . four very general categories into which fictional works seem to fall in terms of their approximation or otherwise of their fictional worlds to the actual world; that is I move from those works which are closest to the actual world in the sense of relating fairly specifically to actual historical events, to those which self-evidently could never be states of affairs of the actual world. (Maitre 1983: 79)

Because of Maitre's decision to exemplify her categories by referring to relatively little-known novels (Maitre 1983: 10), I will use my own examples. The first category includes works which give accounts of or make references to actual historical events (Maitre 1983: 79, 81–9). Historical novels, such as Tolstoy's *War and Peace* are prototypical members of this class. The second category includes works dealing with states of affairs, that, although imaginary, could conceivably be actual. Maitre's criterion here seems to be a general notion of verisimilitude, encompassing not just physical laws, but also the psychological generalizations that underlie people's judgements of what constitutes 'normal' and 'abnormal' behaviour (Maitre 1983: 79, 89–96). David Lodge's novels may be taken as representatives of this class. The works belonging to the third category project worlds that lie on the borderline between what could be actual and what could never be actual. They involve ambiguities as to whether the causes for some of the narrated events are natural or supernatural (Maitre 1983: 79, 96–111). James's story *The Turn of the Screw* presumably falls here, considering that no final decision can be made regarding the existence of the ghosts. Finally, Maitre's fourth category includes works whose worlds could never be actual, and therefore corresponds to the first type of fantastic literature mentioned above (Maitre 1983: 80, 111–13).

Maitre's framework can be seen as an attempt to deal with fictional worlds in terms of a scale from a high degree of overlap with the actual world to outright impossibility. Although she does not take into account the fact that the notions of actuality and verisimilitude are also a matter of degree, Maitre interestingly relates her categories to the readers' interpretative strategies. She argues that, when interpreting works belonging to the first category, readers are invited to engage in frequent cross-referencing between the fictional world and the actual world, and to import large amounts of their knowledge of reality into the construction of the fictional world (Maitre 1983: 81). As one moves away towards the impossible end of the scale, however, such cross-referencing and gap-filling become increasingly less adequate. Pavel also observes that works of fiction vary in their 'permeability with respect to extra-textual information' (Pavel 1986: 101) depending on their degree of overlap with what is taken as actual. This same notion is brought up by Ryan in an attempt to link the applicability of her Principle of Minimal Departure to the degree of resemblance between fictional worlds and the actual world (Ryan 1991a: 57–8). What is lacking from all frameworks is a more accurate account of the way in which readers perceive the distance between fictional worlds and their models of reality during text processing. I will return to this issue in Part III, where I approach text worlds as mental constructs arising in the interplay between the text and the reader's background knowledge.

4.6.3 Ryan's typology of fictional worlds in relation to genre

In her attempt to develop a typology of fictional worlds that can be relevant to a theory of genres, Ryan starts by reconsidering the notion of possibility. Clearly, the logical interpretation of possibility is too general to account for the differences between the worlds associated with different genres. On the one hand, the category of logically possible worlds subsumes very different types of worlds, including the worlds of realistic novels, the worlds of fairy tales, the worlds of science fiction, and so on. On the other hand, as I have shown, the class of fictional worlds is wider than that of logically possible worlds, since fictional worlds may include logical impossibilities. Starting from Kripke's premise that possibility means accessibility from the world at the centre of a given system, Ryan develops a catalogue of the types of accessibility relations that link the actual world to the worlds projected by texts belonging to different genres (Ryan 1991a: 32, 1991b: 553–4). An extended quotation is the best way to do justice to Ryan's framework [AW stands for 'actual world' and TAW for 'textual actual world']:

> In decreasing order of stringency, the relevant types of accessibility relations from AW involved in the construction of TAW include the following:
>
> (A) *Identity of properties* (abbreviated A/properties): TAW is accessible from AW if the objects common to TAW and AW have the same properties.
>
> (B) *Identity of inventory* (B/same inventory): TAW is accessible from AW if TAW and AW are furnished by the same objects.
>
> (C) *Compatibility of inventory* (C/expanded inventory): TAW is accessible from AW if TAW includes all the members of AW, as well as some native members.
>
> (D) *Chronological compatibility* (D/chronology): TAW is accessible from AW if it takes no temporal relocation for a member of AW to contemplate the entire history of TAW. (This condition means that TAW is no older than AW, i.e. that its present is not posterior in absolute time to AW's present. We can contemplate facts of the past from the viewpoint of the present, but since the future holds no facts,

only projections, it takes a relocation beyond the time to regard as facts events located in the future.)

(E) *Physical compatibility* (E/natural laws): TAW is accessible from AW if they share natural laws.

(F) *Taxonomic compatibility* (F/taxonomy): TAW is accessible from AW if both worlds contain the same species, and the species are characterized by the same properties. Within F, it may be useful to distinguish a narrower version F' stipulating that TAW must contain not only the same inventory of natural species, but also the same type of manufactured objects as found in AW up to the present.

(G) *Logical compatibility* (G/logic): TAW is accessible from AW if both worlds respect the principles of non-contradiction and of excluded middle.

(H) *Analytical compatibility* (H/analytical): TAW is accessible from AW if they share analytical truths, i.e. if objects designated by the same words share the same essential properties.

(I) *Linguistic compatibility* (I/linguistic): TAW is accessible from AW if the language in which TAW is described can be understood in AW.

(Ryan 1991a: 32–3, author's italics)

At the top end of the list, the framework accounts for non-fictional genres, whose worlds respect the first two principles, A/properties and B/same inventory, which, in turn, entail all the other relationships. In this case, TAW is identical with AW. In the genre of 'true fiction', on the other hand, either A/same properties or B/same inventory is relaxed. In Plato's dialogues, for example, the characters are historical figures but the conversations in which they engage are imaginary. In historical and realistic novels, A/same properties holds, but C/expanded inventory replaces B/same inventory. Both *War and Peace* and Conan Doyle's Sherlock Holmes stories give accurate accounts of historical events and geographical locations, but they also include imaginary entities and situations (Ryan 1991a: 33–6, 1991b: 561–3).

The relaxation of C/expanded inventory results in worlds such as Kafka's *The Castle*, which feature the same laws of nature, species and objects as the actual world, but no shared individuals, locations or events. As a result, Ryan argues, no cross-referencing is possible between the people and places of TAW and those of AW: these worlds are described as being 'located in a geographic and historical no-man's-land' (Ryan 1991a: 36). Science-fiction worlds, on the other hand, not only break D/chronology but also the narrow version of F/taxonomy: they usually contain the same natural species as AW, but a different range of manufactured objects. If space travel in a science-fiction novel leads to the discovery of new planets with new forms of life, however, the whole of F/taxonomy is violated. If E/physical compatibility and F/taxonomy are both lifted, we get the worlds of fairy stories, which include witches and unicorns as well as talking animals and magical transformations. The relaxation of the relations G/logic and H/analytical obviously leads to the types of worlds that have been described as logically impossible in the preceding discussion. In particular, lifting G/logic results in worlds including contradictory states of affairs (e.g. a character is simultaneously dead and alive), while lifting H/analytical leads to worlds including married bachelors and colourless green ideas. These worlds are characteristic, for example, of nonsense verse. Finally, the relation I/linguistic is severed in the world of rhymes such as *Jabberwocky*, or, more dramatically, in sound poetry, where the lack of linguistic overlap with AW leads to the disappearance of the text world itself (Ryan 1991a: 36–9, 1991b: 563–6). I will return to these distinctions in the next chapter, where I will apply them to the description of the worlds of different types of poetry.

The main strength of Ryan's framework is that it treats possibility as a graded notion, which accounts for the differences between the possible worlds of different fictional genres. Although her list of accessibility relations cannot in itself result in a comprehensive theory of genre (Ryan does in fact try to complement it by adding some additional factors (Ryan 1991a: 43–4)), her typology of fictional worlds is both detailed and, as I will show in the next chapter, amenable to application in text analysis. What problems it raises are in fact inherent in the possible-world approach itself. These will be briefly introduced below, and will be discussed in more detail in the following chapters.

4.7 A preliminary critique of possible-world approaches

Possible-world theories provide a comprehensive and stimulating framework for the study of literary text worlds. However, a number of shortcomings have started to emerge in the course of the preceding discussion:

(a) The notion of 'actual world'. While logicians can afford to take the concept of actuality as a fixed and unproblematic notion, those dealing with cultural phenomena such as fiction and literature are less justified in doing so. What is taken as 'actual' is not an absolute notion, but is dependent on historical, cultural and ideological factors. This has ramifications for the border between reality and fiction, and for the degree of fictionality that is attributed to individual worlds.

(b) The relationship between fiction and non-fiction. While these notions can be separated in theory, in practice they tend to shade into one another in many different ways. One only has to think of television audiences' attitudes to the characters of soap operas, or of the ambivalent status of the stories presented as part of political propaganda. More specifically, possible-world theorists point out that fantastic worlds can be used to comment directly on the actual world (think of Aesop's fables, for example), but they do not account for the way in which we relate fantastic characters and events to the world that we regard as actual. I will return to this issue in Chapter 6.

(c) Fictional worlds as the result of text processing. Because of their origin in logic, possible-world frameworks are not concerned with the cognitive processes whereby interpreters arrive at the construction of text worlds by interacting with the language of texts. They therefore need to be complemented by linguistic and cognitive approaches to the construction of text worlds, such as the one proposed in Part III of this book.

NOTES

[1] In the next chapter I will consider the ideological factors involved in assigning truth-values to propositions. For the purposes of the present chapter, I will follow possible-world theorists in largely ignoring the relative nature of the notion of 'actual' world.

[2] The notion of incompleteness corresponds to Ingarden's claim that the objects represented in literary works inevitably present 'gaps' or 'spots of indeterminacy' (Ingarden 1973: 246–54; see also Iser 1978: 170–9; McHale 1987: 30–3):

> If, e.g. a story begins with the sentence: 'An old man was sitting at a table', etc. it is clear that the represented table is indeed a table and not, for example, a 'chair'; but whether it is made of wood or iron, is four-legged or three-legged, etc. is left quite unsaid and therefore – this being a purely intentional object – *not determined*. The material of its composition is altogether unqualified, although it must be some material. Thus, in the given object, its qualification is *totally absent*: there is an 'empty' spot here, a 'spot of indeterminacy'.
>
> (Ingarden 1973: 249; author's italics)

[3] It could be argued that the notion of incompleteness also applies to the actual world, since the truth-value of sentences such as *Napoleon intended to flee from St Helena* is destined to remain undetermined. There is, however, an important difference. Fictional worlds are *ontologically* incomplete:

there is and never has been an answer to the question about the number of Lady Macbeth's children. The actual world, on the other hand, is *epistemologically* incomplete: the truth-value of the sentence *Napoleon intended to flee from St Helena* may be impossible to determine for us, but would have been obvious to Napoleon and anybody familiar with his intentions (see Ingarden 1973: 246–54; McHale 1987: 31).

[4] Talking about this novel, McHale observes that:

> the projected world is completely destabilized. Here there is no identifiable center of consciousness through which we may attempt to recuperate the text's paradoxical changes of level and other inconsistencies. (McHale 1987: 14)

Insofar as it centres around ontological issues, *La Maison de Rendez-vous* represents for McHale an 'exemplary postmodernist novel' (McHale 1987: 15). I will return to the problems posed by the worlds of postmodernist literature in the next chapter.

[5] The illocutionary force of an utterance can be defined as the act that the speaker performs by producing that utterance. So, for example, the utterance *I'll see you outside* may, depending on the context, have the illocutionary force of a promise, a warning, a threat, and so on. In order for a particular type of illocutionary act to be performed successfully, it has to fulfil a set of requirements known as felicity conditions. A promise, for example, needs to involve something that is beneficial to the addressee and that the speaker can and wants to do (see Austin 1962; Searle 1969).

[6] As Ronen points out, the fact that the worlds of fiction may, and often do, possess a modal structure constitutes another distinguishing feature of fictional worlds as opposed to the possible worlds of logic (Ronen 1994: 8–9).

[7] It can be argued that the distinction between more or less authoritative world versions also applies to what we regard as the actual world. Ronen puts it thus:

> The cultural effects of more or less authoritative versions of the fictional world (presented by an omniscient narrator, by an unreliable narrator, and so forth) are analogous to gradations of authority revealed when we compare the reality-version of a scientist or a logician to that of a sham or a politican.
>
> (Ronen 1994: 175–6)

[8] Maitre's classification seems to take it for granted that events such as the interventions of the dead in the world of the living are unanimously regarded as impossible. It is important to recognize, however, that such beliefs and assumptions are not universally shared.

5

Possible-world theory and the analysis of poetic text worlds

5.1 Introduction

By and large, poetry has been neglected within possible-world approaches to the study of fiction. Poems do tend to be mentioned among the types of texts that fall within the scope of a possible-world semantics of fictionality (e.g. Doležel 1989: 235–6; Wolterstoff 1980: 108; Maitre 1983: 10), but they are rarely selected as the object of analysis (see Meneses 1991 for an exception). The main reason for this neglect can be identified in the closeness of the link between possible-world approaches to fiction and narrative analysis, which leads to privileged attention being devoted to texts with a strong narrative element, such as stories and novels. In fact, some possible-world theorists have gone as far as arguing that, unlike prose fiction and drama, poetry does not involve the projection of fictional worlds, but rather the expression of moods, themes and atmospheres, which are not amenable to possible-world analysis. In such cases it is lyric poetry in particular that is singled out as the mode of literary discourse that falls outside the boundaries of fictionality (Ryan 1991a: 83–7).[1]

In this chapter I will demonstrate the relevance of possible-world frameworks to the study of poetic text worlds. In particular, I will adopt a possible-world perspective in order to consider:

(i)   the internal structure of the world projected by a particular poem;
(ii) the projection of deviant discourse situations;
(iii) the description of different types of poetic text worlds.

The extension of possible-world models to the analysis of poetry is not simply a matter of practical expediency. On the contrary; it is theoretically unsatisfactory to limit the applicability of analytical concepts and frameworks to some literary genres and to exclude others. Ryan, for example, suggests that narrative and nonsense poetry are fictional genres that can be approached in possible-world terms alongside stories and novels, while lyric poetry is nonfictional and cannot be analysed in the same way (Ryan 1991a: 37–9; 83–7). This results in the imposition of an awkward onto-logical and descriptive boundary within the limits of a single overarching genre. More positively, it is difficult to see why poetry, like novelistic prose, cannot be regarded as displaying a wide range of relationships between text worlds and actuality, from a high to a low degree of overlap. Saying that poems may project fictional worlds does not imply that Wordsworth's 'I Wandered Lonely as a Cloud' cannot be treated as a representation of an autobio-graphical experience, in the same way as the fictionality of Orwell's *1984* does not detract from the claims to historical accuracy of Balzac's novels. As Leech (1969: 196) has argued:

> . . . it would be more accurate to say, not that all poems are fictitious, but that they leave the choice between fact and fiction open.

In individual cases, a variety of factors to do with the text, the world it projects, the poetic genre it belongs to, the availability of historical or biographical information, and so on, may lead the reader to make a more definite decision in one direction or the other.

5.2 Complex modal structures in poetry

In the previous chapter I began to show how fictional worlds may possess complex modal structures, in which an 'actual' domain is surrounded by a number of alternative subworlds corresponding to the characters' beliefs, wishes, moral obligations, dreams, hypo-theses, fantasies and so on. I also pointed out that such unrealized alternatives to the actual domain can be related to the systems of epistemic, deontic, axiological and alethic modality (Doležel 1976a, 1976b; Ryan 1985, 1991a). I will now show how these notions can be applied to the analysis of non-narrative worlds, such as that projected by the following poem by Andrew Marvell.

TO HIS COY MISTRESS

Had we but world enough, and time,
This coyness, Lady were no crime.
We would sit down, and think which way
To walk and pass our long love's day.
Thou by the Indian Ganges' side

Should rubies find; I by the tide
Of Humber would complain. I would
Love you ten years before the Flood;
And you should, if you please, refuse
Till the conversion of the Jews.   10
My vegetable love should grow
Vaster than empires, and more slow.
An hundred years should go to praise
Thine eyes, and on thy forehead gaze;
Two hundred years to adore each breast,
But thirty thousand to the rest.
An age at least to every part,
And the last age should show your heart.
For, Lady, you deserve this state,
Nor would I love at lower rate.   20
    But at my back I always hear
Time's winged chariot hurrying near;
And yonder all before us lie
Deserts of vast eternity.
Thy beauty shall no more be found,
Nor, in thy marble vault, shall sound
My echoing song: then worms shall try
That long preserved virginity:
And your quaint honour turn to dust,
And into ashes all my lust: 30
The grave's a fine and private place,
But none, I think, do there embrace.
    Now, therefore, while the youthful hue
Sits on thy skin like morning dew,
And while thy willing soul transpires
At every pore with instant fires,
Now let us sport us while we may;
And now, like amorous birds of prey,
Rather at once our time devour,
Than languish in his slow-chapped power.   40
Let us roll all our strength, and all
Our sweetness up into one ball:
And tear our pleasures with rough strife
Thorough the iron gates of life.
Thus, though we cannot make our sun
Stand still, yet we will make him run.

Marvell's poetic *persona* is one of the most famous representatives of a tradition of frustrated lovers attempting to persuade a reluctant addressee to surrender to the pleasures of sexual love (another well-known example is the speaker in John Donne's 'The

Flea' discussed in 3.3.1). In this particular poem, the conventional *carpe diem* exhortation to enjoy the present moment is combined with a macabre reminder of the inevitability of death and decay (Patrides 1978; Rajan 1978). The rhetorical organization of the speaker's argument involves the projection of a complex world structure involving three main domains, each roughly corresponding to one of the three paragraphs into which the poem is divided:

(a) a hypothetical domain representing the kind of scenario in which, according to the speaker, the coyness of the addressee would constitute legitimate behaviour (first paragraph);
(b) the domain of the poetic *persona*'s knowledge and beliefs, which functions as the actual domain of the world projected by the text (second paragraph);
(c) the domain of the speaker's wishes, in which his sexual desires are realized (third paragraph).

The force of the argument lies in the contrast between the hypothetical and actual domains, which provides support for the speaker's claim that the realization of his wish world is the most appropriate course of action.

The poem opens with a declarative sentence with subject–verb inversion, *Had we but world enough, and time*, where the past tense of the verb *to have* is used hypothetically to introduce what the speaker regards as a counterfactual state of affairs (Quirk *et al.* 1985: 108, 1006). This results in the projection of what Ryan calls an alternate or fantasy world (Ryan 1985: 730–2, 1991a: 111, 119), which is governed by a different system of alethic modality from what counts as the actual domain (Doležel 1976a: 9ff.):

> These creations comprise dreams, hallucinations, fantasies, games of pretense, fictions read or composed by the characters, and *worlds created through counterfactual statements.* (Ryan 1985: 730; my italics)[2]

The nature of this fantasy world is only briefly sketched in the first line: we are invited to contemplate a scenario where the *persona* and his addressee enjoy a life-span and freedom of movement beyond the constraints of the actual world. From line 3 to the end of the paragraph, the speaker explores and specifies in more detail the opportunities that are available to the two lovers in a world where the proposition expressed in the first line is true. The modal auxiliaries *would* and *should* are here used to mark the unreal nature of the hypothesis and its consequences (Quirk *et al.* 1985: 234)[3]: *Thou by the Indian Ganges' side/ <u>Should</u> rubies find; I by* *the tide/ Of Humber would complain* (lines 5–7); *I would love you ten years before the Flood;/ And you should, if you please, refuse/ Till the conversion of the Jews* (lines 7–10); *My vegetable love should grow/ Vaster than empires* (lines 11–12); *An hundred years should go to praise/ Thine eyes* (lines 13–14), and so on. The length of the list and the size of the exaggerations serve to highlight the distant and improbable nature of the world where the woman's coyness would be *no crime*. In the fantasy world the two lovers' courting ground extends across different continents, and their lives span over past and future history.

At the beginning of the second paragraph, the adversative conjunction *But* marks a transition to the domain of actuality, where time is short and death certain. This domain is governed by the system of epistemic modality – expressing what the speaker knows or believes to be the case – and consists of two parts:

(a) the current state of the speaker's actual world, described by means of present tenses, as in *at my back I always hear* (line 21) and *yonder all before us lie* (line 23);

(b) a future state of the speaker's actual world, where both he and his beloved are dead (in fact he emphasizes the consequences of *her* death as part of his persuasive strategy); this is introduced by means of the modal auxiliary *shall*, which in Early Modern English (more than today) was used to express future predictions with an element of fatal necessity independent of human will, as in *Thy beauty shall no more be found* (line 25), *worms shall try/ That long preserved virginity* (lines 27–8), and so on (Jespersen 1954: 267; Barber 1976: 259–60; Görlach 1991: 114).

Strictly speaking, these states of affairs correspond, respectively, to the speaker's knowledge world and to a prospective extension of that knowledge world (Ryan 1985: 722–5, 1991a: 114–16). The reader, however, has no difficulty in recognizing the uncomfortable actuality of the *persona*'s description of his present and future predicament. The strength of the images of decay (lines 27–30) reinforces the contrast between what is presented as real and the carefree fantasy world of the first paragraph.

At the beginning of the third paragraph, the adverb *now* indicates another transition, this time to the speaker's wish world, whose realization depends on the success of his attempt at persuasion. Before the transition is complete, however, the speaker lingers on those aspects of the current state of the actual domain that are absent from the future projection of the previous paragraph, i.e.

the living and youthful state of his addressee: *while the youthful hue/ Sits on thy skin like morning dew,/ And while thy willing soul transpires/ At every pore with instant fires* (lines 33–6). This clearly contrasts with the horrific description of her dead body in lines 25–30. From line 37 onwards, the use of imperatives introduced by the verbal particle *let* outlines an axiological world governed by the realization of what the speaker regards as desirable for himself and his beloved: *let us sport us while we may* (line 37); *Let us roll all our strength, and all/ Our sweetness, up into one ball* (lines 41–2).

The actualization of the speaker's desires will not, however, free the lovers from the constraints of time. On the contrary, they would speed up their perception of the passing of time by engaging in pleasurable activities: *Thus, though we cannot make our sun/ Stand still, yet we will make him run* (lines 45–6). Here lies what some critics have seen as the paradoxical nature of the poem:

> If the sun runs, then time reasserts itself even in our command of it. We declare ourselves only in what we can accomplish; but the accomplishment is always a betrayal of the intention.
>
> (Rajan 1978: 163; see also Carey 1978: 138–9)

The speaker's position, however, is clear: given that there is no escape from time, he prefers a situation where he and his addressee actively take charge of their own destinies and enjoy a transient period of happiness, rather than passively and unenjoyably awaiting the inevitable end. In the last line, the realization of the *persona*'s wish world is described by means of the auxiliary *will*, which, unlike *shall*, carried strong volitional overtones (Jespersen 1954: 244; Barber 1976: 259–60; Görlach 1991: 114): this is a future that is brought about by the individual's initiative, not one that inevitably results from the human condition.

Of the four modal systems considered by Doležel (1976a, 1976b) and Ryan (1985, 1991a), the only one that is absent from the world structure of the poem is that of deontic modality, which would produce an obligation world governed by moral principles and social conventions (Ryan 1985: 729–30, 1991a: 116–17). In fact, it is not difficult to imagine that the addressee's coyness derives, at least in part, from the pressures of her own obligation world, which presumably prohibits the pursuit of sexual pleasure outside wedlock and for its own sake. It is therefore consistent with the *persona*'s objectives that such a domain of permission and obligation is excluded from the world structure of the poem, since it would undermine the conclusion that the actualization of his wish world is not only the most pleasurable, but also the most sensible and dignified option. In fact, the use of the word *crime* in reference to the woman's attitudes (line 2) seems to suggest that, in the speaker's world-view, the deontic system of conventional morality and external authority has been replaced by the axiological system of the individual's personal wishes and desires. A deontic world of moral rules and obligation does nevertheless act as a backdrop to the poem, since, without it, the speaking *persona*'s attempt at persuasion would not be needed.

5.3 Possible worlds and deviant situations of address

In Chapter 3 I considered the way in which poems project different types of situations of address and I pointed out that the degree of overlap between poetic speakers and real-life authors may vary considerably from poem to poem. In the case of William Wordsworth's 'I Wandered Lonely as a Cloud', for example, the speaker is likely to be closely identified with the poet, while in Browning's dramatic monologues the various personages who act as first-person speakers are clearly separate from the author (see 3.3.1 above). Poems such as 'To His Coy Mistress' lie somewhere between these two extremes: although we feel that the poet is adopting a particular type of voice, we have no reason to exclude some degree of identification between Marvell and his love-stricken *persona*.[4]

Poets may also choose as first-person speakers entities that, in the real world, are not endowed with linguistic abilities (Leech 1969: 197–8; Widdowson 1975: 47ff.). In such cases the projected discourse situations belong to alternative possible worlds which can be described by means of the typologies introduced in the previous chapter, and particularly by means of the classification developed by Ryan (1991a, 1991b). As I showed in the previous chapter, Ryan has proposed an inventory of the types of accessibility relationships that connect the actual world with different kinds of fictional worlds. By adopting her model, one is therefore able to specify what kind of accessibility relations need to apply in order for a particular fictional world to be possible and, conversely, in what respects individual worlds may be described as impossible.

A fairly common type of deviation in poetic situations of address occurs where the speaker is a living but non-human entity. This is the case in Sylvia Plath's 'Elm', where the eponymous tree speaks in the first person (see the opening of the previous chapter). According to Ryan's framework, the world projected by this poem is linguistically, analytically, logically and taxonomically compatible with the actual world. However, the inclusion of a speaking tree breaks the rule of physical compatibility (see 4.6.3), the lifting of which, as Ryan puts it, 'makes it possible for animals to talk, people to fly, and princes to be turned into frogs' (Ryan 1991a: 37). This type of impossibility applies to a wide variety of deviant poetic *personae*, including, for example, those of Tennyson's 'The Brook' (see Leech 1969: 198) and Shelley's 'The Cloud' (see Widdowson 1975: 48).

A similar situation occurs where the poetic *persona* is a dead human being, like the speaker in the poem by Emily Dickinson that opens: *I heard a Fly buzz – when I died.* Here it can again be argued that the projected world is physically impossible in Ryan's sense, but this implies two assumptions that may not be universally accepted: firstly, that verbal communication is precluded to dead people, and, secondly, that the dead do still enjoy some kind of existence. If the latter did not apply, the world projected by the poem would break the rule of taxonomic compatibility, which requires that text worlds contain the same species as the actual world. Taxonomically impossible poetic speakers, however, seem to be less common than physically impossible ones. A rare example is provided by Ted Hughes's 'Wodwo', which revolves around the very problem of the speaking voice's nature and identity. The poem's *persona* repeatedly asks questions such as *What am I, what shall I be called, what shape am I*, while it wanders with apparently equal ease through air, water and dry land. The term *wodwo* goes back to the fourteenth-century poem *Sir Gawain and the Green Knight*, where wodwos are among the wild creatures fought by the knight (Sagar 1975: 98; West 1985: 59). No consensus, however, exists on the precise nature of these beings:

> 'Wodwos' is sometimes translated 'trolls', sometimes 'satyrs', some- times 'wildmen of the woods'. It is this uncertainty of status – man or beast or monster or goblin – which attracts Hughes. Introducing a reading of the poem Hughes described his wodwo as 'some sort of satyr of half-man or half-animal, half kind of elemental little things, just a little larval being without shape or qualities who suddenly finds himself alive in this world at any time'. (Sagar 1975: 98)

The theme of the quest for individual identity in relation to the outside environment is therefore conveyed by projecting a world that appears to be the same as our actual world except for the presence of an intriguing amphibious being, whose main property seems to be that it does not belong to any existing species. The violation of the principle of same taxonomy by means of the choice of speaking *persona* is here at the centre of the poem's significance.

5.4 Possible worlds and poetic text worlds

In the previous section I began to show how the approaches to the description and classification of fictional worlds introduced in Chapter 4 may be applied to the study of different types of poetic discourse situations. In this section I will demonstrate the more general relevance of possible-worlds frameworks to the analysis of poetic text worlds. I will first of all discuss the applicability to poetry of Ryan's typology of fictional worlds based on her inventory of accessibility relations (1991a, 1991b; see 4.6.3 above); where relevant, I will also apply other typologies discussed in the previous chapter. I will then demonstrate in some detail a possible-world approach to the analysis of two postmodernist poems. This choice is motivated by the fact that the worlds of postmodernist literature pose rather peculiar problems, and have therefore received a considerable amount of attention from possible-world theorists (see 4.3.2 and 4.5.2 above).

5.4.1 Ryan's typology of fictional worlds and poetry

As I mentioned in 4.6.3, the accessibility relations included in Ryan's framework are listed 'in decreasing order of stringency' (Ryan 1991a: 32). In other words, fictional worlds that only break rules from the top of the list are closer to the actual world than fictional worlds that also break rules from the bottom of the list. This will become clearer as I discuss specific examples. The crucial point, however, is that Ryan's model makes it possible to describe fictional worlds in terms of a scale of increasing distance from the actual world. In my discussion I will start from the top of the list and consider Ryan's nine accessibility relations in groups of three.

The top of Ryan's typology: identity of properties, identity of inventory and compatibility of inventory

The first three accessibility relations considered by Ryan are to do with the extent to which fictional worlds are populated by the same objects as the actual world, and with whether shared objects possess the same properties (see 4.6.3). By 'objects' Ryan means all types of entities that count as members of a world, including people, things, places, and so on. If a text upholds the first two criteria (identity of properties and identity of inventory), it possesses the same truth status as what Ryan calls 'accurate nonfiction' (Ryan 1991a: 34): the text world overlaps exactly with the actual world; it contains the same objects, and these objects have the same properties as their actual counterparts. In principle, this applies to a wide range of poems, including, for example, Matthew Arnold's 'Dover Beach' and Philip Larkin's 'The Whitsun Weddings': in both cases the world of the poem is 'anchored', as it were, to a specific actual setting, and involves objects, situations and thoughts that could accurately reflect a specific real experience. The extent to which this is the case, however, is not as crucial to the interpretation and appreciation of poetry as it is to the reading of newspaper reports, biographies or travel guides. As I have repeatedly pointed out, it is in the nature of poetry to remain ambiguous as to its faithfulness to actual-world detail, particularly when it comes to the relationship between the *I* of a poem and its real-life author. The accuracy of the experiences represented in poetry is nevertheless often the focus of much attention and speculation on the part of critics and readers alike (see, for example, note 4) .

Where the criterion of identity of properties is openly relaxed, the result is a world where real people, places and events are described in terms of largely imaginary details. Below are some extracts from T.S. Eliot's 'Journey of the Magi':

> A cold coming we had of it,
> Just the worst time of the year
> For a journey, and such a long journey:
> . . .
> Then at dawn we came down to a temperate valley,
> Wet, below the snow line, smelling of vegetation;
> With a running stream and a water mill beating the darkness,
> And three trees on the low sky,
> . . .
> Then we came to a tavern with vine-leaves over the lintel,
> Six hands at an open door dicing for pieces of silver,
> And feet kicking the empty wineskins.

The poem can be described as an imaginary first-person account of a documented event – the three kings' visit to the newly born

Jesus.[5] Its focus, however, is on the kind of detail that is absent from historical records, and therefore unverifiable: the conditions of the journey, some trivial occurrences, and, more importantly, the state of mind, thoughts and impressions of one of the participants. In Ryan's terms, therefore, all types of accessibility relations can be said to apply to the text world except for the first one on the list, i.e. the identity of properties between text world and actual world: the people and places to which reference is made can be accepted as actual, but the features, actions and thoughts attributed to them (although plausible) are unlikely to be interpreted in the same way, given that the author of the poem had no privileged access to such information. This type of world is not dissimilar from Ryan's category of 'true fiction', which includes dramatized history, romanced biographies and so on:

> True fiction exploits the informational gaps in our knowledge of reality by filling them in with unverified but credible facts for which the author takes no responsibility (as would be the case in historiography). The textual world is epistemically accessible from the real world, in so far as everything we know about reality can be integrated into it.
>
> (Ryan 1991a: 34)

Maitre accounts for this kind of world in her first category, which includes fictional works reporting or referring to actual events (Maitre 1983: 79, 81–9). As I mentioned in the previous chapter, Maitre also points out that, in reconstructing worlds of this type, readers are expected to rely heavily on their knowledge of real-world people, places and events (Maitre 1983: 81). This is certainly the case with 'Journey of the Magi', where the title alerts the reader as to the background knowledge that is relevant to the interpretation of the speaker's identity, the destination of the journey, the experience described in the final stanza, and the various allusions to Christ's life (*three trees on the low sky; hands . . . dicing for pieces of silver*).

A similar case to 'Journey of the Magi' may be found in Yeats's 'Long-legged Fly': the first and the third stanzas of the poem dramatize moments from the daily lives of two historical figures – Caesar and Michelangelo respectively. The second stanza, however, breaks Ryan's criterion of identity of inventory:

> That the topless towers be burnt
> And men recall that face,
> Move most gently if move you must

in this lonely place.
She thinks, part woman, three parts a child,
That nobody looks; her feet
Practice a tinker shuffle
Picked up on a street.
Like a long-legged fly upon the stream
Her mind moves upon silence.

The reference here is to Helen of Troy, who is a member of the world of Homer's *Iliad*, but not of the actual world. In cases such as these the rule of identity of inventory is replaced by that of compatibility of inventory, which applies to worlds where real people and events are presented alongside fictional ones. This is typically the case in historical ballads or in narrative poems such as Pope's 'Rape of the Lock', where historically documented figures exist alongside fictional characters.

If the criterion of compatibility of inventory is also relaxed, but all subsequent accessibility relations still apply, the result is what Ryan defines as 'realistic fiction' set in 'a geographic and historical "no-man's land"' (Ryan 1991a: 36). The reference here is to fictional worlds that have no people, places or events in common with the actual world, but are otherwise the same as the world of reality. Because she restricts her attention to prose fiction, Ryan treats this as a somewhat unusual category, and only mentions as examples Kafka's novels *The Trial* and *The Castle*. Indeed, realistic novels are usually tied both historically and geographically to the actual world, so that the absence of any such connection at all leads to what Ryan describes as an 'eerie atmosphere' and an 'absolutely foreign world' (Ryan 1991a: 36). This is not true of poetry, however, where the tendency for texts to be shorter and the smaller importance of plot reduce the demands for the specification of settings and characters. As a consequence, poetry includes a great variety of text worlds that do not ostensibly overlap with the inventory of objects found in the actual world, but that still fulfil all other accessibility relations from chronological compatibility onwards.

This applies, for example, to the poems 'The Jaguar' and 'Charlotte: Her Book' which I discussed in 2.3.3 and 3.3.2. Both project realistic text worlds that, unlike 'Dover Beach' or 'Long-legged Fly' have no explicit connection with members of the actual world.[6] In both cases, however, the effect does not seem to be that of presenting a 'geographic and historical "no-man's land"'. On the one hand, such worlds may be perceived to have a similar relationship with specific portions of the actual world as those of 'Dover Beach' and 'The Whitsun Weddings'. On the other hand, the lack of obvious references to specific actual objects may well reduce the relevance of the real-world identification of the characters and situations presented in the poems, as well as increase the readers' awareness of their general or universal significance. Ted Hughes's jaguar, for example, may be seen as a symbol of the thirst for freedom, and Charlotte as a prototypical representative of disadvantaged children. In any case, Ryan's claim as to the historical and geographical indeterminacy of worlds that break the rule of compatibility of inventory ignores the role of inferencing in the construction of text worlds: the fact that Ted Hughes's jaguar is in a zoo rather than in his native environment strongly suggests a Western, perhaps metropolitan, context. Similarly, the fact that Charlotte was run over by a car indicates a contemporary historical setting for the world of the poem.

Where the relaxation of compatibility of inventory does seem to produce a sense of historical and geographical indeterminacy is in the worlds of some nursery rhymes:

> Higglety, pigglety, pop!
> The dog has eaten the mop;
>   The pig's in a hurry,
>   The cat's in a flurry,
> Higglety, pigglety, pop![7]

Here readers (or listeners) may well imagine a specific rural setting in a specific society, but the world of the text is uncomplicated and generic enough to elude any precise connections with a particular portion of the actual world.

To some extent, the same might apply to lyric poems such as Shakespeare's 'Shall I compare thee to a summer's day?', which express feelings and situations that transcend historical and geographical boundaries.[8] Here, however, the readers' perception of the poem's world crucially depends on their decisions as to the status of the speaking *persona* (see 3.3.1). Where the first-person speaker is strongly identified with the author, as in Wordsworth's 'I Wandered Lonely as a Cloud', the rule of compatibility of inventory is upheld: we imagine the poem's setting to be the English Lakes' District, even if it is not explicitly mentioned in the text.[9] On the other hand, if the first-person speaker is constructed as a fictional character, as I suggested of Frost's 'Stopping by Woods', the criterion of compatibility of inventory is relaxed, and the world of the poem is less closely connected to actual settings and events.

The middle of Ryan's typology: chronological compatibility, physical compatibility and taxonomic compatibility

The next three accessibility relations proposed by Ryan capture more general and fundamental ways in which fictional worlds may depart from the actual world (see 4.6.3). If chronological compatibility is lifted, but all subsequent relations are maintained, the result is anticipation fiction such as Orwell's *1984* (although this novel does not, strictly speaking, count as anticipation for post-1984 readers; see Ryan 1991a: 36). If taxonomic compatibility is also relaxed, the outcome is science fiction. The peculiar world of Craig Raine's 'A Martian Sends a Postcard Home' can be partly captured in terms of these principles: the text humorously assumes a hypothetical future state of the actual world where Martians have landed on earth and are able to have mail delivered to their own planet. I will return to this poem in Chapter 8.[10]

It is, however, the principles of physical and taxonomic compatibility that, separately or in combination, account for a wide range of fantasy worlds in poetry. Consider, for example, the following poem by Wallace Stevens:

EARTHY ANECDOTE

Every time the bucks went clattering
Over Oklahoma
A firecat bristled in the way.

Wherever they went,
They went clattering,
Until they swerved
In a swift, circular line
To the right,
Because of the firecat.

Or until they swerved
In a swift, circular line
To the left,
Because of the firecat.

The bucks clattered.
The firecat went leaping,
To the right, to the left,

And
Bristled in the way.

Later, the firecat closed his bright eyes
And slept.

The poem opens with a real-world reference to an existing geo-graphical location – Oklahoma – but the world it projects turns out to be rather different from that of poems such as 'Dover Beach'. The presence of the firecat, like that of the wodwo in Hughes's poem, signals that the world of the text is exempt from Ryan's principle of taxonomic compatibility with the actual world: although unmistakably feline, the firecat is an imaginary creature, not a fictional member of an actual species. The lifting of the constraint of same taxonomy in the world of 'Earthy Anecdote' has interest-ing interpretative implications: critical accounts of the poem show a consistent tendency to give the firecat symbolic significance, whether as a symbol of the poet's ability to form order out of chaos (e.g. Betar 1972: 252–3), or of the constraining force of reality over spiritual freedom (e.g. Nassar 1965: 49). In other words, the introduction of a fantastic element in an apparently realistic setting appears to act as a trigger for non-literal interpretations of the taxonomically deviant entity.

Nonsense verse often thrives on the creation of imaginary beings, as well as on the stretching of natural laws. This is the opening stanza of Edward Lear's 'The Jumblies':

They went to sea in a sieve, they did;
  In a sieve they went to sea;
In spite of all their friends could say,
On a winter's morn, on a stormy day,
  In a sieve they went to sea.
  . . .
    Far and few, far and few,
      Are the lands where the Jumblies live.
    Their heads are green, and their hands are blue;
      And they went to sea in a sieve.

Here the lifting of the principle of same taxonomy via the intro-duction of the multi-coloured (and presumably minute) Jumblies, is combined with the violation of natural laws, since the protagon-ists' attempt to sail in a sieve turns out to be successful. In this type of poetry, the realm of the counterfactual is explored for its potential of playfulness and diversion. The humorous tone of the poem is enhanced by the fact that the friends mentioned in the first stanza seem to share the readers' scepticism about the Jumblies' enterprise, and, like the readers, are forced to face a reality different from their expectations.

The bottom of Ryan's typology: logical compatibility, analytical compatibility and linguistic compatibility

The breaking of Ryan's last three accessibility relations threatens the very essence of the process of text-world construction (see 4.6.3). As I mentioned in the previous chapter, the rule of logical compatibility is violated in a number of postmodernist novels. As far as poetry is concerned, Ryan states that this principle is typically transgressed in popular nonsense verse, and particularly in children's rhymes. Significantly, however, Ryan does not provide any examples. It is in fact very difficult to find poems of any kind which violate the principles of non-contradiction and of the excluded middle. A rare example is quoted in Stewart (1978: 72–3), who is briefly referred to by Ryan (1991a: 37–8):

> Ladies and jellispoons:
> I come before you
> To stand behind you
> To tell you something
> I know nothing about.
> Last Thursday
> Which was Good Friday
> There will be a mothers' meeting
> For Fathers only.
> Wear your best clothes
> If you haven't any,
> And if you can come,
> Please stay at home.
> Admission is free
> So pay at the door.
> . . .
> The next meetings will be held
> At the four corners of the round table.

In this case it is possible to argue that the world projected by the speaking voice's discourse contains a number of logical contradictions: the day referred to as *Last Thursday* both was and was not a Thursday, admission to the meeting is both free and not free, and so on. This is how Stewart (1978: 73) captures this aspect of the poem:

The paired oppositions that the narrative presents are states that cannot tolerate each other, yet that in the frame of the discourse are allowed to be and not to be at the same time.

A world of this kind, where contradictory propositions can be simultaneously true, is not only logically impossible, but also unimaginable – a point to which I will return below. The main effect of texts such as this lies in playfully and repeatedly frustrating the interpreter's attempts to construct a coherent text world.

A different type of logical impossibility can be found in Robert Graves's 'Welsh Incident', which involves a conversation about some extraordinary creatures that the main speaker has seen emerge from *the sea-caves of Criccieth yonder*. These beings are not simply taxonomically deviant, insofar as they appear to belong to non-actual, imaginary species: *All sorts of queer things,/ Things never seen or heard or written about,/ Very strange, un-Welsh, utterly peculiar.* They also seem to be concrete, physical entities which, in some cases, lack size and colour: *All various shapes and sizes, and no sizes*; *some had no colour.* This undermines the application of necessary truths concerning the essential properties of objects (Bradley and Swartz 1979: 19–20), and therefore leads to the projection of a world that violates Ryan's principle of analytical compatibility. Whether we decide to place these analytically impossible creatures in the 'actual' domain of the fictional universe or in a fantasy world that only exists in the mind of the speaker, the world of the poem is, again, difficult to conceive. Clearly, poems such as 'Welsh Incident' and 'Ladies and Jellispoons' pose a more fundamental challenge to our imaginative faculties than any of the poems discussed in the previous sections. Eco's claim concerning the interpretative impasse caused by logically impossible worlds seems to apply here (cf. 4.5.2 above): a world that defeats necessary truths can be mentioned, but it cannot be constructed (Eco 1990: 76), or, at least, it cannot be as easily pictured in our minds as the world in which the Jumblies safely sail in a sieve.

Finally, the breaking of the principle of linguistic compatibility completely blocks the possibility of constructing a text world at all. Ryan associates this type of violation with sound poetry (Ryan 1991a: 39). The following example is a poem by the Russian modernist poet Aleksey Krucenyx, discussed by Enkvist (1991):

dyr bul ščl
ubeššč
skum

vy so bu
r l ez

As Enkvist puts it, the words of the poems 'have no referential meaning even in the sense in which the words of "Jabberwocky" carry mimetic associations' (Enkvist 1991: 3). To some extent at least, the poem is nevertheless interpretable: Enkvist argues that it can be read as a symptom of the poet's rejection of tradition and of his intention to experiment with new ways of expression. All this, however, takes place at the expense of the projection of a text world. As Ryan points out in her discussion of a sound poem by Hugo Ball,

> With the last linguistic connection to AW [Actual World] vanishes the possibility of knowing or saying anything about TAW [Textual Actual World]. Vanishing with this possibility is the very notion of textual universe. (Ryan 1991a: 39)

On the whole, the above discussion has shown that Ryan's framework can be usefully applied to poetry. Although, as I have suggested, one needs to allow for differences across literary genres, it seems clear that the adoption of a possible-world approach does not necessarily lead to a split within literary studies, with the study of poetry set totally apart from that of prose fiction and drama. Rather, poetic text worlds can also be described and classified in terms of their distance from what we take to be the world of reality. In this respect, however, what has consistently emerged from my analyses is the fact that Ryan's typology should not be applied simply as a set of abstract categories, but rather needs to be related to the readers' activities during text processing. On a number of occasions I have shown how the nature of a particular text world cannot be defined in absolute terms, but may vary depending on the background knowledge and interpretative decisions of different readers. In the final chapter I will show how possible-world analysis can be usefully complemented by a more cognitive approach to the description of text worlds.

5.4.2 Postmodernist poetry and ontological instability

Just as it is possible to project fictional worlds that are freed from the laws that govern the actual world, it is also possible to create worlds where the boundaries between ontologically separate domains are transgressed. This is the case in the following poem by Roger McGough:

FRAMED

In the Art Gallery
it is after closing time
everybody has left
except a girl
who is undressing   5
in front of a large painting
entitled: 'Nude'

(The girl undressing
is the girl in the painting)

naked now she faces   10
the girl who gazes
out at the girl
who naked faces
the girl who
naked gazes out   15

of the picture
steps the nude
who smiles, dresses and walks away
leaving the naked girl
gazing into the empty space   20
Framed by this poem.

The first stanza of the poem establishes a textual universe consisting of the 'actual' world of the Art Gallery (apparently overlapping with our actual world) and the fictional world of a particular
painting. At this point the only laws that are violated are the social
conventions that should prevent the 'real' girl from removing her
clothes in a public place. As the poem progresses, a relationship
of identity is established between the 'real' girl in the Art Gallery
and the 'fictional' girl who inhabits the world projected by the
painting: although the bracketed second stanza could be stretched
into a logical contradiction, the most likely interpretation is that
the 'real' girl acted as a model for the creation of the 'fictional'
girl. The verbal whirlpool of the third stanza builds up to the
surprise of the final stanza, where the 'fictional' girl crosses the
boundary between the 'fictional' and 'actual' worlds of the textual
universe. The word *out* at the end of the third stanza provides a
linguistic counterpart of the moment in which the threshold is
crossed, since it acts simultaneously as an adverbial particle following the verb *gazes*, and as part of a complex preposition in the prepositional phrase *out of the picture*. The unexpected enjambment

between lines 15 and 16 reinforces the surprise effect caused by the 'fictional' girl stepping out of the painting.

The violation of ontological boundaries is a typical device of postmodernist fiction (McHale 1987: 119ff.). The situation presented by McGough's poem has many parallels in contemporary cinema: in Woody Allen's *The Purple Rose of Cairo* a character from a film-inside-the-film steps out of the screen into the 'actual' domain; in *Ladri di Saponette* by the Italian director Maurizio Nichetti an accidental exchange of characters occurs between a film-inside-the-film and the advertisements that interrupt it while it is being shown on television in the 'actual' domain. Equally typical of postmodernist fiction is the final twist in McGough's poem, where the girl that had been constructed as 'real' within the boundaries of the textual universe is exposed in her true nature as a fictional construct projected by the poem itself. This is a poetic example of what Doležel calls 'self-disclosing narratives' (cf. 4.5.2), in which, as with John Fowles's *The French Lieutenant's Woman*, the act of fiction-making is laid bare, and somehow encroaches upon the fictional universe (Doležel 1989: 238).

Another typically postmodernist technique is the projection of indeterminate or ambiguous worlds, where it is difficult to distinguish between what is and is not the case in the 'actual' domain. As I mentioned in the previous chapter, Doležel characterizes this strategy in terms of the blocking of authentication in narrative texts (Doležel 1980, 1988, 1989). Referring particularly to postmodernist poetry, McHale (1992) talks about a consistent tendency to frustrate the readers' sense-making attempts, by making it impossible to arrive at any definite conclusions about the contents of the world projected by a particular text. A primary technique for this particular purpose, McHale points out, is the blurring of the line that divides literal and figurative language, so that readers are unable to distinguish between the tenor and the vehicle of figurative expressions (McHale 1992: 11–14, 1987: 133ff.).

McHale draws particularly on the work of Hrushovski (1984), who highlights the ontological implications of the interpretation of figurative language: what belongs to the tenor of a metaphor or simile (Hrushovski's 'primary frame') exists in the fictional world; what belongs to the vehicle (Hrushovski's 'secondary frame') is non-existent from the point of view of the text world. In T.S. Eliot's 'Love Song of J. Alfred Prufrock', the evening is said to be *spread out against the sky like a patient etherised upon a table.* Hrushovski points out that of the two frames of reference that are activated

by the simile – the evening (tenor) and the hospital (vehicle) –
only the former is actualized in the world projected by the text:
the world of the poem, in other words, includes no etherized
patient (Hrushovski 1984: 15ff.; see also McHale 1987: 133–4).
The relative status of the two domains involved in figurative language, therefore, carries a potential for ontological ambiguity
(Hrushovski 1984: 39).

The work of the poet John Ashbery is often associated with
the postmodernist tendency towards the creation of ontological
uncertainty (Waggoner 1984; Konuk 1987; McHale 1987). Here is
one of Ashbery's poems:

THE ABSENCE OF A NOBLE PRESENCE

If it was treason it was so well handled that it
Became unimaginable. No, it was ambrosia
In the alley under the stars and not this undiagnosable
Turning, a shadow in the plant of all things

That makes us aware of certain moments,   5
That the end is not far off since it will occur
In the present and this is the present.
No, it was something not very subtle then and yet again

You've got to remember we don't see that much.
We see a portion of eaves dropping in the pastel book   10
And are aware that everything doesn't count equally–
There is dreaminess and infection in the sum

And since this too is of our everydays
It matters only to the one you are next to
This time, giving you a ride to the station.   15
It foretells itself, not the hiccup you both notice.

The speaker in the poem seems to be striving to make sense of a
past experience, anaphorically referred to by *it* in the first line. It
is difficult, however, to see through the images and thoughts that
flit through the speaker's mind in order to identify their source
in the actual domain of the world projected by the poem. This
difficulty arises from a number of factors. Firstly, the speaker himself seems to be confused about the nature of the event he is
reflecting upon, since his statements carry a low degree of cer-
tainty and tend to contradict one another. The first sentence opens
with the hypothetical conjunction *if*, introducing a first attempt
at rationalizing his experience; the second and third sentences
open with the negative adverb *No*, which in both cases denies the

validity of the previous statement and introduces a new attempt at making sense of the past: *it was . . .* (lines 2 and 8). Furthermore, *it was something not very subtle* in line 8 contradicts *it was so well handled* in line 1, while the positive connotations of *ambrosia* in line 2 conflict with the negative associations of *treason* in line 1.

Secondly, the poem overflows with metaphors but it is difficult to pin down exactly what is metaphorical and what is not, and, more importantly, what constitutes the tenor of each metaphor. Let us consider, for example, the expressions in the poem to do with roads and movement. Is *the alley under the stars* in line 3 a literal alley existing in the text world or a metaphor for something else? The chances are that it will be interpreted literally, but the same does not apply to the *undiagnosable turning* of the following lines: although the heads of the two noun phrases (*alley* and *turning*) belong to the same semantic field, the latter is likely to be read as a metaphor of some change in the speaker's life, largely as a result of the collocational clash with the premodifying adjective *undiagnosable*. The reference to *a ride to the station* in the final stanza is equally ambiguous: is it part of an extended metaphor where life is presented as a series of crossroads and journeys, or is it just an example of a trivial happening in everyday life? It is difficult to say. In fact, it is even harder to interpret some expressions that are definitely metaphorical, partly because of the poet's tendency to produce 'compound' metaphors, i.e. expressions containing more than one metaphor (Leech 1969: 159–60). One of the many examples is *a shadow in the plant of all things* (line 4), where both the shadow and the plant appear to be metaphorical. Overall, we are left with a large number of potential vehicles of figurative expressions, but not much clue as to what the tenors might be.

In Hrushovski's terms, this results in an ontological vacuum. We are aware of the images that the speaker uses to think and talk about his experiences, but we have little access to the experiences themselves. Only some general themes can be identified: the nearness of death (lines 6–7), the limits of human knowledge (lines 9–10), the fleeting nature of human relationships (lines 14–15). In fact, the critics have claimed that the central aim of Ashbery's poetry is to convey the poet's own scepticism about the possibility of arriving at any knowledge of the world, and of using words to refer to anything other than to the words themselves (Waggoner 1984: 613ff.; Konuk 1987: 200ff.). McHale claims that postmodernist poetry in general can be interpreted as an attempt to arrive at a 'cognitive mapping' of the postmodernist world, i.e. to represent the fragmented and chaotic nature of contemporary reality (McHale 1992: 26–9). An obvious limitation of this type of critical statement, however, is that it seems to imply that all postmodernist poems have roughly the same interpretation.

Whatever one may think of the critics' statements and of the poet's intent, it is undeniable that this type of poetry challenges the whole notion of text world, by impeding the readers' world-constructing efforts. As the title of Ashbery's poem seems to anticipate, nothing is definitely present in the world projected by the text. The speaker's knowledge world, in other words, is too opaque for us to be able to reconstruct much beyond an impression of a rather confused train of thoughts. In Ryan's terms, this is a case of a fictional universe with an 'empty centre', i.e. with an indeterminate actual domain:

> The text limits its assertions to worlds at the periphery, avoiding the representation of an actual world. (Ryan 1991a: 39)

As a consequence, accessibility relations between the text world and the readers' actual world remain largely undecidable (Ryan 1991a: 39).

5.5 Possible-world theory: evaluation and prospect

The above analyses have shown how possible-world frameworks can be made relevant to the study of poetry, particularly as regards the description of the internal structure of poetic worlds and the analysis of the different types of relationships that may exist between text worlds and actuality. Not all poems, however, can be usefully analysed in terms of their modal structure or of the accessibility relations that link the worlds they project to the actual world. Poems may achieve their significance not by creating alternative states of affairs, but by proposing particular world-views, i.e. particular ways of approaching the world that is taken as real. In order to deal adequately with such texts, one needs a framework in which actuality is seen as a relative notion, so that different effects can be achieved by proposing certain views of reality rather than others.

The idea that the distinction between the actual and the non-actual is problematic does receive a certain amount of consideration on the part of possible-world theorists. Eco, for example, points out that what is referred to as the 'real' world is a cultural construct, and that possibility is more an ideological rather than an ontological matter (Eco 1979: 222–3; see also Pavel 1986: 139ff.). In practice, however, possible-world models tend to operate on the basis of a clear-cut distinction between what is actual and what is not, in line with the logician's postulate that any given proposition is either true or false in a particular world. This obviously requires a certain amount of simplification. Even in the case of the apparently uncontroversial propositions that I used as examples in the previous chapter (4.2), truth-values may be a matter of opinion. The idea that the sentence *Iraq invaded Kuwait in 1990* expresses a true proposition may be questioned by those who agree with Sadam Hussein's claim that his military action was aimed at regaining possession of a lost Iraqi province and not at invading the legitimate territory of another nation. A less extreme example is provided by the debate over the truth value of the proposition 'The recession is over' in relation to the economic situation of Britain in 1994. In these and many other cases, what is taken to be the case in the actual world may be a matter of ideological stance, previous experience and cultural background.

In defence of possible-world approaches, one has to recognize that some degree of simplification in these matters is often justified, or even necessary. After all, in order to function efficiently in our daily lives, we often have to assume that we share an objectively given reality with our fellow human beings. Moreover, possible-world theorists tend to focus on relatively uncontroversial aspects of reality, such as those captured by natural and logical laws. On the other hand, this not only obscures the problematic nature of the notion of actuality, but also tends to limit the scope of analysis to text worlds containing obviously counterfactual elements, as is the case with the majority of the poems analysed in this chapter. In Part III of this book I will introduce an alternative approach to the study of text worlds, one that focuses on the world-views that are projected by different texts, rather than on the degree of possibility of fictional worlds in relation to a world that is taken as actual.

NOTES

[1] This clearly goes against the more general tendency in literary studies to talk about the 'worlds' of poems, and to regard such worlds as, at least potentially, fictional (e.g. Leech 1969; Levin 1976; see also 1.2 above).

[2] Ryan points out that constructs of this kind are better seen as complete universes, i.e. systems made up of a world counting as actual and a variety

of unrealised possible worlds (Ryan 1985: 730, 1991a: 119). For the purposes of my analysis, however, it is convenient to ignore this aspect of fantasy domains, which will therefore continue to be referred to as 'worlds'.

[3] This use of *should*, although rare today, was common in Early Modern English (Jespersen 1954: 329).

[4] In fact this poem has been at the centre of a debate over Marvell's own virility and heterosexuality (see Ellrodt 1978: 219–20).

[5] The historicity of the Kings' visit to Jesus is itself a matter of dispute (see Douglas 1980: 930). For the purposes of the present discussion, however, I will assume that the relevant Gospel narrative describes an actual event.

[6] It should be noted that the world of 'Charlotte, Her Book' is realistic according to my interpretation of the poem, but not according to other possible interpretations. For those readers who see the dead Charlotte herself as the main speaking voice, the world of the poem breaks Ryan's principle of physical compatibility.

[7] From *The Oxford Book of Nursery Rhymes*, edited by Iona and Peter Opie (1955).

[8] It should be noted, however, that the association between May and the beginning of summer in Shakespeare's poem suggests that it is set in the Northern hemisphere. Below the Equator, May leads towards the winter.

[9] Even if read in an autobiographical mode, Wordsworth's poem does not, however, uphold the rule of identity of properties. The poet was not wandering 'lonely as a cloud' when he came across the daffodils: if we are to believe Dorothy Wordsworth's diaries, she was with him.

[10] Although Ryan makes no mention of this, the principle of chronological compatibility can also be lifted in non-fictional discourse. This is the case in hypotheses and speculations about the future, which frequently occur in everyday conversations, political discourse, the media, and so on.

Part II: Suggestions for further analysis

1. The internal structure of text worlds and plot

James Joyce's short story 'Eveline', which is contained in *Dubliners*, focuses on a young Irish woman who is at a crossroads in her life. She has agreed to elope with Frank in order to start a new life with him in Argentina, but she is also reluctant to leave the life she has always known – a rather dreary existence dedicated to her younger siblings and to an uncomprehending and potentially violent father. As she is musing over the past, present and possible future, she lingers on memories of her dead mother, and particularly on the promise she made to her on her deathbed, that she would 'keep the home together as long as she could'. When the moment of truth comes, Eveline goes as far as meeting Frank at the harbour but eventually fails to join him.

Clearly, Eveline's inability to take action in order to change her life is due to conflicts and inconsistencies in her own private worlds. How can her impasse be described in terms of the framework introduced in 4.5.1? More specifically: What is the internal structure of the fictional universe projected by the story? What types of subworlds are involved? What relationships exist between them? How can Eveline's indecisiveness and ambiguous attitude towards a possible future with Frank be captured by means of Ryan's catalogue of private worlds? Which of her private worlds does Eveline eventually privilege when she decides not to leave? In answering these questions, you may also want to consider the way in which changes in mood, tense and aspect in verb phrases mark transitions between the worlds that make up the fictional universe of the story (see my discussion of Marvell's 'To His Coy Mistress' in 5.2 for an example of this type of analysis). A detailed analysis of the language and plot structure of 'Eveline' from a range of different perspectives can be found in Toolan (1988, chapters 2 and 4).

2. Different versions of famous stories and accessibility relations between worlds

Well-known stories have often been told by different authors in different texts: think, for example, of the case of Tiresias – the blind Theban prophet who appears in Homer's *Odyssey* and other Greek legends, as well as in Apollinaire's play *Les Mamelles de Tirésias* and Eliot's *The Waste Land* (for a discussion of the complexities arising when the same characters/individuals are members of different worlds, see Eco (1979: 228ff.)). In such cases a web of accessibility relations can be established between the different worlds involved: we can study the way in which each fictional world relates to our 'actual' world and we can consider how the various fictional worlds relate to each other. This can lead to interesting insights into the texts involved, the different cultures in which the texts were produced and the intentions of different authors.

Here I want to focus on a series of poems by Carol Ann Duffy which are included in the collection 'The World's Wife'. These poems are entertaining and often tongue-in-cheek retellings of the stories of famous men from the point of view of their (supposed) wives in a contemporary context. 'Mrs Midas', for example, has as its background the ancient legend of the king who was granted the wish of turning into gold everything he touched. In the poem, his wife focuses on the consequences this had for their relationship and their daily life. Similarly, in 'Mrs Tiresias' the wife of the Theban prophet gives her own account of the consequences of his sex change from man to woman. And in 'Mrs Lazarus' the wife of Jesus's friend in the Gospel gives a bewildered and not altogether enthusiastic account of her husband's return from the dead.

In studying these poems from a possible-world perspective, you may want to adopt Ryan's catalogue of accessibility relations (see 4.6.3 and 5.4.1). What accessibility relations link the world of each of Duffy's poems with the worlds of the original classical version(s) of the story? What accessibility relations link the worlds of the classical stories with our own 'actual' world? What accessibility relations link the worlds of Duffy's poems with our own 'actual' world? You will need to consider, among other things, the entities who populate each world, the physical laws that apply to each world, the details that are included or excluded in Duffy's poems, and issues to do with the chronological setting of the stories. Out of Ryan's list of accessibility relations, the following will be particularly

relevant: Identity of Inventory, Compatibility of Inventory, Chronological Compatibility, Physical Compatibility. What does this type
of analysis contribute to your understanding of the texts involved?
You can adopt a similar procedure to compare different versions
of any story, including, for example, contemporary rewritings of
traditional fairy stories such as those by Angela Carter and James
Finn Garner.

3. Complex world structures and the violation of ontological boundaries in postmodernist fiction and advertising

(a) Luigi Pirandello's play *Six Characters in Search of an Author*
opens with a group of actors preparing to start the rehearsal of a
play under the direction of their producer. Suddenly, their activities are interrupted by the entrance into the theatre of a myster-
ious group of people, who plead that the producer and the actors
listen sympathetically to their case. They turn out to be six characters who carry in themselves the potential for a complete and tragic
play, which was however never completed by the playwright who
originally conceived of them. The author's decision to abandon
the writing of their story has left the characters in a painful limbo
of unrealized existence. As a consequence, they are now looking
for another author who is willing to turn the plot they are part
of into a script for a play. After some negotiation, the characters
manage to persuade the producer to allow them to 'perform' their
story on stage so that it can be watched by the actors and written
up by the prompter. After a few scenes, however, the height of
emotions involved in the plot and the conflict between characters
and actors lead to a dramatic and inevitable failure.

   In this play, Pirandello deals with issues and boundaries that
are central to possible-world theory. How can the ontological plight
of the six characters be described in the light of the discussion in
4.3.1? How can Doležel's notion of authentication introduced in
4.5.2 be applied to the six characters' 'need' for an author? Consider the internal structure of the world of the play in the light
of the discussion in 4.5.1. What types of subworlds are involved?
What relationships are established between them? What are the
implications of the contact between the six characters and the
actors who inhabit the 'actual' domain of Pirandello's play? How
does this text compare with the poem by Roger McGough discussed

in 5.4.2 or with other postmodernist texts that you are familiar with? In what ways does the play question conventional assumptions about the distinction between reality and fiction? See McHale (1987: 35, 121) for some useful comments on this play.

(b) The breakdown of boundaries between ontologically incompatible domains can be exploited for less profound effects than those pursued by Pirandello's play. A few years ago, a car manufacturer ran a television advertisement that went roughly as follows. An ordinary-looking young man approaches a brand new car in a rather nondescript setting. As soon as he enters the car, his hair stands up on his head, the dull suit he is wearing turns into a multi-coloured Hawaian-style shirt, and his surroundings change into an exotic setting with beaches, palm trees and colourful birds. The strikingness of the transformation is enhanced by a switch to bright cartoon-like colours for the scene inside the car. When the young man gets out of the vehicle, everything reverts to its original dullness. However, a split-second later a bright (and cartoon-like) pineapple drops from the sky and falls on the young man's head.

In what way(s) can the relationship between the 'ordinary' and the 'exotic' settings be captured by the framework for the description of complex world structures outlined in 4.5.1? Why is the sudden appearance of the pineapple surprising in terms of boundaries between different subworlds? Consider the effects of the projection of a complex world structure and of the violation of the boundary between two different domains: in what ways do they relate to the advertisers' objectives? You may want to consider whether you have come across any other advertisements that work in a similar way.

4. Impossible worlds and humour

(a) The projection of impossible worlds can be exploited simply as a vehicle for humour. Consider the following jokes – both translated from Italian:

(1) Question: How do you fit four elephants into a FIAT Cinquecento? Answer: Two in the front and two in the back.

(2) A mute says to a deaf man: 'Careful: there's a blind man spying on us!'

In example (1), what kind of world is suggested by the presupposition carried by the first utterance? (For a brief definition of the notion of presupposition, see 2.2, and especially note 4 in

Chapter 2.) What kind of world is projected by the punchline? How does this world relate to our actual world in terms of Ryan's accessibility relations (see 4.6.3)? The world projected by example (2) is more radically deviant: how can it be described in terms of Ryan's accessibility relations? Eco's comments on worlds that can be mentioned but not constructed may also be relevant here (see 4.5.2 and 5.4.1). How does the projection of impossible worlds potentially result in a humourous effect? Can you think of any other jokes that achieve their effects by projecting impossible worlds of different kinds?

(b) The nursery rhyme below raises an interesting ambiguity as to the kind of world it projects:

> Yesterday upon the stair
> I met a man who wasn't there.
> He wasn't there again today.
> I wish that man would go away!

Consider the implications of taking the expression 'who wasn't there' literally. Which of Ryan's accessibility relations (see 4.6.3) is violated by the contrast between the claims that the man 'wasn't there' on the one hand and the statement 'I met a man' together with the presupposition carried by the final line on the other hand? What kind of world does the rhyme project according to this interpretation? How does it compare with the worlds projected by 'Ladies and Jellispoons', 'Welsh Incident' and 'The Absence of a Noble Presence' (see 5.4.1 and 5.4.2)? Eco's comments on worlds that can be mentioned but not constructed are also relevant here (see 4.5.2 and 5.4.1).

You may also have become aware of a different reading of the rhyme, which results from relating the expression 'wasn't there' to the idiom 'not to be all there', which means 'to be simple' or 'to be silly in the head'. How does this interpretation affect the world that the rhyme projects? How does the presence of this ambiguity contribute to the overall effect of the rhyme?

Part III

POETIC TEXT WORLDS AS COGNITIVE CONSTRUCTS

Schema theory and literature

6.1 Introduction

The possible-world frameworks discussed in the last two chapters rely on logical and philosophical concepts in order to describe and categorize different types of text worlds. In this and the next two chapters I will introduce an alternative (although not incompatible) approach, based on the models of the organization of human knowledge which have been developed in cognitive psychology and artificial intelligence under the general framework of schema theory. The focus will be on how text worlds are constructed in the interaction between the readers' prior knowledge on the one hand and the language of texts on the other. My central claim will be that the reader's perception of the world projected by a text depends on the way in which his or her existing background knowledge is reinforced or challenged during the process of interpretation.

As a preliminary example, consider the opening of the story 'Love in a Colder Climate' by J.G. Ballard, to which I will return in the course of the chapter:

> Anyone reading this confession in 1989, the year when I was born, would have been amazed to find me complaining about a state of affairs that must in every respect have resembled paradise. However, yesterday's heaven all too easily becomes today's hell. The greatest voluptuary dream of mankind, which has lifted the spirits of poets and painters, presidents and peasants, has turned only twenty-two years later into a living nightmare. For young men of my own generation (the word provokes a shudder in the heart, if nowhere else), the situation has become so desperate that any escape seems justified. The price that I have paid for my freedom may seem excessive, but I am happy to have made this serious, if curious, bargain.
>
> Soon after I reached my twenty-first birthday I was ordered to enlist for my two years of national service, and I remember thinking how much my father and grandfather would have envied me. On a

pleasant summer evening in 2010, after a tiring day at the medical school, I was ringing the doorbell of an apartment owned by an attractive young woman whose name I had been given. I had never met her, but I was confident that she would greet me in the friendliest way – so friendly that within a few minutes we would be lying naked together in bed. Needless to say, no money would change hands, and neither she nor I would play our parts for less than the most patriotic motives. Yet both of us would loathe the sight and touch of the other and would be only too relieved when we parted an hour later.

Sure enough, the door opened to reveal a confident young brunette with a welcoming, if brave, smile. According to my assignment card, she was Victoria Hale, a financial journalist on a weekly news magazine. Her eyes glanced at my face and costume in the shrewd way she might have scanned a worthy but dull company prospectus.

'David Bradley?' She read my name from her own assignment card, trying to muster a show of enthusiasm. 'You're a medical student . . . how fascinating.'

'It's wonderful to meet you, Victoria,' I riposted. 'I've always wanted to know about . . . financial journalism.'

I stood awkwardly in the centre of her apartment, my legs turning to lead. These lines of dialogue, like those that followed, had seemed preposterous when I first uttered them. But my supervisor had insisted that I stick to the script, and already, after only three months of national service, I was aware that the formalised dialogue, like our absurd costumes, provided a screen behind which we could hide our real feelings.

I was wearing the standard-issue Prince Valiant suit, which a careful survey of the TV programmes of the 1960s had confirmed to be the most sexually attractive costume for the predatory male. In a suit like this Elvis Presley had roused the Las Vegas matrons to an ecstasy of abandon, though I found its tassels, gold braid and tight crotch as comfortable as the decorations of a Christmas tree.

Victoria Hale, for her part, was wearing a classic Playboy bunny outfit of the same period. As she served me a minute measure of vodka her breasts managed both to be concealed and exposed in a way that an earlier generation must have found irresistibly fascinating, like the rabbit tail that bounced over her contorted buttocks, a furry metronome which already had me glancing at my wristwatch.

'Mr Bradley, we can get it over with now,' she remarked briskly. She departed from the script but quickly added: 'Now tell me about your work, David. I can see you're such an interesting man.'

She was as bored with me as I was uneasy with her, but in a few minutes we would be lying together in bed. With luck my hormonal and nervous system would come to my rescue and bring our meeting to a climax. We would initial each other's assignment cards and make a thankful return to our ordinary lives. Yet the very next evening another young man in a Prince Valiant suit would ring the doorbell of the apartment, and this thoughtful journalist would welcome him in her grotesque costume. And I, in turn, at eight o'clock would put aside my anatomy textbooks and set out through the weary streets to an arranged meeting in an unknown apartment, where some pleasant young woman – student, waitress or librarian – would welcome me with the same formal smile and stoically take me to bed.

(Ballard 1991: 65–7)

The narrator goes on to explain that this dramatic change in people's sexual attitudes and behaviour was caused by the spread of the AIDS pandemic in the last decade of the twentieth century. The fear of the disease had so completely alienated people from marital and sexual relationships, that serious measures had to be taken to reverse the resulting drop in the birth-rate. Hence the institution of a two-year national service for all young men and women, who were forced to engage in regular intercourse with multiple partners in order to guarantee the survival of the nation. The instruction and supervision of the sexually disaffected conscripts was entrusted to the Christian churches, who had to impose carefully selected scripts and costumes in order to ensure the successful outcome of all encounters. Not entirely surprisingly, the narrator ends up falling in love with one of his 'assignments', thereby breaking one of the central rules of the system, and finally has to accept the prospect of surgical castration as punishment for his crime.

The oddity of the world of 'Love in a Colder Climate' can be accounted for, to some extent at least, in terms of the possible-world frameworks discussed in the previous chapters. Three of Ryan's accessibility relations are broken (see 4.6.3): firstly, identity of inventory – since the story involves fictional characters who do not exist in the actual world; secondly, chronological compatibility – since the story presents a hypothetical *future* state of our actual world; thirdly, and more tentatively, physical compatibility – insofar as the apparent disappearance of sexual urges contradicts the natural instincts of real human beings. The strange status of sexual relationships in the story can also be captured by means of Doleželʼs distinction between deontic, axiological, epistemic and alethic narrative worlds (see 4.6.1). In the actual world – or, at any rate, in the current state of the Western world – sex primarily belongs to the individual's axiological world of personal pleasures and desires (with some encroachments of the deontic world of prohibition and obligation when it comes to moral restrictions, vows of celibacy, marital duties, and so on). In the world of the story, on the other hand, sex is firmly entrenched within the deontic domain of external restrictions and obligations, and is no longer part of the individual's axiological world. It is significant in this respect that the affair between the narrator and the woman he falls in love with is never consummated in the physical sense: even in the context of a romantic relationship, sex does not appear to become part of the characters' wish worlds, and therefore never takes place in the actual domain.

In other words, the world of 'Love in a Colder Climate' is strange, interesting and amusing because it goes against many of the assumptions and expectations that readers are likely to have about the attitudes and behaviour of individuals and the structure of society. This is where a theory of the organization of human knowledge can provide a useful complement to possible-world models in the study of text worlds. Ballard's story assumes that readers have a certain amount of knowledge about sexual encounters, national service, people's sexual goals and attitudes, and so on. These are some of the areas of background knowledge – or schemata – that are relevant to the understanding of the story. The effect of the story lies in the fact that the expectations that result from such knowledge are frustrated in a variety of ways.

Some highly predictable components of familiar domains turn out to have been replaced by very different or even opposite ones in the world of the story: in sexual encounters, personal satisfaction has been replaced by patriotic duty, and pleasure by repulsion; conversely, the national service involved does not require that people receive military training, but that they engage in sexual activities. Some variable elements of familiar situations have become fixed and stereotyped: sexual encounters involve compulsory costumes and scripted conversations. New objects and roles have become part of familiar social activities: the choice of sexual partner is determined by an assignment card, and the progress of the individual's sex life is under the control of a supervisor. Clearly, much of the irony depends on the relationship between what readers are likely to expect and what turns out to be the case in the world of the story. The imposition of regular sexual intercourse as part of the national service in the world of the story contrasts with the restrictions on sex in army life in the real world; the mutual interest that the fictional conscripts are forced to feign in order to adhere to the script is sometimes strategically feigned by real people in order to attract potential sexual partners; the clergy's role in enforcing compulsory sex in the fictional world is the reverse of the churches' condemnation of sexual promiscuity in the actual world.

A theory of the organization of knowledge and of its use in comprehension can help to explain how it is that text worlds may be perceived as more or less familiar, conventional, surprising, disturbing and so on. The crucial factor will be the way in which the reader's existing knowledge applies to a particular text. In the rest of this chapter I will provide an overview of schema-based theories of comprehension and I will introduce a number of attempts to apply such theories to the study of literature in general. In the next chapter I will show how schema theory can be used to analyse text worlds in poetry.

6.2 Comprehension, background knowledge and the notion of schema

It is one of the basic tenets of cognitive psychology that comprehension crucially depends on the availability and activation of relevant prior knowledge. We make sense of new experiences – and of texts in particular – by relating the current input to pre-existing mental representations of similar entities, situations and events. A well-known empirical investigation of the role of background knowledge in comprehension and memory involved the following passage:

> The procedure is actually quite simple. First you arrange items into different groups. Of course one pile may be sufficient depending on how much there is to do. If you have to go somewhere else due to lack of facilities that is the next step; otherwise, you are pretty well set. It is important not to overdo things. That is, it is better to do few things at once than too many. In the short run it may not seem important but complications can easily arise. A mistake can be expensive as well. At first, the whole procedure may seem complicated. Soon, however, it will become just another facet of life. It is difficult to foresee any end to the necessity of this task in the near future, but then, one can never tell. After the procedure is completed one arranges the material into different groups again. Then they can be put into their appropriate places. Eventually they will be used once more and the whole cycle will have to be repeated. However, that is part of life.
>
> (Bransford and Johnson 1972: 722)

As it stands, the passage is somewhat obscure, and it is not surprising that the subjects of Bransford and Johnson's experiment rated it as low in comprehensibility and showed poor levels of recall. On the other hand, much higher comprehension and recall scores were achieved by subjects who were provided with a title before listening to the text. The title was 'Washing Clothes'. Clearly, in a case such as this the contribution of the title is very important, since it spells out what portion of the readers' background knowledge is relevant to the interpretation of an otherwise elusive text. Although such relevant knowledge was potentially available to all of Bransford and Johnson's subjects, only those in the second group were able to activate it during the processing of the text. This explains the differences in comprehension and recall between the two groups. A large amount of similar empirical evidence highlights the link between understanding and prior knowledge (see, for example, Bransford 1979: 130ff.; Bransford *et al.* 1984; Abbott *et al.* 1985).

The term **schema** is generally used to refer to a portion of background knowledge relating to a particular type of object, person, situation or event (Eysenck and Keane 1990: 275). The passage in Bransford and Johnson's experiment, for example, requires the activation of a WASHING CLOTHES schema. Each schema contains generic information about the component elements of a particular domain and about the relationships between such elements. A WASHING CLOTHES schema, for example, will include information about things that are used to deal with dirty clothes (e.g. washing powder, washing machines), about the way in which such elements relate to one another (e.g. the washing powder goes into a drawer in the washing machine), and about the sequencing of the actions in which one has to engage (e.g. the powder is placed in the washing machine *before* starting it). Clearly, the content of schemata will vary from individual to individual, and, more dramatically, from culture to culture. My WASHING CLOTHES schema and that of a woman living in a rural area of a developing country are unlikely to have more than a few central elements in common (see also 2.2 above).

The activation of schemata allows us to make predictions and to draw inferences in the process of comprehension. We are likely to assume, for example, that the 'procedure' described in Bransford and Johnson's passage involves washing powder even if the text makes no reference to it. According to schema theory, therefore, meanings are not 'contained' within the text but are constructed in the interaction between the text and the interpreter's background knowledge (see, for example, Carrel and Eisterhold 1988). This interaction is often described as a combination of **bottom-up** or **stimulus-driven** processing and **top-down** or **conceptually-driven** processing (Rumelhart and Ortony 1977: 128; Carrel and Eisterhold 1988; Eysenck and Keane 1990: 8). Bottom-up processing is guided by the external input: an example is the visual perception of black marks on the page while reading. Top-down processing is guided by the interpreter's prior knowledge: an example is the inference to do with the washing powder while reading Bransford and Johnson's text on the basis of the active WASHING CLOTHES schema. Bottom-up and top-down processing are inextricably linked with each other: recognizing and interpreting words while reading a text involves an interaction between visual perception (bottom-up) and previous knowledge of the shapes and meanings of words (top-down); similarly, inferences result from the fact that particular elements in the text trigger the activation of certain schemata (bottom-up), and that activated schemata generate expectations that fill in what is not explicitly mentioned in the text (top-down). You may have noticed that in this book I alternate between expressions such as the *projection* and the *construction* of text worlds. The former expression highlights the bottom-up dimension of text world creation (i.e. texts *project* worlds); the latter emphasizes the top-down component (i.e. readers *construct* worlds while reading).

Schemata arise from repeated exposure to similar objects and situations; they are formed by abstracting common elements from different individual experiences. As such they are part of what psychologists call **semantic memory**, i.e. 'our de-contextualised memory for facts about the entities and relations between entities in the world' (Eysenck and Keane 1990: 250). This is normally distinguished from **episodic memory**, i.e. our memory about specific situations and events that occurred at a particular time (Rumelhart and Ortony 1977: 116; Bransford 1979: 168–9; Eysenck and Keane 1990: 250). My memory of the time when my tumble-drier broke down, for example, is part of my episodic memory, whereas my knowledge of how to operate a tumble-drier is part of my semantic memory. Although in practice such a distinction is less clear-cut than these definitions seem to imply (Eysenck and Keane 1990: 250), it is nevertheless useful in pointing out the difference between autobiographical memories and schemata.

6.3 The origins and development of schema theory

The notion of schema as a mental representation goes back at least to Kant's *Critique of Pure Reason* (1787) – see Kant (1963). According to the *Oxford English Dictionary*, Kant used the term to refer to:

Anyone of certain forms or rules of the 'productive imagination' through which the understanding is able to apply its 'categories' to

the manifold of sense-perception in the process of realizing knowledge or experience. (Quoted in Rumelhart 1980: 33)

In other words, Kant describes schemata as structures of the mind
that represent concepts such as 'dog' or 'triangle', and that guide
our perception and comprehension of the world (Rumelhart and
Ortony 1977: 100–1; Thorndyke and Yekovich 1980).

The origin of modern schema theory, however, is usually traced
back to the work of the Cambridge psychologist Bartlett (1932),
who, in his turn, attributes the notion of schema to the neuro-
physiologist Head (1920).[1] In his empirical investigations of the
processing of visual and verbal stimuli, Bartlett found evidence
that perception, understanding and memory are shaped by the
expectations that people form on the basis of their prior knowledge. In the terms introduced in the previous section, Bartlett
highlighted the pervasive influence of top-down processing in all
mental activities; in his own terms, he showed that perception and
memory are not simply reduplicative, but constructive (Bartlett
1932: 204 and throughout; Thorndyke and Yekovich 1980: 25).
A classic and much quoted example of this is the way in which
Bartlett's British informants responded to a North American Indian
folktale, *The War of the Ghosts*, whose setting and structure were
alien to Western minds. In recall, subjects consistently altered the
story to match their own cultural assumptions about the world:
unfamiliar objects were remembered as familiar ones (e.g. canoes
became boats); links were made between apparently unrelated
elements (e.g. apparently unmotivated characters' actions were
explained as direct effects of previous events); puzzling details
were omitted or transformed (e.g. ghosts were transformed into
human beings or regarded as part of a dream).

Like the gestalt psychologists of the 1920s and 1930s (Anderson
and Pearson 1988), Bartlett used his findings to question the idea
that each experience leaves its own individual trace in memory, so
that remembering simply amounts to mere 're-excitation, or pure
reproduction' of such traces in the mind (Bartlett 1932: 197). On
the basis of his work on perception and cognition, he claimed that:

> . . . in all relatively simple cases of determinations by past experiences
> and reactions the past operates as an organised mass rather than as a
> group of elements each with its own specific character.
>
> (Bartlett 1932: 197)

The basic unit of prior knowledge is the schema, which Bartlett
(1932: 201) describes as:

... an active organisation of past reactions, or past experiences, which must always be supposed to be operating in any well-adapted organic response.

In fact, Bartlett was unhappy with the use of this term to refer to the generic representations in which past knowledge is organized. He felt that 'schema' suggests some static 'form of arrangement', and therefore plays down the fact that human knowledge structures are dynamic constructs, playing an active role in comprehension and constantly changing in the light of new experiences (Bartlett 1932: 201). I will return to this issue in the course of the chapter.

Apart from the basic principle that comprehension depends on the activation of appropriate areas of existing knowledge, Bartlett made a number of further claims, the import of which has not been fully realized in subsequent developments of schema theory. He stressed, for example, that the organization and activation of knowledge is crucially affected by factors such as emotions, interests and attitudes, although he did not attempt a clear description of the operation of these elements within cognitive activities (Bartlett 1932: 206–7 and throughout). In fact, the relationship between cognition and affect was largely ignored for several decades after Bartlett's observations, and has only very recently become the focus of some specific attention (see 6.6 below). Bartlett also highlighted the social origin of schemata (Bartlett 1932: 303) and attempted to sketch a global theory of the functioning of the mind, which included not just remembering, but also the imagination and constructive thought (Bartlett 1932: 312–13).

In the forty years that followed its publication, Bartlett's theory had hardly any impact on the work of psychologists: the dominance of behaviourism and psychoanalysis resulted in a general neglect of the study of cognitive processes and in a lack of interest in the notion of schema in the sense proposed by Bartlett (Neisser 1976: 4ff.; Cook 1994: 18). It was only in the 1970s that schema theory gained a central position as a model of human knowledge, due to the growth of artificial intelligence and its impact on cognitive psychology. The adoption of the computer as a metaphor for the mind gave rise to what is known as the 'information-processing paradigm', where cognition is seen as a sequence of processing stages, from the perception of stimuli to the storage of information in long-term memory (Neisser 1976: 5–6; Eysenck and Keane 1990: 7ff.). Over the last few decades, schema theory has developed as a result of the ongoing cross-fertilization between speculations on the nature of human cognition on the one hand, and attempts to simulate human intelligence by machine on the other. Its range of application includes a wide variety of areas, such as anthropology (Tannen 1984), story processing (e.g. Rumelhart 1975; Mandler and Johnson 1977), second and foreign language teaching (e.g. Anderson and Pearson 1988; Carrel and Eisterhold 1988), semantic theory (e.g. Fillmore 1985), language acquisition and neurolinguistics (Arbib *et al.* 1987).

The adoption of schema-based models of comprehension by cognitive psychologists and computer scientists has led to a proliferation of terms for what I have so far referred to as 'schemata'. The term 'schema' has continued to have wide currency, particularly in cognitive psychology (e.g. Neisser 1976; Rumelhart 1980), and is largely accepted as the most general label for knowledge structures (Cook 1994: 20; Eysenck and Keane 1990: 275). The term 'scenario' has also been used to refer generally to cognitive representations in semantic memory (Sanford and Garrod 1981). Two terms originally coined by computer scientists have gained considerable currency: 'frame' and 'script'. The former was introduced by Minsky (1975) to refer to stereotypical knowledge about settings and situations used in visual perception (e.g. knowledge about different types of rooms); the latter was introduced by Schank and Abelson (1977) to refer to knowledge about sequences of related actions used in the comprehension of complex events (e.g. knowledge about going to a restaurant). Both terms, however, are sometimes used as general labels for knowledge structures as an alternative to 'schema'.

In the rest of this book I will continue to use 'schema' as the most general and basic term, following particularly the version of the theory proposed by Rumelhart and his collaborators (Rumelhart 1975, 1980, 1984; Rumelhart and Ortony 1977; Rumelhart and Norman 1978, 1981). Where appropriate, I will also adopt the terminology proposed by Schank and Abelson (1977) and Schank (1982) to refer to particular types of schemata. These three versions of schema theory will be discussed in more detail in the next section.

6.4 Three versions of schema theory

The versions of schema theory, proposed by Rumelhart on the one hand and Schank and Abelson on the other, provide a comprehensive view of the nature and power of this framework. Rumelhart is primarily a cognitive psychologist; Schank and Abelson are concerned with both artificial and human intelligence. All have produced highly influential models of the organization of human knowledge. More specifically, both Rumelhart (e.g. Rumelhart and Norman 1978) and Schank (1982) focus on the issue of schema change, which, as I will show, is often regarded as particularly relevant to the study of literary text processing.

6.4.1 Schemata in Rumelhart's theory of cognition

The notion of schema as a generic knowledge structure that plays an active role in a variety of mental activities is central to Rumelhart's view of cognition:

> Schemata are data structures for representing the generic concepts stored in memory. They exist for generalized concepts underlying objects, situations, events, sequences of events, and sequences of actions. Schemata are not atomic. A schema contains, as part of its specification, the network of interrelations that is believed to generally hold among the constituents of the concept in question.
>
> (Rumelhart and Ortony 1977: 101)

> [Schemata] are the fundamental elements upon which all information processing depends. Schemata are employed in the process of interpreting sensory data (both linguistic and non-linguistic), in retrieving information from memory, in organizing actions, in determining goals and subgoals, in allocating resources, and, generally, in guiding the flow of the processing system. (Rumelhart 1980: 33–4)

According to Rumelhart, schemata may represent knowledge at all levels of abstraction, from the meaning of words to the structure of complex events and ideologies (Rumelhart and Ortony 1977: 109–10; Rumelhart 1980: 41 and throughout).

Each schema contains a number of variables which may be realized by different aspects of the environment in different applications of the schema. The schema for BUYING, for example, has four main variables – a seller, a buyer, some merchandise and some method of payment – which may take on a variety of different specific values when the schema is used in comprehension (Rumelhart 1980: 35–7). A schema also specifies the constraints that usually apply to each variable, i.e. the types of entities that typically realize the variable. In the case of the BUYING schema, for example, the buyer and the seller are strongly expected to be human. Variable constraints have two main functions: firstly, they guide the comprehender's search for the entities that realize the variables of an active schema; secondly, they provide default values for variables that are not specified by a particular input (Rumelhart and Ortony 1977: 103; Rumelhart 1980: 36). In our culture, for example, money can be taken as the default method of payment within the BUYING schema, even if it is not explicitly mentioned[2] (Minsky (1975) also talks about variable nodes or 'slots' and default values in frames). Rumelhart envisages schemata as flexible structures, taking into account the 'human tolerance for vagueness, imprecision, and quasi-inconsistencies': although the schema for FACE predicts the presence of two eyes, a face with only one eye is still recognized as a face (Rumelhart and Ortony 1977: 111). Variable constraints, as a consequence, are not to be seen as fixed and clear-cut requirements on the application of the schema, but as indications of the normal range of values associated with a specific variable.

Communication crucially depends on shared expectations about the default elements of schemata. Consider, for example, Philip Larkin's poem 'Talking in Bed', which I discussed in 3.3.2. Nowhere does the text explicitly tell us that the poetic *persona* is talking about couples who have sexual and possibly marital relationships. Yet most readers draw conclusions to that effect when they interpret the poem. How can this be explained? Clearly, the references to people who share the same bed over a long period of time (cf. *more and more time passes silently*) evoke schemata whose default participants are people who are (or have been) sexual partners, live together, belong to different sexes, are probably married to each other, and so on. Differences in default expectations may lead to differences in interpretation: for example, some readers may not assume that the people involved are necessarily a man and a woman, in which case marriage may not come into the picture and the poem concerns homosexual relationships as well.

Some of the components of schemata may be schemata in their own right. A FACE schema, for example, will include subschemata for NOSE, MOUTH, EYE and so on. Each subschema may in turn contain further subschemata. Although this could in principle lead to infinite regression, in practice one rapidly reaches a level at which no further subdivision of a concept is possible or necessary in normal cognitive activities: most people's HAIR schema, for example, is unlikely to contain any further subschemata (Rumelhart and Ortony 1977: 106–9; Rumelhart 1980: 38–40).

When a schema is activated during processing, an attempt is made to associate its variables with elements of the input. If a configuration of values is successfully found for the variables, the schema is instantiated, i.e. applied to the particular input (be it a real-life experience or a scene imagined while reading). In order for a situation to be interpreted as an instance of BUYING, for example, the variables of the schema need to be matched with specific people and objects, or, where appropriate, with default values (Rumelhart 1980: 36). Comprehension can thus be described as the selection and instantiation of a configuration of schemata that successfully accounts for the input, whether linguistic or non-linguistic.

> We say that a schema 'accounts for' a situation whenever that situation can be interpreted as an instance of the concept the schema represents. Thus the bulk of processing in a schema-based system is directed towards finding those schemata which best account for the totality of the incoming information. On having found a set of schemata which appears to give a sufficient account of the information, the person is said to have 'comprehended' the situation.
>
> (Rumelhart and Ortony 1977: 111–12)

Clearly, if a comprehender lacks or fails to activate adequate schemata for a particular input, comprehension is impaired. This was the case with the subjects who unsuccessfully read the 'Washing Clothes' passage in the experiment discussed earlier: because the text did not provide enough clues for the activation of the relevant schema, they found it hard to understand (see Rumelhart 1980: 48–9). The difficulties posed by Ashbery's poem 'The Absence of a Noble Presence' (see 5.4.2) can be explained along similar lines. In this case different parts of the text may potentially activate a wide range of schemata (e.g. a TREASON schema, a JOURNEY schema, a DEATH schema), but it is difficult to find a schema or a set of interconnected schemata that can account for the overall coherence of the poem as a whole.

One of the strengths of Rumelhart's framework in relation to other versions of schema theory is the attempt to account for the way in which schemata change and develop in the light of new experiences, or, in other words, the attempt to account for learning. Rumelhart and his collaborators identify three main modes of learning within a schema-based system: **accretion**, or 'fact-learning', **tuning**, or schema modification, and **restructuring**, or schema creation (Rumelhart and Norman 1978, 1981; Rumelhart 1980).

Accretion, which is described as the most common form of learning, involves the accumulation of new information within existing schemata. It occurs when existing knowledge turns out to be adequate to the processing of new input, so that no schema change is required. In an ordinary visit to a supermarket, for example, I may learn the current price of iceberg lettuce, but I will not need to modify my SUPERMARKET schema. Typical instances of learning by accretion include the memorization of lists, telephone numbers, people's names, and so on (Rumelhart and Norman 1978: 38–9, 44–5; Rumelhart 1980: 52–3).

Tuning occurs when new experiences lead to the modification of existing schemata (Rumelhart and Ortony 1977: 123–7; Rumelhart and Norman 1978: 47–50; Rumelhart 1980: 53–4). This may involve:

- further specification of variable constraints and default values
- the replacement of a fixed element with a variable (generalization)
- the replacement of a variable with a fixed element (specialization).

The Church of England's decision in 1992 to allow the ordination of women, for example, led to a situation where people had to modify their schema for Anglican priests, by converting gender from a constant into a variable. On the other hand, if I suddenly found myself living in the world of 'Love in a Colder Climate', I would have to turn some variable elements of my SEXUAL ENCOUNTER schema – such as clothes, verbal exchanges and so on – into constants (in the story, sexual partners wear bizarre uniforms and engage in scripted conversations). I would also have to discard some default elements of my existing schema (e.g. that both partners willingly engage in intercourse) and introduce new ones (e.g. the assignment card).

Restructuring involves the creation of new schemata when existing ones prove to be inadequate. This may happen in two ways:

- by modelling a new schema on old ones (patterned generation)
- by inducing a new schema directly from experience (schema induction).

This is the mode of learning that Rumelhart and his collaborators discuss in the vaguest terms (Rumelhart and Norman 1978: 45–7, 1981; Rumelhart 1980: 54). As an example of patterned generation, Rumelhart and Norman (1981) refer to the way in which their students learnt how to execute new procedures on computer by analogy with old ones they had already mastered. Turning to my own experience, patterned generation could apply to the way in which my HOTEL schema provided the basis for the formation of a more specific BED AND BREAKFAST schema after I moved to Britain from Italy. With schema induction, finding examples is much more problematic. As Rumelhart and his collaborators point out, the ability to discover some regularity in experience tends to require the application of a pre-existing schema – no matter how general – in which case, however, patterned generation occurs. This seems to suggest that patterned generation is the most common mode of learning through restructuring. On the other hand, some form of schema induction must occur at least in the early stages of cognitive development (Rumelhart and Norman 1978: 46–7; Rumelhart 1980: 54).[3] I will return to this problem in the next section.

Finally, Rumelhart's pioneering work on story grammar in the 1970s (Rumelhart 1975) was influential in drawing attention to the study of schematic representations of different types of discourse. Empirical investigations have shown that the comprehension and recall of narratives relies upon schemata of typical story structures, and that such schemata can be represented in terms of the grammar proposed by Rumelhart (Mandler and Johnson 1977; Thorndyke 1977). More generally, it is common for schema-based approaches to discourse comprehension to include a distinction between **formal schemata** (i.e. knowledge about properties of texts) and **content** or **world schemata** (i.e. knowledge about properties of extralinguistic reality) (e.g. van Dijk 1980; Carrel and Eisterhold 1988; Cook 1994). The ability to recognize a poem simply by glancing at it on the page, for example, results from the possession of a formal schema for poetry, which includes information about the characteristic visual appearance of verse as opposed to prose or drama.

During the 1980s Rumelhart participated in the development of an alternative model of cognition known as Parallel Distributed Processing, or PDP (McClelland *et al.* 1986; see Eysenck and Keane 1990: 19–23). Within this framework, knowledge is not divided into separate high-order chunks, but is distributed across networks of low-level neuron-like units. Our knowledge about rooms, for example, is not stored within schemata such as KITCHEN, BEDROOM or BATHROOM, but is contained within a network whose units correspond to objects such as chairs, tables, cupboards, coffee-pots, beds, bathtubs, etc. (see Rumelhart *et al.* 1986). Each unit is activated when some input stimulates it above a certain threshold, and can in its turn activate or inhibit other units to which it is connected. The unit for bath, for example, will activate units such as sink and toilet-roll, and inhibit units such as bed and coffee-pot. Schemata, within this model, are not pre-existing structures in memory, but correspond to patterns of activation of units within a network:

> Schemata are not 'things'. There is no representational object which is a schema. Rather, schemata emerge at the moment they are needed from the interaction of large numbers of much simpler elements all working in concert with one another. (Rumelhart *et al.* 1986: 20)

The schema for BATHROOM, for example, will emerge as a result of the activation of a particular configuration of strongly connected units within the network relating to different types of rooms. It is clear that, as Rumelhart *et al.* (1986) point out, the central claims of schema theory concerning the activation and use of knowledge are totally compatible with PDP approaches. In particular, the idea that complex schemata may not be stored in memory on a permanent basis but rather are assembled during processing will receive further consideration in the present and the following chapters.

6.4.2 Schank and Abelson's typology of schemata

The version of schema theory developed in Schank and Abelson's *Scripts, Plans, Goals and Understanding* (1977) is one of the most detailed, comprehensive and influential. Schank and Abelson's aim was to produce a model of the organization and use of human knowledge that could also be implemented in artificial intelligence. Their primary concern was to describe the kind of knowledge and cognitive mechanisms that enable people to understand texts like the following:

> John went to a restaurant. He asked the waitress for coq au vin. He paid the check and left. (Schank and Abelson 1977: 38)

Although the passage may not make very rewarding reading, it is likely to be perceived as coherent by all (American) English-speaking readers who have some experience of restaurants. Such readers have no difficulties in dealing with the use of the definite article to introduce previously unmentioned referents (*the waitress, the check*), and are likely to infer a variety of further details about the described event, such as, for example, that John sat down, that he ate the coq au vin, that he used cutlery to do so, that he probably had something to drink, and so on.

Schank and Abelson use the term **script** to refer to the memory structures that contain our knowledge of familiar types of events:

> A script is a structure that describes appropriate sequences of events in a particular context . . . Scripts handle stylized everyday situations . . . [A] script is a predetermined, stereotyped sequence of actions that defines a well-known situation. (Schank and Abelson 1977: 41)

Thus, the understanding of the short passage above relies on the application of a RESTAURANT script, which supplies the information that is not explicitly mentioned (e.g. that John ate his food after ordering it and before paying the bill), and therefore enables the reader to perceive the text as a coherent whole.

According to Schank and Abelson, a script consists of slots (Rumelhart's variables) and requirements about what kind of entities can fill those slots (Rumelhart's variable constraints). The slots are to do with roles (e.g. waiter, cook, cashier), props (e.g. tables, menus, food), entry conditions (e.g. wanting to eat), results (e.g. not being hungry), and scenes (e.g. entering, ordering, eating). Each scene consists of a number of actions: in the RESTAURANT script, for example, ordering involves reading the menu, selecting dishes, giving orders to the waiter, and so on. When a script is activated, its component parts become available to be connected to elements of the input. This explains why reference to such elements is made by means of the definite article, as in the case of *the waitress* and *the check* above: both have been implicitly introduced by the initial instantiation of the RESTAURANT script (see 2.2 above). Similarly, reliance on shared scripts allows speakers to omit, and hearers to infer, default roles, props, actions, and so on. This explains why most people would agree that John ate his coq au vin even if this information is not explicitly provided in the text.

Schank and Abelson identify three types of scripts: **situational scripts** (such as going to a restaurant, taking the bus, etc.), **personal scripts** (such as wooing the waitress, being a jealous spouse, etc.), and **instrumental scripts** (such as starting the car, lighting a cigarette, etc.).[4] Each individual script may have a number of different tracks, with slightly different slots and requirements: the RESTAURANT script, for example, may include a 'fast food' track, a 'Chinese restaurant' track and so on. A script also implies a particular point of view, corresponding to one of the roles included within the script. The RESTAURANT script as described so far reflects the perspective of a customer. A cook's RESTAURANT script would, of course, be rather different.

In discourse comprehension, scripts are activated by **headers**, i.e. textual references to entities and actions related to the script. Headers may be more or less strongly associated with a particular script, and therefore vary as to their predictive power. The following are the four categories of headers identified by Schank and Abelson (1977: 49–50), in increasing order of predictive strength:

- **Precondition headers**, i.e. references to a precondition for the application of the script, as in *John was hungry.*
- **Instrumental headers**, i.e. references to actions that can be interpreted as the means towards the realization of a script, as in *John took the subway to the restaurant.*
- **Locale headers**, i.e. references to the setting associated with a particular script, as in *John was sitting at a window table in the Chinese restaurant.*
- **Internal Conceptualization headers**, i.e. references to any action or role from the script, as in *John started reading the menu.*

Schank and Abelson claim that at least two items from a script need to be mentioned in a text in order for the script to be instantiated by the comprehender. The 'Restaurant' story discussed above, for example, contains references to several elements of the RESTAURANT script (*restaurant, waitress, check*), so that the script is fully instantiated. This means that 'a copy of some of its general details is made, with slots filled in by the known properties of the story at hand' (Schank and Abelson 1977: 47). On the other hand, in processing the sentence *John took the bus to New York,* comprehenders do not need to fully instantiate their BUS script, but simply need to assume that the sequence of actions predicted by the script has taken place. Schank and Abelson describe such non-instantiated scripts as **fleeting scripts**. Clearly, such clear-cut rules and distinctions are necessary in computer programming, but cannot amount to more than speculations in relation to human cognition. It is nevertheless reasonable to assume the operation of some mechanism of cognitive economy, whereby comprehenders do not spend unnecessary effort on unimportant elements of the input. In Relevance theory (Sperber and Wilson 1986, 1995), such balancing between processing effort and meaning production is seen as the central principle of all cognitive activities.[5] I will return to this issue in the textual analyses contained in the next three chapters.

The smooth operation of scripts in comprehension may be blocked in a variety of ways. Interferences and distractions may occur, which require the comprehender to abandon or suspend currently active scripts in favour of others. If a fire breaks out in a story while the characters are eating in a restaurant, a new script needs to be activated, and some parts of the RESTAURANT script will become redundant. In other cases, it may be difficult to determine which of a number of possible scripts needs to be activated, or whether any existing script applies at all. More generally, it is common for more than one script to be active at the same time. A simple example would be a story about people having a meal in the dining car of a train: here both the RESTAURANT script and a TRAIN script may be active at the same time, so that both function as sources of expectations and inferences in the processing of the text.

It is not uncommon for jokes to achieve their effect by leading interpreters to activate a particular script and then forcing them to switch to another, often leading to absurdity. Consider the following example (taken from Chiaro 1992: 14):

'Mummy, Mummy, I don't like Daddy!'
'Then leave him on the side of your plate and eat your vegetables.'

In order for the joke to work, the first utterance needs to be interpreted in the light of our knowledge about 'normal' relationships between family members, which, in Schank and Abelson's terms, might be captured by something like a FAMILY RELATIONSHIPS script or a PARENT–CHILD ARGUMENT script: we imagine a highly familiar world where a child complains to one parent about the other, presumably as a result of some trivial conflict or disagreement. The second utterance proves these inferences to be inappropriate and forces us to switch to a different area of world knowledge, which could be described as a FAMILY MEAL script. The humorous effect results not just from the unpredictable shift from one script to another, but from the peculiar instantiation of the FAMILY MEAL script triggered by the second utterance, where the slot for FOOD is filled by a close family member. The ordinary world suggested by the first utterance has been replaced by a rather absurdist world, where it is apparently normal for mother and child to eat the father at the dinner table with vegetables as an accompaniment!

Schank and Abelson claim that most understanding is script-based, i.e. depends on the application of specific knowledge about familiar types of situations and events. On the other hand, they recognize that stories can make sense even if they do not trigger any scripts. Consider the following example:

> John knew that his wife's operation would be expensive. There was always Uncle Harry.... He reached for the suburban phone book.
>
> (Schank and Abelson 1977: 70)

Here readers would easily infer that John is going to phone Uncle Harry to ask for the money needed for the operation. One cannot, however, postulate the application of a PAYING FOR AN OPERATION script which includes ringing up wealthy relatives as a likely course of action (although it is of course possible for someone to have a script for such a situation). Clearly, some of our knowledge is organized in looser and more general structures, which are used when no script applies to a particular input. Schank and Abelson postulate three further types of knowledge structures in memory apart from scripts: **plans**, **goals** and **themes**.

Plans contain information about the sets of actions that some-one may perform in order to accomplish a certain objective, such as funding an expensive operation or reaching one's destination after breaking down in the middle of nowhere. While scripts are quite specific as to what can fill up their slots, plans are much more general. The plan for gaining possession of something, for example, allows for possibilities such as asking, bargaining, stealing, and so on. Plans can therefore be used to tackle infrequent or unfamiliar situations, and, more specifically, to interpret texts dealing with events the reader has no script for. In the case of the text given above, we assume that John has opted for the strategy of 'asking' in order to gain possession of the money he needs. Plan-based com-prehension may also involve scripts: the understanding of John's strategy requires the application of a TELEPHONE script, of which *He reached for the suburban phone book* is an instrumental header.

If a sequence of actions contained in a plan becomes routinized as a result of multiple occurrences, the plan turns into a script. As Schank and Abelson put it, 'plans are where scripts come from' (Schank and Abelson 1977: 72). On arrival in a foreign country, for example, a tourist's knowledge about how to find cheap accom-modation for the night may be held by a plan; after some time, the same knowledge may have become part of a script. Clearly, the same area of knowledge may be part of a plan for some people and part of a script for others. A story about daily life during an expedition to the North Pole will mostly activate plans in the present writer, but is likely to be processed by means of scripts by experienced Arctic explorers (see Cook 1994: 85).[6]

Goals are schemata that contain knowledge about the aims and objectives that people are likely to have. They provide explanations for the behaviours captured by scripts and plans. Schank and Abelson provide a typology of seven overarching goals. The first three are to do with achieving desired states; the next two with avoiding undesired states; and the final two are intermediate goals for the achievement of the first five:

- **Satisfaction goal** (e.g. hunger, sex, sleep, addiction)
- **Enjoyment goal** (e.g. travel, entertainment, exercise, competition)
- **Achievement goal** (e.g. possessions, power, good job, social relationships, skill)
- **Preservation goal** (e.g. health, safety, family, property)
- **Crisis goal** (e.g. health, fire, storm)
- **Instrumental goal** (aimed at enabling the achievement of another goal: e.g. getting a baby sitter)
- **Delta goal** (like an instrumental goal, but realized by general plans rather than scripts)

John's behaviour in the story about the restaurant makes sense in the light of a SATISFACTION OF HUNGER goal, and/or of an ENJOYMENT OF FOOD goal. The 'Uncle Harry' story makes sense if one attributes to John a HEALTH CRISIS HANDLING goal, which is instrumental to a FAMILY HEALTH PRESERVATION goal. Rather like the distinctions between different types of scripts, the different classes of goals tend to merge into one another (there seems to be some overlap, for example, between satisfaction goals and enjoyment goals). It is also obvious that Schank and Abelson's typology captures the priorities of a particular cultural and social group (notice particularly the enjoyment goals of travel and exercise, and the achievement goal of power). As Cook (1994: 89) puts it,

> it might be unkindly observed that there are many ways in which the list reflects the goals of a male middle-aged North American academic – though to be fair, the authors often show humorous recognition of this.

As a consequence, a computer equipped with Schank and Abelson's typology would have difficulties handling stories in which characters operate on the basis of a different set of goals. This would be the case, for example, in a story about religious martyrs, where the goals of upholding one's faith and achieving eternal salvation take precedence over self-preservation. The limitations of Schank and Abelson's list do not, however, undermine the general claim that some set of main overarching goals needs to be assumed in order to predict and explain people's behaviour in both real-life experience and text processing.

Finally, themes provide background information about the origin of people's goals. For example, if we know that someone is a vegetarian Animal Rights campaigner we have no difficulties dealing with the news that he or she is demonstrating outside an abattoir. If the same behaviour is attributed to someone we know as a keen hunter and meat-eater, further effort may be expended in trying to ascertain his or her motivation. Schank and Abelson postulate three categories of themes: **role themes, interpersonal themes** and **life themes**. Role themes provide information about the goals associated with particular societal positions, such as being a sheriff, being a lawyer, and so on. Interpersonal themes contain information about the consequences of social and emotional relationships, such as lover–lover, husband–wife, prisoner–guard, employer–employee. Finally, life themes are to do with the general position that a person aspires to in life. Schank and Abelson identify the following types of life themes: personal qualities (e.g. honesty), ambitions (e.g. having a particular job), life style (e.g. luxury living), political attitude (e.g. communist), approval (e.g. being liked by parents), physical sensations (e.g. having constant sex).

The notions of plans, goals and themes can be used to explain, for example, our ability to make sense of Browning's poem 'Meeting at Night', which I discussed in 2.3.3. The behaviour of the poem's first-person narrator makes sense in the light of the interpersonal theme of lover, which generates the goal of being with one's loved one. In 'Meeting at Night', this goal is achieved by means of a plan involving travel by sea and land. The fact that the journey takes place at night may also suggest that the relationship between the two protagonists is secret, which generates the additional goal of not being discovered.

To sum up, Schank and Abelson provide a typology of schemata based on varying degrees of generality. Scripts are the most specific schemata: they have high predictive power but a limited range of application. Plans, goals and themes are increasingly more general: they provide less precise expectations but they can be applied to a wider variety of situations. The main advantage of the model is that it is detailed, comprehensive and powerful: as the examples have shown, many types of inferences and comprehension problems can be explained with reference to the different levels of schematic knowledge. On the other hand, the theory gives a rather rigid representation of background knowledge, particularly as far as scripts are concerned. In particular, it makes it difficult to explain how knowledge about one domain can be applied to a different domain, and, more importantly, it does not explicitly account for how knowledge structures evolve once they have been formed. It is to deal with some of these drawbacks that Roger Schank developed a further version of the theory in his *Dynamic Memory* (1982).

6.4.3 Schank's dynamic theory of cognition

Schank's dissatisfaction with the version of schema theory proposed in Schank and Abelson (1977) lies, first of all, in its failure to account for people's ability to change their memory structures in order to deal more efficiently with new experiences. Moreover, the 1977 definition of script does not easily account for the possibility that existing knowledge could be used to process situations that are similar but not identical to the one captured by the script. These problems were particularly acute in artificial intelligence applications, where computer programs applied their knowledge base in a rigid fashion, and were unaffected by any input that contradicted their expectations. The way forward, therefore, was to develop a model of a *dynamic* memory, i.e. a flexible and open-ended memory that was able to adapt and develop in the light of new experiences. This would lead to more plausible hypotheses about human cognition and to more successful implementations in machine understanding.

The subtitle of Schank's *Dynamic Memory* (1982) is *A theory of reminding and learning in computers and people.* The term 'reminding' is used to refer to the phenomenon whereby a person, situation or event reminds us of another. The doctor's waiting room, for example, may remind us of the dentist's waiting room; or the plot of *West Side Story* may remind us of the plot of *Romeo and Juliet.* Schank aims to explain not only such reminding experiences, but also the kind of memory failure whereby one may confuse what happened in the doctor's waiting room with what happened in the dentist's waiting room, or even with what happened in the solicitor's waiting room (see Bower *et al.* 1979 for empirical evidence of memory problems of this kind). The 1977 version of the theory, besides failing to consider learning, could not account for either of the above phenomena: if knowledge about visits to doctors and visits to dentists is contained in different discrete scripts, it is hard to see how events stored within one script could trigger, or be confused with, events stored within the other. Yet, the ability to perceive such similarities (which has memory confusions as an inevitable side-effect) is central to people's ability to cope efficiently with the world they live in. Schank also points out that reminding is much more central to cognition than one might think: if we make sense of new experiences by matching them with memory representations of old ones, understanding can be claimed to depend on the occurrence of appropriate remindings. Reminding, Schank argues, can therefore be used as a way into the investigation of human knowledge structures.

What kind of knowledge organization is suggested by the remindings mentioned above? More specifically, how can memory be both abstract enough to allow remindings and confusions between different types of waiting rooms, and specific enough to provide expectations that apply particularly to the dentist's waiting room? Schank makes two main suggestions. The first is that memory structures containing knowledge about specific situations (e.g. the routine in a particular dentist's waiting room) are embedded within memory structures containing knowledge about more general situations (e.g. waiting rooms in general). These memory structures are called, respectively, **scripts** and **scenes**. The second is that a further type of high-level structure exists in memory, whose function it is to organize other memory structures into appropriate sequences (e.g. on a visit to the doctor one goes from the waiting room to a surgery, while on a visit to the solicitor, one goes from the waiting room to an office). Schank calls these structures **Memory Organization Packets**. I will now consider each of these structures in turn.

Scenes are general schemata containing information about different types of situations and what happens in them.

> A scene defines a setting, an instrumental goal, and actions that take place in that setting in service of that goal. . . . As long as there is an identifiable physical setting and a goal being pursued within that setting, we have a scene. Two kinds of information are present in a scene. First, we have physical information about what the scene looks like. . . . Second, we have information about the activities that go on in a scene. (Schank 1982: 86)

Examples of scenes are WAITING ROOM, ORDERING IN A RESTAURANT, GETTING ONE'S BAGGAGE IN AN AIRPORT, and so on. Schank distinguishes between three types of scenes: physical, societal and personal scenes. **Physical scenes** are defined in terms of a particular physical setting: all the examples given above are physical scenes. **Social scenes** are defined in terms of a particular social setting, i.e. a particular social relationship between people for a particular purpose. ARGUMENT can be taken as an example of a social scene. **Personal scenes** are defined in terms of the pursuit of a goal that is private and idiosyncratic to a particular person. A person's own strategy to get one's spouse to do the washing up is an example of a personal scene.

What is a script, then, within this framework?

> A script, in our new, narrower, sense, is a sequence of actions that take place within a scene. Many scripts can encode the various possibilities for the realisation of a scene. (Schank 1982: 86)

A WAITING ROOM scene, for example, may contain a number of different scripts providing specific knowledge about the doctor's waiting room, the dentist's waiting room, the solicitor's waiting room, and so on. An ORDERING IN A RESTAURANT scene will have different scripts for fast-food restaurants, Chinese restaurants and so on. Scripts, in other words, are scene-specific sequences of actions that represent common instantiations of the scene.

Memory Organization Packets (MOPs) are organizers of scenes. They contain information about how different scenes are linked together in frequently occurring combinations.

> A MOP consists of a set of scenes directed towards the achievement of a goal. (Schank 1982: 97)

Our knowledge about flying on aeroplanes, for example, can be thought of in terms of a MOP (M-AIRPLANE) containing the following scenes:

> PLAN + GET MONEY + CALL AIRLINE + GET TICKETS + DRIVE TO AIRPORT + CHECK IN + WAITING AREA + BOARDING + FLYING + DEPLANING . . . (Schank 1982: 100)

Many of these scenes are not specific to this particular MOP, but are shared by a number of other MOPs. CHECK IN, for example, also occurs in M-PROFESSIONAL OFFICE VISIT and M-HOTEL, where, however, it is instantiated by different scripts. The whole M-AIRPLANE can in its turn occur as part of a larger structure organizing our knowledge about trips. Schank calls such structures **meta-MOPs**. Their function is to organize sequences of MOPs in the same way as MOPs organize sequences of scenes. The meta-MOP for trip (mM-TRIP) may include the following MOPs:

> PLAN + GET RESOURCES + MAKE ARRANGEMENTS + PREPAR-ATORY TRAVEL + PREPARATION + PRIMARY TRAVEL + ARRIVAL + DO. (Schank 1982: 100)

Like scenes, MOPs can be physical, societal and personal. Because most events have physical, societal and personal aspects, an individual experience may involve the simultaneous activation of different types of MOPs. As an example, Schank points out that a visit to the doctor may be understood, recalled and remembered in terms of its physical aspects (M-DOCTOR VISIT or M-PROFESSIONAL OFFICE VISIT), its personal aspects (M-HEALTH PRESERVA-TION), and its societal aspects (M-CONTRACT).[7]

Like the 1977 version of the theory, this model involves what Schank calls 'a natural progression of structures' (Schank 1982: 100), including, in increasing order of generality, scripts, scenes, MOPs and meta-MOPs. What is new about *Dynamic Memory* is the idea that, while scripts contain knowledge that is specific to particular situations, scenes can be applied more flexibly to a variety of experiences. Another significant development is the notion that higher level structures like MOPs and meta-MOPs do not exist in a fixed form prior to processing, but are assembled along familiar paths according to processing needs (see also my summary of PDP models in 6.4.1 above). The cognitive system described by the model, therefore, organizes its knowledge more efficiently and uses it more flexibly than suggested by Schank and Abelson (1977). It is not necessary, for example, to postulate the existence of separate WAITING ROOM scenes for a DOCTOR VISIT script, a DENTIST VISIT script and a SOLICITOR VISIT script, but rather of a single scene that can be instantiated within a number of different MOPs. This explains the possibility of remindings and reminding confusions between different types of instantiations of the same scene. The flexible nature of MOPs and meta-MOPs also explains why people do not grind to a halt if a new input does not perfectly match their expectations.

A dynamic memory does not simply need to tolerate expectations failures, but also to learn from them. Schank suggests that, when processing predictions fail, a notation is made in the relevant part of the currently active schema, providing details of the deviant occurrence. This notation will then be referred to in the event of another similar failure. If the same deviation occurs several times, it will become part of the schema.[8] A recent experience of mine can be described in terms of Schank's account of learning. While watching the news on Italian television in December 1993, I was surprised to notice that the newscaster got up from his chair and delivered most of the news standing up in front of his desk, or occasionally sitting on it. This behaviour contradicted the expectations derived from my TV NEWS schema. My reaction was to try to work out why he did it (this occurred during an industrial dispute between the national TV employees and the government), and to wonder whether this behaviour represented an exception or a new rule. The same newscaster behaved in the same way the following day, and so did a different newscaster the day after that. If this trend had continued (which it did not) a standing newscaster would have entered my schema for the (Italian) television news. In Schank's terms, what had started as a rather surprising deviation would have gradually become part of the relevant schema. It is, however, rather simplistic to describe learning in terms of a single invariant mechanism. The particular circumstances where an expectation failure occurs must contribute to determine whether we ignore it completely, we take note of it pending further evidence, or we incorporate it immediately within an existing schema. This applies particularly to the difference between genres in discourse comprehension. The expectation failures experienced while reading 'Love in a Colder Climate', for example, would have rather different effects if they occurred while reading a text that the reader regarded as non-fictional.

In his attempt to account for the phenomenon of reminding, Schank came across instances where an explanation in terms of scenes and MOPs also proved to be inadequate. For example, a sunbather lying naked on a secluded spot on a beach, unaware that he could be easily seen from the cliffs above him, reminded someone of an ostrich hiding its head in the sand. What kind of knowledge organization can make this possible? Schank suggests that similarities across situations can not only be perceived on the basis of scripts and scenes, but also on the basis of goals, plans and themes (these terms are used in the sense of Schank and Abelson (1977)). The main similarity between the sunbather and the ostrich lies in the fact that both are unaware that their hiding goal has failed. A further similarity is due to the presence of sand in both contexts.

Table 6.1

Reminding	Goal	Conditions	Features
Sunbather/ Ostrich	Goal blocked	Planner unaware	Sand; hiding

(After Schank 1982: 114)

Table 6.2

Reminding	Goal	Conditions	Features
R&J/ West Side Story	Mutual Goal Pursuit	Outside Opposition	Young lovers; false report of death

(After Schank 1982: 113)

Extrapolating from a variety of similar instances of cross-contextual reminding, Schank introduces a further type of high-level memory structure, that highlights similarities and parallels between different areas of knowledge. He calls such structures **Thematic Organization Points** (TOPs).

> TOPs are convenient collections of memories involving goals and plans, written in terms of a sufficiently abstract vocabulary to be useful across domains. . . . For any reminding experience that crosses contexts, we can expect that the two experiences share a goal type, some planning or other conditions, and one or more low level identical features.
>
> (Schank 1982: 113)

Schank points out that, like MOPs, TOPs are not permanent structures in memory, but arise during processing, and are only preserved as long as they turn out to be useful. Schank's representation of the TOP involved in the sunbather/ostrich reminding is given in Table 6.1.

Table 6.2. illustrates the TOP that accounts for the reminding experience involving the plots of *Romeo and Juliet* and *West Side Story*. Here, Schank argues, the similarity is due to the presence of two young lovers whose desire to be together meets external opposition. In both cases a tragic end results from a false report of death.[9]

While it is inevitable to feel a certain amount of scepticism at the way in which Schank postulates different types of knowledge structures, it is undeniable that his notion of TOP attempts to capture something important about cognition, that other theories fail to consider. The ability to draw parallels across quite different domains is a central feature of human intelligence, and plays a central role in comprehension, reasoning and learning. According to Schank, TOPs do not simply account for accidental remindings, but also for our ability to actively search our memories for suitable parallels to a situation or issue under consideration. For example, Schank uses the notion of TOP to explain how in 1979 President Carter could propose a parallel between the behaviour of the Soviet Union in Afghanistan and that of Nazi Germany in pre-war Europe. Perceiving such similarities has momentous implications for the prediction of possible outcomes, the planning of future behaviour and the general notion that we can learn from history. Schank also claims that TOPs can explain our understanding of abstract concepts such as imperialism, in terms of sets of goals, conditions and themes (Schank 1982: 111–12).

In the next two chapters I will show how TOPs can be applied to the analysis of metaphorical connections. Here I want to argue that the notion of TOP can be used to deal with an important issue in the study of fiction, namely how fictional texts can be interpreted as making comments on the real world, even when the worlds they project are fantastic. As I mentioned at the end of the previous chapter, this is a problem that is not adequately handled by possible-world theory. Consider, for example, the following fable by Aesop:

A LESSON FOR FOOLS

A crow sat in a tree holding in his beak a piece of meat that he had stolen. A fox which saw him determined to get the meat. It stood under the tree and began to tell the crow what a beautiful big bird he was. He ought to be king of all birds, the fox said; if only he had a voice as well. The crow was so anxious to prove that he *had* a voice, that he dropped the meat and croaked for all he was worth. Up ran the fox, snapped up the meat, and said to him: 'If you added brains to all your other qualifications, you would make an ideal king.'

The world projected by this text is physically impossible in Ryan's sense, since it contains animals who can talk with one another. Like all Aesop's fables, however, the story conveys a moral that is meant to apply to the reader's world, namely that giving in to flattery can have unpleasant consequences. The title of the story ('A Lesson for Fools') clearly suggests that the story is intended to have general significance, well beyond the specific episode involving the fox and the crow. This general relevance of the story's plot to real-world situations can be explained in terms of TOPs. The fable applies generally to situations that involve similar goals (a person A wants an object X), similar conditions (another person

B has possession of X), similar plans (A flatters B) and similar features (A is cunning, B is naive). A similar account can be provided of the significance of Ted Hughes's poem 'Wodwo'. As I argued in 5.3, the speaker in the poem is a member of an unspecified non-actual species, who is uncertain about its own identity and its relationship with the world around it. Although the world of the poem is taxonomically impossible, the plight of the poetic speaker can be made relevant to the situation of human beings in our world. This can be explained in terms of the universality of the wodwo's condition of doubt about its identity, and its goal of continuing to explore its origin and place in the world. In other words, the situation of the wodwo can be related by means of a TOP to the self-doubts and attempts at self-discovery of real people (e.g. an artist trying to define his or her role in society or a teenager negotiating the transition between childhood and adulthood).

6.5 Schema theory: a preliminary assessment

The central claims of schema theory concerning knowledge, comprehension and memory are highly plausible. It is intuitively acceptable that we cope with the complexity and variety of our experiences by discovering and remembering regularities in them, and that we use such regularities as the basis for our subsequent categorizations, predictions and actions (see Thorndyke and Yekovich 1980: 39). Overall, schema theory provides a remarkably flexible and powerful framework for the explanation of inferences, expectations, default assumptions and the perception of coherence in comprehension. The operation of schema-like structures in memory has also been confirmed by a large amount of empirical evidence (for overviews see, among others: Brewer and Nakamura 1984; Abbott et al. 1985; Eysenck and Keane 1990: 279–80, 323ff.; Cook 1994: 12–14). Experiments such as the ones discussed in section 6.2 indicate that the activation of appropriate portions of background knowledge facilitates comprehension and guides recall. Further studies have shown that, after reading a text, people often confuse what was explicitly mentioned in the text with what they have inferred on the basis of their expectations (see Spiro 1980; Brewer and Nakamura 1984: 147; Tannen 1984; Cook 1994: 12–13). This confirms that understanding and remembering involve an interaction between current input and previous knowledge, in which default elements of active schemata are automatically included in our mental representations of the content of texts.

In fact, it is virtually impossible to find empirical evidence that contradicts schema theory, which, paradoxically, highlights the greatest weakness of the model. Schema theory is not sufficiently constrained to generate predictions that can easily be disproved by empirical means. Because no precise principles are provided as to what can be a separate knowledge structure in memory, it is always possible to postulate the existence of a schema that accounts for a particular empirical finding (Thorndyke and Yekovich 1980: 41– 3; den Uyl and van Oostendorp 1980; Eysenck and Keane 1990: 283–5). In *Dynamic Memory* Schank partially tackles this problem by providing a precise typology of memory structures, but the issue of what can and what cannot constitute a schema remains open:

> There can be no correct answer to what kind of content a MOP can have and therefore to what is and is not a MOP. Any prototype that provides expectations can be a knowledge structure in memory.
>
> (Schank 1982: 101)

Elusive as it may sound, Schank's statement could also indicate that the underspecified nature of schema theory is an inevitable consequence of the complexity and inscrutability of human knowledge. In fact, as *Dynamic Memory* shows, an attempt to provide an inventory of all possible schemata may not only be impossible, but also misguided. Our schemata probably do not constitute a limited and fixed set, but are likely to be constantly reshaped and reorganized in the course of our cognitive activities.

For the purposes of this book, the main advantage of schema theory is that it provides a powerful descriptive and explanatory heuristic for observed interpretative activities (see Thorndyke and Yekovich 1980: 39–40). In the analyses contained in the next chapters, I will make references to specific schemata in order to explain particular interpretations of particular texts.

6.6 Cognition, affect and schema theory

As I mentioned in 6.3, the importance of emotional and attitudinal factors in cognitive activities was highlighted by Bartlett at the onset of modern schema theory. The adoption of the computer metaphor within the information-processing paradigm, however, has resulted in a general neglect of affective phenomena in contemporary cognitive science (Ortony *et al.* 1988: 5; Eysenck and Keane 1990: 465). Schema theory has been no exception in this respect: no version of the theory has so far considered the affective dimension of schematic knowledge and its role in comprehension and recall. It is only in recent years that the relationship between cognition and affect has begun to receive the attention of cognitive psychologists, and that a growing body of empirical evidence has been gathered showing the close interdependence between the two. As far as literary text processing in particular is concerned, the need to consider affective phenomena alongside cognitive ones is being highlighted with increasing frequency (e.g. Spiro 1982; Schmidt 1982: 146; Abelson 1987; Lehnert and Vine 1987; Meutsch and Viehoff 1989: 22ff., 99, 188; Miall 1988, 1989; Tsur 1992).

The systematic study of affect, and particularly of its relationship with cognition, is still in a relatively early stage of development. Little consensus has been reached, for example, over the existence of a set of basic or primary emotions, and over the composition of such a set (Isen 1984: 183). The only widely accepted distinction is between positive affective states (e.g. happiness), and negative affective states (e.g. sadness) (Isen 1984; Lehnert and Vine 1987; Ortony *et al.* 1988). As far as terminology is concerned, 'affect' tends to be used as the most general term, 'emotion' is often reserved for intense but relatively brief experiences, and 'mood', 'state' or 'feeling' for more persistent but less intense experiences (see Eysenck and Keane 1990: 466; Isen 1984: 185). A major area of debate is the issue of whether affect and cognition can occur independently of each other. While some scholars argue that cognitive appraisal is always a necessary prerequisite of any affective response, others claim that emotions can be generated independently of cognitive processes (for overviews of this debate, see Leventhal and Scherer 1987; Eysenck and Keane 1990: 466–9). Whatever the answer to this question, empirical evidence shows that affect has a profound influence on cognitive activities (for overviews see Isen 1984; Eysenck and Keane 1990: 472–8).

A considerable amount of interdependence has been found to exist between subjects' affective states at the time of learning something and at the time of recalling what they learnt: people in a certain affective state remember more easily information that they learnt when they were in a similar state. More interestingly, it has been proved that positive affective states lead to better retrieval of positive material (e.g. people feeling happy have a tendency to remember happy experiences). Negative affect states, on the other hand, generally result in decreased recall of positive experiences, but do not consistently lead to an increase in recall of negative material. This asymmetry can been attributed to the fact that people in positive affective states aim to maintain their current mood, while people in negative affective states may wish to change their mood to a positive one (see Isen 1984: 200; Eysenck and Keane 1990: 477). What is crucial, in any case, is the fact that if affective states can act as retrieval cues, material in memory must be marked according to the feelings that are associated with it (see Isen 1984: 218).

Conway and Bekerian (1987) conducted a systematic investigation of the relationship between emotions and knowledge about different types of situations. They found that people tend to perceive similarities between emotions that are likely to arise in similar circumstances, and that members of the same culture share a high degree of consensus over the affective states associated with different situational contexts. When presented with brief descriptions of settings and events, subjects tended to agree about the emotions that people would experience in them, and showed priming effects for related emotion words (i.e. they were faster in recognizing a word presented to them if the word referred to an emotion associated with the situation they had just read about). Conway and Bekerian point out that their findings are particularly compatible with the models of the organization of knowledge proposed by Schank and Abelson (1977) and Schank (1982). The suitability of these versions of schema theory to incorporate an affective component is in fact highlighted in a number of studies (Isen 1984; Lehnert and Vine 1987; Ortony *et al.* 1988).

In applying schema theory to the analysis of poetic text worlds in the next chapters, I will therefore consider the likely emotional associations of different schemata, and their role in the interpretation of the poems. Following Lehnert and Vine (1987), I will adopt a basic distinction between circumstances typically associated with positive affective states (e.g. meeting a loved one), circumstances typically associated with negative affect states (e.g. losing a loved one), and circumstances that would typically involve low or neutral emotionality (e.g. going to the supermarket) (see also Conway and Bekerian 1987: 185). The distinction between positive and negative states will not however be presented in terms of an opposition between the two extremes of a single continuum, as has traditionally been suggested. As Isen (1984: 202) points out, there is increasing empirical evidence that positive and negative affect are separate feeling states, which should be captured by separate scales. Highly emotional situations may involve a mixture of the two: getting married, for example, may give rise to a combination of happiness and sadness, and can therefore score highly in terms of both positive and negative affect.

6.7 Schema theory as an approach to literature

Since the early 1980s a number of studies have applied schema theory to the analysis of literary texts and literary reading. This has resulted from an increased interest in the process of literary interpretation, and from an increased awareness of the connection between differences in readers' background knowledge and differences in interpretation (Freundlieb 1982; Müske 1990).

As I will show in this section, a common thread in studies applying schema theory to literature is the claim that literary texts tend to challenge and modify the readers' existing schemata. This leads to a cognitive approach to the definition of literariness, whereby the main common characteristics of literary texts are their ability to disrupt the ordinary application of schemata and their potential for causing schema change. Such an approach is part of a wider recent tendency to regard literariness as a property of text processing rather than as a formal property of a certain type of texts. Culler's notion of 'literary competence' (1975) and Schmidt's 'aesthetic' and 'polyvalence' conventions for literary reading (Schmidt 1982) are among the most influential representatives of this trend within contemporary literary studies.

For the purposes of this book, however, the relevance of any application of schema theory to literature lies in its implications for the analysis of text worlds. With this in mind, I will now introduce in detail the theory of literariness proposed by Cook (1990, 1994).

6.7.1 Cook's 'schema refreshment'

In Cook's recent work (Cook 1990, 1994), schema theory and literary theory complement each other to produce a comprehensive approach to the definition of literariness. Cook argues that literary theory has failed to account satisfactorily for the nature of literature because of its almost exclusive concentration on linguistic and text-structural features. In particular, the Russian Formalists' notions of deviation and de-automatization have been unwisely restricted to the linguistic make-up of texts, rather than being extended to include the extra-linguistic knowledge that readers employ to achieve coherence in interpretation. Schema theory can provide a framework in which to account for the interaction between the language and structure of texts on the one hand, and the readers' knowledge on the other. It is only in relation to this interaction, Cook argues, that literariness can be successfully defined. He states his overall aim as follows:

> to propose a theory of literariness as a dynamic interaction between linguistic and text-structural form on the one hand, and schematic representation of the world on the other, whose overall result is to bring about a change in the schemata of the reader. I shall call this dynamic interaction 'discourse deviation'. [. . .] In particular, I wish to suggest that in certain types of discourse, change in high-level schemata takes place through linguistic and text-structural deviation, but that (as is the case in many advertisements) such deviation is no guarantee of such change. (Cook 1994: 182)

Literariness, the argument goes, typically arises when deviations at the level of language and text pose a challenge to the reader's schemata (**schema disruption**), and result in schema change (**schema refreshment**). According to Cook, such change may involve the destruction of old schemata, the creation of new ones, or the establishment of new connections between existing schemata (Cook 1994: 191ff.). It is this complex phenomenon that Cook describes as discourse deviation, and that he sees as the essence of literariness.[10]

By means of this approach, Cook proposes an explanation as to why, for example, advertisements are not considered to be literary even if they often display linguistic deviation and patterning. In advertising discourse, he argues, linguistic experimentation does not usually correspond to deviation at the level of the background knowledge that is likely to be shared by the audience. Cook's analyses aim to show how advertisements tend to rely on and confirm stereotypical assumptions about people and the world. Their effect is therefore described as **schema reinforcing**, if they strengthen existing schemata, **schema preserving** if they simply confirm existing schemata, or **schema adding**, if they provide new information (usually about the advertised product) to be incorporated within existing schemata.[11]

On the other hand, Cook argues, literary texts typically evoke conflicting and open-ended schemata, and establish complex and novel relationships between them. In Cook's reading of Blake's 'The Tyger', for example, the following schemata are activated: TIGER, FORESTS, NIGHT, BLACKSMITH, ARTIST, GOD, SPEAR THROWER, TEARS. These schemata are brought together and related to one another by means of deviations, patterns and ambiguities in the language of the text:

> The overall effect of the poem, then, is to bring together these schemata either by choosing elements which they already have in common, or by establishing new links between them. (Cook 1994: 220)

In summarizing his theory, Cook (1994: 206) points out that:

> The idea of 'schema refreshment' through discourse deviation is essentially the Russian formalist concept of defamiliarization restated in the light of AI text theory and discourse analysis.

In other words, the theory builds on the notion of defamiliarization by using tools that were not available to its original creators. As I mentioned earlier, Cook's central claim is that literary discourse performs the crucial cultural function of creating the conditions for schema change. This, he argues, is due to the fact that literature is a type of discourse with 'no immediate practical or social consequence' (Cook 1994: 191). As a result, it provides readers with an opportunity to reorganize their schemata without the risk of incurring social sanctions and inconvenient practical consequences.

Clearly, Cook's argument captures something that is central to the notion of literariness, at least in contemporary Western cultures. It is true that, by and large, we tend to associate literature (or at least some types of literature) with both linguistic creativity and with innovative, original thinking. A high degree of discourse deviation, in other words, may well be the distinguishing feature of works that are considered prototypically literary (although this is probably more true of poems than of novels and plays). On the other hand, it is also true that discourse deviation is not limited to literature, and that not all texts that are considered to be literary display discourse deviation. Cook explicitly and repeatedly acknowledges this, but he does nevertheless seem to imply the existence of an almost necessary link between literary texts and, minimally, schema refreshment. The problem with this is that it leads to the conclusion that texts that confirm dominant assumptions have a weaker claim to literariness than schema refreshing ones, which is hard to maintain even within the boundaries of twentieth-century Western culture.[12] Rather, I would argue that, although discourse deviation may be a central property of prototypically literary texts, in practice texts that are regarded as literary range on a continuum from schema reinforcement at one end to schema refreshment at the other end. My analyses in the next three chapters will contrast poems that I regard as occupying different positions on such a continuum. In order to account for such differences, I will suggest some adjustments to Cook's definition of schema refreshment.

Cook's theory has interesting implications for the analysis and description of text worlds. These are partly highlighted by Cook himself:

> A reader's feeling that the text structure or linguistic choices of a given discourse are normal or deviant derives from a comparison of its text structure (T) and its language (L) with the reader's pre-existing text schemata S(T) and language schemata S(L). The interaction of these interactions creates the illusion of a 'world' in the discourse (W), which can then be compared with the world schemata of the reader, yielding a judgement as to the normality or deviance of that illusory world. (Cook 1994: 201)

If a text reinforces the reader's schemata, the world it projects will be perceived as conventional, familiar, realistic and so on. If a text disrupts and refreshes the reader's schemata, the world it projects will be perceived as deviant, unconventional, alternative, and so on. It is important to notice that this enables us to account for readers' perceptions of text worlds without being restricted to the presence or absence of impossible or counterfactual elements. A text world may be regarded as deviant or alternative because it presents a view of reality that goes against the readers' existing assumptions, or the assumptions shared by a particular cultural group. In this respect, a schema-theory approach to the analysis of text worlds goes beyond some of the limitations of possible-world models. Another advantage is the possibility of accounting for the fact that different readers may construct and perceive the world of the same text in different ways. As Cook repeatedly points out, discourse deviation and schema refreshment are reader-dependent phenomena (Cook 1994: 192 and throughout): what is schema refreshing for one reader, or one culture, may not be schema refreshing for another reader, or another culture.

Finally, Cook's framework achieves another important result: that of showing in detail how schema theory can be sensitively and usefully applied to the analysis of texts that are much more complex and rewarding than those traditionally discussed within artificial intelligence and cognitive psychology.[13] This involves, first and foremost, considering a link that was consistently ignored by schema theorists, namely the role of linguistic choice and text structure in the activation, application and modification of schemata (Cook

1994: 188–9 and throughout). The interaction between the linguistic features of texts and the readers' background knowledge will be the main focus of my analyses in the following chapters.

6.7.2 Other applications of schema theory to literature

Similar attempts at defining literariness in terms of schema theory have been made by de Beaugrande (1987) and Weber (1992). De Beaugrande claims that, although literature is processed by means of the same schemata that apply to other types of discourse, the application of such schemata is made more flexible by the activation of a special higher-order ALTERNATIVITY schema. The influence of this schema leads to greater flexibility in the range of values that can be taken by the variables of other schemata, and therefore creates the conditions for constructing worlds that stand in a relationship of alternativity to what readers regard as the 'real' world (see also de Beaugrande 1980: 198; de Beaugrande and Dressler 1981: 185). Although de Beaugrande explicitly denies that this definition of literature implies the inherent fictionality of all literary texts (de Beaugrande 1987: 58–9), his approach does nevertheless sound more like an account of fiction than of literature. Moreover, no empirical backup is provided for the existence of high-level schemata that control the application of lower-level ones. What is interesting for the purposes of this book is that de Beaugrande recognizes that literary text worlds may be more or less alternative, deviant or innovative and that he defines such potential for alternativity within the framework of schema theory.

Weber (1992) has developed a framework similar to Cook's from a critical linguistic perspective. Like Cook, Weber argues that the interaction between readers and texts may result in their schemata being reinforced or challenged. If the outcome is the strengthening of existing schemata, he talks about 'negative manipulation'. If the outcome is questioning and changing existing schemata, he talks about 'positive manipulation'. Like Cook, Weber sees the latter as a marker of literariness. In addition, Weber explicitly links positive manipulation with literary and aesthetic value, as is evident from the choice of the adjectives 'positive' and 'negative' for the two different modes of interaction between texts and readers' schemata (Weber 1992: 161–5). Clearly, these claims raise a number of problems. First of all, the attribution of value is a subjective matter, and, as such, cannot be decided upon in absolute terms: while some readers may enjoy reading texts that challenge their assumptions, others may prefer texts that confirm their view of the world (in fact the same reader may prefer one or the other in different circumstances). Secondly, and more importantly, Weber's framework seems to take it for granted that the reader's existing schemata are always narrow-minded, intolerant and stereotyped, and that literary texts always work towards the establishment of non-classist, non-racist and non-sexist views. This is, in my view, too restricted a picture of both readers and literature. In spite of these problems, Weber's work helps to show how schema theory is increasingly being extended beyond its original boundaries, and also how similar ideas about schemata and literature are at the present time being developed from different perspectives.

Apart from the definition of literariness, a popular area of application of schema theory is the study of story processing (see 6.4.1). Although the texts discussed within this tradition tend to be very simple and artificially constructed, some studies have focused on literary narratives (e.g. Rumelhart 1975; Lenders 1989). Here the emphasis tends to be on issues such as inferencing, the disambiguation of anaphoric references, and story schemata. More generally, a number of literary scholars have used schema theory as a model for the analysis of literary works. For example, Freundlieb (1982) discusses various interpretative possibilities of Poe's stories from a schema-theory perspective; Miall (1988, 1989) highlights the difficulties involved in applying schema theory to the interpretation of a story by Virginia Woolf; Müske (1990) analyses a story by the German author Heli Busse; and Gladsky (1992) considers the role of world and language schemata in the comprehension of Anthony Burgess's 'A Clockwork Orange'. Only Cook (1994) and Tsur (1992), however, apply schema theory to the analysis of poetry as well as literary prose.

As I mentioned earlier, many of these studies agree in one way or another with Cook's and Weber's view that literary texts make special interpretative demands which may lead to schema change (Freundlieb 1982; Miall 1988, 1989; Müske 1990; Tsur 1992). This, of course, is a way of expressing in terms of schema theory the expectation that texts that are regarded as literary convey original ideas and provide new and challenging insights into reality. A partially alternative approach is proposed by McCormick and Waller (1987) in a paper called 'Text, reader, ideology: the interactive nature of the reading situation'. McCormick and Waller argue that the interaction between readers and literary texts may result in three types of outcomes: what they call a **matching of repertoires**, when the reader's assumptions and expectations are fulfilled by the text; a **mismatching of repertoires**, when the reader's assumptions and expectations are not fulfilled by the text because of a lack of relevant knowledge on the reader's part; and a **clashing of repertoires**, when the reader disagrees with or opposes the assumptions expressed by the text.

In the rest of this book, I will largely adopt Cook's terminology, but, rather like McCormick and Waller, I will focus on the differences between schema-reinforcing and schema-refreshing texts *within* the domain of literature (or more specifically poetry), and on their implications for the readers' perception of the worlds projected by different texts.

NOTES

[1] Some sources give historical precedence to gestalt psychologists, who started talking about schema-like mental structures in the second decade of this century (Anderson and Pearson 1988).

[2] To be precise, the position of cash as a default method of payment is being increasingly displaced by cheques and credit cards. What is being transferred by paying, however, is still the same type of 'entity', i.e. credit in a particular currency. This contrasts, for example, with the exchange of goods that takes place in barter.

[3] Rumelhart's account of learning is similar to that proposed by Piaget within a developmental context. Piaget sees intelligence as a form of adaptation to the environment, which involves a combination of **assimilation** and **accommodation**. Assimilation involves the integration of external stimuli into existing schemata, and is therefore analogous to accretion. Accommodation involves the modification of existing schemata to fit new experiences, and is therefore analogous to tuning (Piaget 1953: 6–7 and throughout; Piaget and Inhelder 1969; 5–6 and throughout).

[4] The examples given in brackets (which are all provided by Schank and Abelson (1977: 61–6)) show some unhelpful overlaps between different types of scripts: why, for example, is 'wooing the waitress' a personal and not an instrumental script? Schank and Abelson spell out the differences between the three categories as follows. Situational scripts (such as going to a restaurant) are linked to a specific situational context and involve multiple participants, whose interactions are governed by a shared understanding of the application of the script. Personal scripts, on the other hand (such as wooing the waitress while in a restaurant), are made up of private goals and routines, of which other people may not necessarily be aware. Instrumental scripts (such as starting the car) also involve only one participant, but they are not private and tend to be characterized by highly fixed and relatively uninteresting sequences of actions aimed at the achievement of very specific goals.

[5] Relevance theory is not in fact incompatible with schema theory. Sperber and Wilson define context as 'a psychological construct, a subset of the hearer's assumptions about the world' with which a new input combines to produce contextual effects (Sperber and Wilson 1986, 1995: 15). The most relevant interpretation of an utterance is the one that requires the smallest processing effort and results in the greatest cognitive effects. In schema theory terms, Sperber and Wilson's context can be said to correspond to the configuration of schemata that is activated during the processing of a particular input. As far as the organization of knowledge is concerned, Sperber and Wilson use the phrase 'encyclopaedic entry' in much the same way as I use the term 'schema'.

[6] This can in fact be seen as an account of what Rumelhart calls schema induction. As I mentioned in 6.4.1, Rumelhart and his collaborators have difficulties describing this process (I am grateful to Caroline Clapham for this observation).

[7] This final dimension clearly would not apply to a visit occurring within a national health system.

[8] This results in what Rumelhart calls tuning. Schank's account of learning focuses more on the details of the process that leads to schema change, but is, on the whole, less comprehensive and sophisticated than Rumelhart's. It is worth remembering, however, that Schank aimed to produce a model of human cognition that could be applied in artificial intelligence.

[9] In this example the parallels are in fact considerably more profound than Schank points out, given that *West Side Story* originated as a deliberate modern version of *Romeo and Juliet.*

[10] It may be useful to emphasize the difference between schema refreshment and discourse deviation. Schema refreshment is change at the level of schemata. Discourse deviation is the phenomenon whereby linguistic patterns and deviations cause schema refreshment. Schema refreshment, therefore, can occur independently of discourse deviation.

[11] Cook's notion of schema refreshment clearly corresponds to Rumelhart's tuning, while schema adding corresponds to accretion (see 6.4.1 above). It is surprising, however, that Cook's impressively detailed overview of schema theory contains no references to Rumelhart's work on schema change.

[12] During 'Poetry week' in October 1995, the BBC invited the British public to vote for their favourite poem. The winner was 'If' by Rudyard Kipling – a poem where a high degree of linguistic parallelism is used, in my view, to express very traditional assumptions about honour, self-control and 'manhood'.

[13] In his analyses, Cook uses a simplified version of the framework proposed in Schank and Abelson (1977) (see 6.4.2. above).

Schema theory and the analysis of poetic text worlds

7.1 Introduction

In this chapter I propose an approach to the analysis of poetic text worlds based on schema theory. I will show how such an approach goes beyond some of the limitations of possible-world frameworks. As I demonstrated in Part II of this book, possible-world theory allows the description and classification of text worlds on the basis of the accessibility relations that link them to the actual world. As a consequence, it is helpful in accounting for the different types of impossibility or counterfactuality that one may encounter in reading literature in general and poetry in particular. This does not, however, go far enough. Firstly, we may perceive a text world as impossible, or – more likely – as strange, puzzling or improbable, not because it breaks any abstract laws of possibility, but rather because it goes against less clearly defined sets of ex-pectations, attitudes and assumptions that we have formed on the basis of our own experience of the world. Secondly, possible-world models do not account for the fact that a considerable amount of variation can be found between text worlds that are linked to the actual world by the same accessibility relations. For example, I will show that texts that fall at the 'realistic' end of typologies such as Ryan's (1991a, discussed in 4.6.3 and 5.4.1 above) may still vary a great deal as to the kind of world they project. These issues require a different type of approach, one that focuses on how text worlds are constructed in the interaction between readers and texts.

The two poems that I will analyse in the course of this chapter ('A Pillowed Head' by Seamus Heaney and 'Morning Song' by Sylvia Plath) are similar in two main respects: they both deal with the birth of a child and they both project worlds that, in possible-world terms, are fully compatible with the world we live in. In other words, according to frameworks such as Ryan's, both text worlds fall within the same category, and cannot therefore be differentiated from one another.[1] Yet, as I will try to show, the two poems differ considerably as to how familiar, conventional, harmonious, etc., their text worlds are likely to be judged by readers. More generally, it is important to account for the fact that worlds that are described as 'realistic' in possible-world terms may still present different perspectives or views of reality, and therefore be perceived differently by readers. These differences, I will argue, can be explained by considering the different configurations of schemata that are activated by different texts, and by applying notions such as Cook's schema reinforcement and schema refreshment (Cook 1994).

From a schema-theory perspective, text worlds are cognitive constructs that arise in the interaction between readers and the language of texts. More precisely, a text world corresponds to the configuration of schemata that are instantiated by a reader during the processing of a text (cf. de Beaugrande 1980: 24; Rumelhart 1980: 37; Cook 1994: 197ff.; Enkvist 1991). The sum of the reader's existing schemata makes up the skeleton of that person's model of reality – what possible-world theorists call the 'actual' world – which serves as a frame of reference in the construction and evaluation of text worlds (Rumelhart 1980: 37; Arbib *et al.* 1987: 7; Weber 1992: 14). The way in which a particular reader will perceive a particular text world will depend on how his or her various instantiated schemata interact with one another in comprehension, and on whether the reader's current model of the world is reinforced or challenged in the process (Cook 1994: 197ff.). Differences in the availability and application of schemata during the processing of the same text will of course lead to differences in the resulting text worlds. This fact needs to be borne in mind during the reading of the present and the following two chapters. My analyses will make use of schema theory to account for textual interpretations that are, inevitably, my own. Readers whose attitudes and background knowledge are different from mine may arrive at different interpretations.

Because text worlds are constructed in the interaction between readers and the *language* of texts, it is important to consider the role of linguistic choices and patterns in the activation, instantiation and potential modification of schemata. This is where, as Cook points out, most schema-theory approaches to discourse processing tend to be lacking (Cook 1994: 188–9 and throughout). Possible-world frameworks are also generally insensitive to the effect of the linguistic make-up of texts in the projection of text worlds. In my discussion of two contemporary poems in the rest of this chapter I will therefore try to show how a schema-theory approach can be usefully and systematically related to a linguistic analysis of the texts.

7.2 'A Pillowed Head' by Seamus Heaney

'A Pillowed Head' is contained in Seamus Heaney's collection *Seeing Things*, which appeared in 1991. In the poem a father gives a first-person account of the birth of his second child, from an early-morning rush to the hospital, to the first moments of relief after the delivery. The identity of the speaking *persona* and the nature of the narrated events are not revealed explicitly, but can be inferred on the basis of a CHILDBIRTH schema, which readers need to activate in order to make sense of the sequence of actions, feelings and objects presented in the text. 'A Pillowed Head', in other words, relies for its comprehension on the availability of a specific but widely accessible area of world knowledge, which will be shared by all those readers who are familiar with pregnancy and birth in general, and with hospital births in particular.[2] More importantly, the poem seems unlikely to challenge or refresh the schemata that are required for its interpretation, since it presents, from a male perspective, a fairly conventional view of childbirth. This, I will argue, explains why the text world projected by the poem can be described not just as 'potentially actual' in possible-world terms, but also as providing a rather familiar, conventional and generally unproblematic view of reality.

In my analysis of the poem I will firstly concentrate on deixis, definite reference and on the occurrence of various types of linguistic patterns and deviations. I will then go on to discuss in more detail the configuration of schemata that are centrally involved in my interpretation of the poem. As I announced in the previous chapter, I will use the term schema to refer generally to knowledge structures in memory. Where appropriate, I will also use more specific terms such as scene, script, MOP and TOP in order to describe particular *types* of schemata.

7.2.1 The poem: a linguistic approach

A PILLOWED HEAD

Matutinal. Mother-of-pearl
Summer come early. Slashed carmines
And washed milky blues.

To be first on the road,
Up with the ground-mists and pheasants.   5
To be older and grateful

That this time you too were half-grateful
The pangs had begun – prepared
And clear-headed, foreknowing

The trauma, entering on it   10
With full consent of the will.
(The first time, dismayed and arrayed

In your cut-off white cotton gown,
You were more bride than earth-mother
Up on the stirrup-rigged bed,   15

Who were self-possessed now
To the point of a walk on the pier
Before you checked in.)

And then later on I half-fainted
When the little slapped palpable girl   20
Was handed to me; but as usual

Came to in two wide-open eyes
That had been dawned into farther
Than ever, and had outseen the last

Of all those mornings of waiting   25
When your domed brow was one long held silence
And the dawn chorus anything but.

Deixis and the projected discourse situation

The poem projects a narrative discourse situation in which a
first-person speaker talks to a specific (but presumably absent)
'addressee' about a past experience that involved them both. Because all references to addresser and addressee are made deictically
(*I/ me, you/ your*), readers need to infer their identities and mutual
relationship from the content of the speaker's narrative. As I mentioned earlier, the activation of a CHILDBIRTH schema results
in the poetic *persona* being constructed as a father recalling his
child's birth and the addressee as the child's mother.[3]

The use of the past tense throughout the poem marks content time (the time of the recounted events) as antecedent with
respect to coding time (the time of the narration), and positions
the first-person speaker in a conventional narrative role. A further

distinction within content time is established by the use of proximal time deixis to refer to the time of the main narrated event,
namely the birth of the couple's second child: _This time you too were
half-grateful_ (line 7), _Who were self-possessed now_ (line 16). This event
is contrasted by the speaker with the birth of the couple's first
child, which is referred to as _The first time_ (line 12) and described,
within brackets, between lines 12 and 15. Distal time deixis is also
used to refer to the time of the woman's second pregnancy in _all
those mornings of waiting_ (line 25). Overall, these deictic choices do
not simply signal the chronological relationships between different
periods and events. They also highlight the speaker's perception
of them: his strong emotional involvement with the second, more
recent birth, his satisfaction with the woman's more controlled
attitude second time round, and his relief that the anxieties of the
pregnancy are a thing of the past. The deixis of the poem, in
other words, can be explained in both temporal _and_ empathetic
terms (see 3.2 above).

Definite reference and schema activation

The use of definite reference in the poem reflects the personal
nature of the projected communicative situation, in which the
speaking _persona_ talks about an experience that he shared with the
person he is apparently addressing. An _in medias res_ effect is created by the occurrence of the definite article to introduce referents that are given for the poetic addresser and addressee, but
new from the readers' perspective (e.g. _the pangs_ in line 8 and _the
pier_ in line 17).[4]

More specifically, definite reference is made to a number of
central components of the narrated event, which can be regarded
as default, or at any rate as highly predictable elements of a schema
to do with childbirth. This applies, for example, to _the pangs_ in
line 8, _the trauma_ in line 10, _the stirrup-rigged bed_ in line 15, _the little
slapped palpable girl_ in line 20 and so on. As I mentioned in 6.4.2,
Schank and Abelson point out that when a schema is in operation
its component elements are implicitly introduced, and therefore
take the definite article even when they are referred to for the
first time (Schank and Abelson 1977: 41, 66; see also Cook 1994:
13 and 2.2 above). This satisfactorily accounts for the simple texts
considered by Schank and Abelson, where an early indefinite
reference unequivocally activates a script, and is then followed by
multiple definite references to default elements of the script (see,

for example, the short passage discussed in 6.4.2). Clearly, in 'A Pillowed Head' the situation is not quite so simple. Here, I would argue, the cumulative effect of the definite noun phrases mentioned above indicates that a schema containing their referents is currently active for the poetic *persona*, and that readers need to activate such a schema in order to interpret the text (cf. Tsur 1992: 227–8). Once the schema is activated, it will justify any further definite reference to its component elements, as argued by Schank and Abelson.

The use of definite reference to introduce the main elements of a schema is not therefore necessarily a *consequence* of the fact that a certain schema has been activated, as suggested by schema theorists, but can also act as a *trigger* causing the activation of the schema. Some of the definite references in 'A Pillowed Head' seem to perform the former role from the point of view of the poetic speaker, and the latter from the point of view of the readers.

The 'dawn' images

The poem opens with three highly elliptical sentences giving a vivid description of a summer dawn:

> Matutinal. Mother-of-pearl
> Summer come early. Slashed carmines
> And washed milky blues.

The first sentence consists only of an adjective, the second sentence of a noun phrase (which also contains an elliptical relative clause), and the third sentence of two coordinated noun phrases. The absence of finite verbs and subjects in the whole of the first stanza, and consequently of any specification of tense and agency, foregrounds the juxtaposition of visual images providing the setting of the opening of the poem. The rare flavour of some lexical choices (*Matutinal, carmines*), and the oddity of the associations between premodifiers and head nouns in sentences 2 and 3 (*mother-of-pearl summer, slashed carmines, washed milky blues*) contribute to the foregrounding of the opening scene and give a graphic and effective portrayal of the mixing and patterning of colours in the early morning sky.

Although the first stanza contains no explicit references to the main topic of the poetic *persona*'s narration, some of the deviant noun phrase premodifiers (*mother-of-pearl, milky*) can be interpreted in retrospect as making indirect references to motherhood and rearing, and thereby anticipating the events that will be the main focus of the poem (in this context, *slashed carmines* could also be seen as an allusion to the spillage of blood during birth). This association between dawn and birth is not restricted to the first stanza, but re-emerges towards the end of the poem. In stanza 8 the speaker describes the moment when, after the emotional turmoil of the birth, he metaphorically regains consciousness at the sight of his partner's eyes. Here a dawn metaphor is used to express the way in which the depth of the woman's experience of bringing about for the second time the beginning of a new life is reflected in her eyes:

> Came to in two wide-open eyes
> That had been dawned into farther
> Than ever,

The fact that the eyes being referred to here are the mother's (rather than the baby's) is indicated by the use of the adverbial phrase *as usual* and by the comparative construction *farther than ever*. These expressions also seem to suggest a parallel between the speaker's relief at the sight of his partner's eyes after the birth, and a more habitual experience, such as that of seeing her face next to him when he wakes up in the morning. This time, however, her eyes have not just been through the dawn of a new day, but the metaphorical dawn of the birth of a new child (*dawned into farther than ever*). Birth, like dawn, is both old and new for the woman: it is the repetition of an old experience, but also represents a new beginning in her life.

In the final line, the tense anticipation experienced during the pregnancy is summed up by the partners' inability to appreciate the singing of the birds at dawn:

> When your domed brow was one long held silence
> And the dawn chorus anything but.

Overall, the association between birth and dawn forms a pattern that runs through the whole poem, thereby constituting an underlying theme. In section 7.2.2 I will discuss the implications of this association for the configuration of schemata that is evoked during the interpretation of the text.

Foregrounding and the crucial moments in the narrative

Various types of linguistic deviations and parallelisms cluster at particular points in the poem, resulting in what Leech calls **congruence**

of foregrounding, i.e. 'congruence between deviations occurring concurrently but at different linguistic levels'[5] (Leech 1985: 50; see also the notion of **nexus of foregrounding** in van Peer 1986). Such clusters of foregrounded features mark some of the crucial moments in the recounted experience, and also highlight the speaker's attitudes and emotional reactions.

In the first stanza, the co-occurrence of ellipsis and unusual collocations foregrounds the description of the initial setting of the story and marks the beginning of a chain of associations between birth and dawn that connects the beginning and the end of the poem. In lines 12–15, the flashback to the birth of the couple's first child also displays foregrounding at different levels. This indicates both its prominence in the speaker's memory and its oddity as compared to the more recent experience:

> The first time, dismayed and arrayed
>
> In your cut-off white cotton gown,
> You were more bride than earth-mother
> Up on the stirrup-rigged bed,

The foregrounding effect of the grammatical and phonetic parallelism between the two past participles *dismayed and arrayed* is emphasized by their position at the end of a run-on line and by their partial contrast in meaning (*dismayed* indicates a negative emotional reaction, particularly in this context; *arrayed* is often used to describe an elaborate and attractive outward appearance). The opposition between *bride* and *earth-mother*, on the other hand, seems to highlight the conflict between the awkwardness and youthful inexperience of the woman, and the dignity and maturity of the role that she is expected to play. The speaker's keen perception of the change in his partner's attitude from her first to her second experience of labour is also conveyed by his emphasis on her newly acquired rationality and self control: expressions such as *half-grateful* in line 7, *prepared and clear-headed* in lines 8–9, *with full consent of the will* in line 11, and *self-possessed* in line 16 form a set of *quasi* synonyms, which are opposed to *dismayed* in line 12.

In lines 19–21 the excitement and emotional intensity of the speaker's first contact with the newborn baby is reflected, in part at least, in the heavy pre-modification of the noun phrase *the little slapped palpable girl* (which is phonetically foregrounded due to the repetition of /l/ and /p/ sounds, the high frequency of plosives, and the onomatopoeia in *slapped*). The three adjectives are concerned, respectively, with the size of the girl, the result of an immediately preceding action (the midwife's slapping of the infant), and a tactile perception of the speaker's. The compression of different kinds of experiences within a single noun phrase contributes to convey the speaker's heightened emotions and overlapping perceptions while he is struggling not to lose control of himself (cf. *I half-fainted* in line 19).

In the following stanza the dawn metaphor discussed above is preceded by the speaker's full recovery of his faculties when he sees himself reflected in his partner's eyes:

> . . . but as usual
> Came to in two wide-open eyes

The foregrounding of this particular scene, and therefore its prominence in the speaker's memory, is increased by its connection with the title. The meaning of 'A Pillowed Head' and its relevance to the rest of the poem can only be fully determined after the speaker's reference to the moment when he first looked at his partner after the birth of the child. This, as I mentioned earlier, can be paralleled to the more usual experience of waking up with her in the morning and seeing himself reflected in her eyes. The image of the woman's head on the pillow is made particularly memorable by the unusual occurrence of the participial adjective *pillowed* in pre-modifying position in the title noun phrase. In the last stanza, the flashback to the anxieties of pregnancy involves an equative metaphor associating the expression on the woman's face with her temporary reluctance, or inability, to speak (*your domed brow was one long held silence*), and ends with the reference to the dawn chorus discussed above.

The following analysis of the poem in terms of schemata will draw upon the above observations concerning the language of the text. I will first of all propose a description of the main knowledge structures that are relevant to the interpretation of the poem. I will then focus on some specific functions of schemata within the processing of the text, and on the way in which different schemata are connected by means of linguistic patterns in the poem. Finally, I will suggest that a schema-theory approach can provide an account of the kind of text world that readers are likely to construct during the reading of the poem.

7.2.2 A schema-theory approach

As I said earlier, the interpretation of 'A Pillowed Head' requires the availability of some prior knowledge about hospital births and the instantiation of such knowledge during the processing of the text. How can this knowledge be described within a schema-theory approach? Schank and Abelson's (1977) notion of script can be used to capture the series of actions and events that are expected to occur during the birth of a child, but it is too rigid to account for the changes in settings and participants (e.g. from the home to the car to the hospital), and for the fact that some elements of a hypothetical CHILDBIRTH script would not exclusively belong to this particular script (e.g. travelling to the hospital and check-ing in at reception).

Schank's notion of MOP works significantly better. The settings and events evoked by the poem, such as the beginning of labour (lines 7–8), the trip to the hospital (lines 4–5), the delivery room (lines 12–15, 19–21) and so on, can be accommodated within Schank's definition of scene. As I explained in 6.4.3, a scene is a memory structure that contains information about a setting and about a series of actions (a script) that takes place in that setting for the achievement of a certain goal (Schank 1982: 95–7). In the framework developed in *Dynamic Memory*, MOPs have the function of arranging scenes into sequences that bring together knowledge about complex events, such as flights, visits to doctors, or, in our case, hospital births. As I said earlier, one of the advantages of this framework is that it accounts for the fact that individual scenes may occur within more than one MOP, although this will affect the properties of the script that is instantiated in each particular case.

'A Pillowed Head' and M-CHILDBIRTH

'A Pillowed Head' can be interpreted as evoking a series of scenes belonging to a CHILDBIRTH MOP (M-CHILDBIRTH), or, more precisely, to the version of such MOP where the birth takes place in a hospital (which may or may not be the dominant version for individual readers). Table 7.1 contains a list of the scenes from this particular version of M-CHILDBIRTH that are *instantiated* in the poem. In other words, the table does not purport to be a

Table 7.1 Scenes from M-CHILDBIRTH instantiated in 'A Pillowed Head'

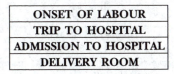

ONSET OF LABOUR
TRIP TO HOSPITAL
ADMISSION TO HOSPITAL
DELIVERY ROOM

complete description of the content of this particular MOP in my background knowledge or anyone else's: it simply shows how the sequence of events presented in the text can be seen as a series of scenes belonging to the same MOP.

How is this MOP triggered by the language of the poem? As I mentioned in 6.4.2, Schank and Abelson (1977: 47) claim that at least two elements of a script need to be mentioned in a text in order for the script to be instantiated. In *Dynamic Memory*, however, Schank (1982) does not attempt to specify the nature and number of headers that are needed to trigger the activation of a MOP. It is often pointed out that schema theory tends to be rather vague as to the mechanisms and conditions that lead to schema activation (e.g. Thorndyke and Yekovich 1980). In this respect, Relevance theory (Sperber and Wilson 1986, 1995) offers a useful contribution. Sperber and Wilson claim that in comprehension we always aim to balance the effort involved in searching and activating background knowledge with the resulting cognitive effects. In schema-theory terms, this is equivalent to saying that we activate a schema when its contribution to interpretation counterbalances the effort expended in activating it. Unfortunately, Relevance theory is also rather vague when it comes to specifying how much processing effort is justified by how many interpretative conclusions, and also ignores any factors that might affect people's willingness to expend different amounts of processing effort in different circumstances.[6]

In any case, there can be little doubt that 'A Pillowed Head' requires the activation of a CHILDBIRTH schema, which I claim is best described as a MOP. In 7.2.1 I have discussed how a number

Table 7.2 Textual triggers for M-CHILDBIRTH

ONSET OF LABOUR lines 7–11 (*the pangs had begun*)
TRIP TO HOSPITAL lines 4–5 (*to be first on the road*)
ADMISSION TO HOSPITAL line 18 (*you checked in*)
DELIVERY ROOM lines 12–15, 19–21 (*the trauma, white cut-off cotton gown, the stirrup-rigged bed, earth mother, the little slapped palpable girl*)

of definite noun phrases in the text function as headers for the activation of such a schema. In Table 7.2 I identify in more detail the parts of the text that are particularly responsible for the selection of M-CHILDBIRTH. The table associates each scene with the lines of the poem that are directly relevant to it, and also highlights those elements in the text that refer to different component elements of M-CHILDBIRTH, and that therefore cumulatively contribute to its activation.

Schema activation and disambiguation

As I pointed out in 7.2.1, many of the definite references in the text are justified by the currently active schema and also responsible for its activation (e.g. *the pangs* in line 8). Similarly, a number of expressions that can only be fully disambiguated in the light of the relevant schema may also function as triggers for its selection. The reference to 'checking in' in line 18, for example, contributes to the activation of a schema that involves a hospital stay. On the other hand, it is only in the light of the schema that one can determine what type of 'checking in' is being referred to. As Schank points out, a CHECK IN scene may occur as part of different MOPs (e.g. M-AIRPORT, M-HOTEL), but will be instantiated by different scripts depending on which MOP happens to be relevant (Schank 1982: 151).

The interpretation of deviant features in general, and of metaphors in particular, is also affected by the schemata that are active during the processing of the text. This applies, for example, to the metaphoric description of the woman's eyes in lines 23–5:

> . . . two wide-open eyes
> That had been dawned into farther
> Than ever

In 7.2.1 I suggested an interpretation of the metaphor that is obviously channelled and constrained by the main active CHILDBIRTH schema: the woman's eyes show how she has been affected by her recent experience of childbirth, which, like dawn, marks a new beginning, and, like dawn, is for her both a new and an old experience.

Schemata and inferencing

Generally speaking, the main function of schemata is to enable understanders to form expectations about what is likely to happen next, either in the real world, or in the world of a text. This does not only contribute to the disambiguation of references and of figurative expressions, but also to the readers' ability to infer what they do not witness directly, or what is not explicitly mentioned in a text.

As I said earlier, the attribution of roles and identities to the poetic *persona* and his addressee largely depends on the selection of a CHILDBIRTH schema, which includes 'mother' and 'father' as default roles (although the latter may not always be instantiated). The activation of relevant prior knowledge is also essential to the gap-filling that readers need to do in order to make sense of the sequence of events narrated in the text. The appearance of the *little slapped palpable girl* in line 20, for example, does not come as a surprise although the text contains no explicit reference to the mother giving birth: the latter event is a default element of the active schema, or more precisely, part of the script relating to the DELIVERY ROOM scene, which is, in its turn, the central scene of M-CHILDBIRTH.

Secondary schemata

My analysis has so far focused on the schema that I see as essential to the interpretation of 'A Pillowed Head'. Not surprisingly, the number of schemata that may be considered to be relevant to the interpretation of the poem increases rather rapidly once we leave the main story-line of the poem and concentrate on the individual images evoked by the text. In my analysis of linguistic deviation and foregrounding in section 7.2.1, I have discussed, for example, the comparison between the addressee and a bride in line 14. In order to interpret this image, readers need to refer to their knowledge about weddings, and to see the analogy between some components of that schema and the main currently active schema. They are unlikely, however, to instantiate their WEDDING schema in full. The same applies to the potential instantiation of a WALK schema and a PIER schema as a result of the reference to *a walk on the pier* in line 17. These schemata are relevant to some limited sections of the text, and will therefore play a relatively minor role in the readers' overall representation of the world projected by the text. In Relevance theory terms, the cognitive effort involved in fully activating these schemata is not justified by their contribution to the interpretation of the text.

Schank and Abelson take this kind of situation into account

when they introduce the notion of 'fleeting scripts', namely scripts that are mentioned without being fully instantiated (see 6.4.2). The distinction between fleeting and non-fleeting scripts is based on the number of linguistic triggers present in the text. For a script to be non-fleeting, Schank and Abelson argue, at least two of its component elements need to be mentioned (1977: 46–7). As I have repeatedly pointed out, this criterion is rather limited, but it does apply to the three examples from 'A Pillowed Head' mentioned in the previous paragraph.[7]

The DAWN schema

In section 7.2.1 I highlighted the patterning of linguistic features in the poem that associate birth with dawn. The opening description of sunrise contains two implicit references to motherhood (*mother-of-pearl summer, milky blues*), while the last two stanzas include two dawn images within the context of birth and pregnancy (*eyes that had been dawned into further than ever; the dawn chorus anything but*). A DAWN schema is therefore activated by means of a variety of headers (lines 1–5, 23, 27), which are consistently related, both literally and metaphorically, to the headers for the main MOP.

The literal relevance of dawn to the topic of the poem is due to the fact that it provides the initial setting of the story. We may say that the TRIP TO HOSPITAL scene instantiated by the text is preceded by, or combined with, the instantiation of a DAWN schema. The metaphorical connection, on the other hand, relies on the association between the beginning of a new day with the beginning of a new life, and on the similarity of some of the feelings that may be aroused by both (e.g. hope, joy, wonder at the power of nature, etc.). It is also significant that both birth and dawn are presented in generally positive terms in the poem. The words used to describe dawn in the first stanza are connected with warmth, light and bright colours (*mother-of-pearl summer, slashed carmines and washed milky blues*); and *mother-of-pearl* also has connotations of beauty and value.[8] As for childbirth, although reference is made to the pain experienced by the mother (*the pangs, the trauma*), the emphasis is on other, more positive aspects of the main narrated event, such as the controlled attitude of the woman (*clear-headed, with full consent of the will, self-possessed*, etc.), and her appearance after the birth (*A Pillowed Head, two wide-open eyes*).

What are the implications of the association between birth and dawn for the configuration of schemata evoked by the poem? I think it is fair to say that the association is not a particularly new or original one. In their work on conventional metaphorical connections, Lakoff and Turner (1989: 11–12 and throughout) point out that the stages of human life are often metaphorically talked about in terms of the daily cycle (consider, for example, expressions such as *He's in his twilight years* to indicate that someone is advanced in age). As a consequence, the establishment of a metaphorical connection between dawn and birth is unlikely to refresh the schemata involved, but rather highlights some similarities that are generally perceived to exist between them. The reference to the *dawn chorus* in line 27 may also trigger a further parallel between the cry of a new baby and the singing of birds at dawn. In Schank's terms, the DAWN schema and the CHILDBIRTH schema can be regarded as sharing a common goal of beginning a new cycle (a new day and a new life respectively), as well as some general features (e.g. the presence of white and red colours, the manifestation of the power of nature, and the noises mentioned above) and generally positive emotional associations.[9] Their connection in the poem can therefore be interpreted in terms of the notion of TOPs (Thematic Organization Points), i.e. of high-level memory structures that associate lower order schemata on the basis of shared themes or goals, and of some other features or conditions (see 6.4.3 above).[10]

A visual representation of the structure of the TOP connecting birth and dawn is suggested in Table 7.3, which is an adaptation of Schank's own framework reproduced in 6.4.3. The inclusion of the additional category 'Emotional Associations' reflects the need to take into account the affective components of cognitive processing, which I discussed in 6.4.3. Clearly the representation of the TOP proposed in Table 7.3 is dependent both on the text which triggers its construction (where, as I said earlier, both dawn and

Table 7.3

Schemata	Goal	Conditions	Features	Emotional Associations
Dawn/ Birth	Beginning something new	New life cycle	Manifestation of nature, noises (baby's cry, birds song), colours (e.g. white, red)	Hope, joy, optimism ...

(Based on Schank 1982: 113ff.)

childbirth are treated as positive and wondrous events), and on the interpretation of an individual reader (myself). In any case, the table shows how the two main schemata evoked by the poem can be related on the basis of a set of fairly conventional and stereotypical associations.

7.2.3 Final considerations

The preceding discussion demonstrates, first of all, the possibility of combining linguistic analysis and schema-level analysis in order to account for the interpretation of texts. By looking in detail at the language of the poem, I have been able to consider the point of view and the attitudes that underlie the activation of different schemata, and I have been able to explicate the way in which connections between schemata are triggered by the text. Secondly, and more importantly, my analysis provides an example of a literary text that seems to reinforce rather than question the areas of knowledge which are relevant to its interpretation, and that therefore triggers the construction of a text world that is not just 'possible', but also fairly conventional and familiar.

As I have shown, the poem requires a straightforward instantiation of a widely shared schema, M-CHILDBIRTH, which accounts for the sequence of settings and events presented in the poem. This contrasts, for example, with the story by Ballard discussed at the beginning of the previous chapter, where schemata such as SEXUAL ENCOUNTER and NATIONAL SERVICE are instantiated in an unusual and defamiliarizing manner. Moreover, the connection between childbirth and dawn in 'A Pillowed Head' results in a harmonious configuration of schemata, since the two main schemata – CHILDBIRTH and DAWN – are frequently associated and tend to reinforce each other's stereotypical properties and emotional associations. In Cook's terms, therefore, the reading of the text is unlikely to cause any significant degree of schema refreshment, but rather largely reinforces the validity of existing knowledge structures. The adequacy of existing schemata in the interpretation of 'A Pillowed Head' can also be captured by Weber's (1992) notion of negative manipulation,[11] and by McCormick and Waller's (1987) notion of matching of repertoires (see 6.7.2).

Like most other discourse types, literary texts may challenge or confirm existing beliefs and assumptions (in this, I go against Cook's and Weber's claim that the reading of literature typically results in schema change). A schema-theory approach helps to pin

down the way in which the reader's background knowledge inter-
acts with the language of the text, and how the former is altered
or reinforced as a result of its interaction with the latter. In other
words, an analysis at the level of schemata contributes to describe
the relationship between the worlds imagined while reading and
the readers' models of reality, and therefore provides a useful
framework in which to account for the degree of alternativity, possibility, conventionality, etc., that readers attribute to text worlds.
As I said earlier, the text world evoked by 'A Pillowed Head' is not
simply 'possible' in the sense of potentially actual, but is also likely
to be perceived as familiar, harmonious, conventional, and so on.
This is not simply due to the lack of obvious violations of physical
laws or of abstract rules of possibility, but rather to the text's compatibility with a number of schemata that are likely to be shared
by the readership of the poem.

7.3 'Morning Song' by Sylvia Plath

I will now discuss a poem that is less easily accounted for in
terms of conventional assumptions and expectations, and that
consequently projects a more challenging and problematic view
of reality. 'Morning Song' was composed in March 1961, and
appeared as the opening poem of Sylvia Plath's posthumous collection *Ariel*. The poem is a first-person address from mother
to baby, and focuses on the mother's experiences and feelings
over a period spanning from the conception of the baby to the
restless nights that followed its birth. 'Morning Song' is similar
to 'A Pillowed Head' in a number of respects. It deals with the
birth of a child from the point of view of one of the parents. Its
interpretation, therefore, crucially depends on the activation of
knowledge to do with childbirth and young babies. Moreover,
both poems project worlds that do not contain any impossible
elements, and therefore fall at the possible, or realistic, end of
possible-world typologies. Minimally, both text worlds fulfil all of
Ryan's (1991) accessibility relations from chronological compatibility onwards (see 4.6.3 and 5.4.1 above). If the poems are read
as faithful reports of autobiographical experiences, the worlds they
project also comply with the rules of identity of properties and
identity of inventories, and therefore overlap completely with the
actual world. In the case of 'Morning Song' in particular, docu-
mentary sources agree in suggesting a closely autobiographical
reading. Plath is generally believed to have written the poem for

her daughter Frieda, who was just under a year old when the poem was written (cf. Hughes 1970: 193; Aird 1973: 70). The poem's composition dates from a few days after Plath's second and much wanted pregnancy ended with a miscarriage (Stevenson 1989: 206–7).

In spite of these general similarities, the text world evoked by 'Morning Song' is rather different from that of Heaney's poem. Whereas 'A Pillowed Head' presents a fairly conventional and harmonious representation of reality, 'Morning Song' gives a more challenging and problematic view of birth and parenthood, by activating a more complex configuration of schemata. From a schema-theory perspective, I will argue, the two poems project different types of text worlds: one largely schema reinforcing, the other potentially schema refreshing.

7.3.1 The poem: a linguistic approach

MORNING SONG

Love set you going like a fat gold watch,
The midwife slapped your footsoles, and your bald cry
Took its place among the elements.

Our voices echo, magnifying your arrival. New statue.
In a drafty museum, your nakedness   5
Shadows our safety. We stand round blankly as walls.

I'm no more your mother
Than the cloud that distils a mirror to reflect its own slow
Effacement at the wind's hand.

All night your moth-breath   10
Flickers among the flat pink roses. I wake to listen:
A far sea moves in my ear.

One cry, and I stumble from bed, cow-heavy and floral
In my Victorian nightgown.
Your mouth opens clean as a cat's. The window square   15

Whitens and swallows its dull stars. And now you try
Your handful of notes;
The clear vowels rise like balloons.

'Morning Song' consists of six three-line stanzas, with no rhymes. All of the stanzas are divided into several sentences except for stanza three, which is made up of a single sentence. With its striking –

and much quoted – metaphorical description of motherhood, the third stanza is, as I will show, particularly central to the poem as a whole.

The discourse situation of the poem

The focus of 'Morning Song' is on the relationship between the poetic *persona* – a mother – and the addressee of her discourse – her child. The poem contains ten occurrences of the second-person pronouns *you/your* referring to the baby, five of the first-person singular pronouns *I/my* referring to the mother, and two of the first-person plural pronouns *we/our* referring, besides the speaker, to other adults involved (presumably the baby's father, and possibly the midwife, friends, relatives, etc.). As I mentioned earlier, what is known about the circumstances of the composition of the poem suggests a strong degree of identification between the author and the poetic voice.

The poem reflects a complex and multifaceted perception of the relationship between mother and child, which mixes joy and tenderness with feelings of distance and separation. The grammatical relationship between the *I* and the *you* of the poem is never a transitive one. The first-person singular pronoun occurs once as subject of the copular verb *to be* (line 7) and twice as subject of intransitive verbs (*wake* in line 11 and *stumble* in line 13). It never occurs as the subject of a transitive verb with *you* as object. The only person who acts directly on the baby is the midwife in line 2. In the second stanza the plural first-person pronouns *we* and *our* are used in an exclusive sense: they associate the speaker with other adults, and exclude the addressee. Like the poetic speaker, the referents of the plural first-person pronoun are the subjects of intransitive verbs, which, furthermore, are predominantly static in meaning: *our voices echo* (line 4) and *we stand round* (line 6). The only potential exception is in the non-finite clause *magnifying your arrival* (line 4), where the implied subject is *our voices* and the object of the transitive verb (*your arrival*) involves the addressee. The transitive nature of the relationship, however, is rather weak, both in syntactic and semantic terms: the first-and second-person pronouns are determiners within the subject-noun phrases (rather than subjects in their own right), the verb (*magnify*) indicates an abstract, non-physical process, and the object is not the baby, but the nominalization of a process of which the baby is subject (*arrival*).

The baby is, on the whole, endowed with a more dynamic role, being the notional subject of verbs such as *took* (line 3), *flickers* (line 11) and *try* (line 16). I use the expression 'notional' subject because, with the exception of *you try* in line 16, the subject noun phrases involving the baby refer to her actions, properties or body parts, rather than to the baby as a whole (e.g. *your bald cry* in line 2, *your nakedness* in line 5, *your moth-breath* in line 10, *your mouth* in line 15). This seems to reflect a tendency on the speaker's part to perceive the baby as a series of separate aspects rather than to relate to her as a whole individual (it is significant, in this respect, that in line 3 the baby's cry is said to have taken its place *among the elements*). Such a tendency is emphasized by the metaphors and similes used to describe the baby, which will be discussed in the next section.

The poem begins in a narrative mode: in the first stanza, the past tense is used to refer to the time of the conception and of the birth (*set, slapped, took*). From the second stanza onwards, however, the present tense is used. This is, in one case, the 'state present' that is used to refer to universal truths or, more generally, to states of affairs that are not limited to a fixed or specific time (Quirk *et al.* 1985: 179): the statement made in the third stanza (*I'm no more your mother/ Than . . .*) describes a permanent relationship between addresser and addressee. In all other cases, the present tense may be variously interpreted as a historic present, providing immediacy to the narration of past events (e.g. *our voices echo* in line 4), as a habitual present, referring to a current routine (e.g. *One cry, and I stumble from bed* in line 13) or as an instantaneous present, reporting actions that occur at the time of utterance (e.g. *Your mouth opens* in line 15) (Quirk *et al.* 1985: 179–84). The latter meaning seems to prevail towards the end of the poem, where the occurrence of *now* in line 16 can be read as an indication that the poetic *persona* is reporting a specific moment that she is experiencing at the time of utterance. On the whole, however, the discourse situation of the poem remains for the most part ambiguous between narration of past events, description of familiar routines, and direct report of current events.

Finally, the title of the poem 'Morning Song' can be interpreted both in relation to the poetic *persona*'s voice and in relation to the baby's: in the former case, it refers to the mode of the speaker's expression of her feelings and experiences – the tone of the poem itself; in the latter case, it is a reference to the baby's own voice, as it is perceived – ironically perhaps – by the mother.

The latter interpretation is particularly plausible in the light of the focus on the sounds produced by the baby in the final stanza of the poem. Whatever the reading, the title carries positive connotations, which, as I will show, are only partly confirmed by the rest of the poem.

Figurative language in the poem

The use of figurative language is the richest and most striking aspect of the language of 'Morning Song'. A variety of metaphors and similes are used to describe the mother, the other adults included in the reference of *we* in the second stanza, and, more than anyone else, the baby. The main common feature of these figurative expressions is that they are all of the 'dehumanizing' type, i.e. they attribute to human beings the properties of animals or inanimate entities (Leech 1969: 158). I will start by considering the two extended metaphors, which, by definition, play an especially prominent role in the meaning of the poem.

In the second stanza, the room where the baby is the centre of the adults' attention is metaphorically described as a museum:

> Our voices echo, magnifying your arrival. New statue.
> In a drafty museum, your nakedness
> Shadows our safety. We stand round blankly as walls.

The description of the baby as a *new statue* is foregrounded by its status as an elliptical sentence at the end of a line, and has at least two main effects: (i) it emphasizes the value of the baby in the eyes of the people who focus their attention on her; and (ii) it creates a sense of distance and lack of communication (statues cannot interact with the people who admire them, and are generally appreciated in aesthetic rather than affective terms). The latter effect is enhanced by the fact that the role attributed to the parents and others by the simile in line 4 is not the predictable one of visitors in the museum, but that of walls who *stand round blankly* (the use of the adverb *blankly* also involves a metaphorical transfer, since the property of blankness relates to the walls – and, therefore, the people involved – rather than to the process of standing). This plays down the possibility of interaction between adults and baby, and clearly reinforces the passivity and ineffectuality of the mother's role that I pointed out in the previous section.

A number of further features of the second stanza add to the negative implications of the museum metaphor in this context.

In line 5 the nakedness of the baby is presented as a threat to the adults' safety (*your nakedness/ Shadows our safety*), presumably because it acts as a reminder of their physical nature, and possibly their vulnerability. In the same line the use of the adjective *drafty* as a premodifier of the noun *museum* confers an unpleasant attribute to the situation, particularly in the light of the baby's nakedness.

In the third stanza (which, as I said earlier, is the only stanza that consists of only one sentence) it is the concept of motherhood that gives rise to a metaphorical description:

I'm no more your mother
Than the cloud that distils a mirror to reflect its own slow
Effacement at the wind's hand.

Giving birth is paralleled to the phenomenon whereby a cloud condenses into rain and thereby forms a watery surface – a puddle – in which the process of its own dissolution under the strength of the wind can be reflected. The puddle, which stands for the child within the main metaphor, is itself metaphorically described as a mirror, because of its ability to reflect visual images.

The implications of the metaphor are rather disturbing. The choice of a purely physical process as vehicle plays down the intentional and emotional dimensions involved in creating a new life (this partly contrasts with the opening *Love set you going*, to which I will return below). More importantly, motherhood is presented as, paradoxically, involving both self-preservation and self-destruction: in the same way as the cloud is reflected in the puddle it creates, the mother produces a child in which she can see an image of herself. The creation of a puddle, however, not only reflects, but also accelerates the disappearance of the cloud. Likewise, we are encouraged to see the production of offspring as something that both records and precipitates the inevitable decline of the mother's life with the passing of time. The metaphor highlights the debilitating effects of the physical process of childbirth, and the connection between having children and growing old. The process that constitutes the vehicle of the metaphor, however, is a cyclical one: the rain water that makes up the puddle eventually evaporates to form a new cloud. This aspect can, by analogy, be applied to the reproduction of human beings, at least insofar as the creation of offspring is the only way in which one's genetic material can survive in future generations.

The view of motherhood suggested by the third stanza of the

poem is, nevertheless, not a positive one: the relationship between mother and child, according to the metaphor, is purely physical, and the process of becoming a mother involves depletion and fading away. It may also be significant that the insertion of a line break after *mother* in line 7 produces at least a temporary impression of a much stronger denial of the speaker's parental role than is suggested by the metaphor itself. *I'm no more your mother* (line 7) could, at a first reading, be read as a complete statement in its own right, rather than as the first part of a comparative construction (*Than the cloud . . .*).

The majority of the remaining figurative expressions in the text focus on the poetic *persona*'s baby, and partly counterbalance the effects of the two extended metaphors. Although they are all dehumanizing, they tend to carry more positive and optimistic connotations. In line 1, the baby is compared to a *gold watch*, which is inanimate but has associations of attractiveness and value. Stanzas 4 and 5 contain two figurative expressions (a metaphor and a simile respectively) with animals as vehicles: *your moth-breath/ Flickers among the flat pink roses* (lines 10–11), and *Your mouth opens clean as a cat's* (line 15). The former emphasizes the baby's vulnerability; the latter associates the child with an animal – the cat – which is perceived (in Western cultures at least) as a cuddly and comfortable pet, but also as fiercely independent (the use of the adjective *clean* in adverbial function adds a further figurative element to the sentence). Stanza 5 also contains an animal metaphor for the speaker herself: *cow-heavy* in line 13. This occurs in the context of a self-mocking description of her clumsiness as she stumbles out of bed, and humorously parallels the heaviness of the speaker's own body to that of an animal typically associated with reproduction. In line 12, the noise of the baby's breathing is metaphorically referred to as *A far sea*. This, again, brings together connotations of attractiveness and distance. The final simile in line 18 gives the poem a positive and cheerful conclusion. The sounds produced by the baby are attributed visual properties of brightness in the synaesthetic metaphor *the clear vowels*, and of colourfulness in *like balloons*.[12]

While human beings tend to be metaphorically described in non-human terms, a number of inanimate entities are treated as animate agents. In lines 15–16 the lightening of the sky in the morning and the consequent fading away of the stars are described from the point of view of somebody who is looking through a window:

... The window square
Whitens and swallows its dull stars.

This results firstly in a synecdoche, whereby it is the window, and not the sky, that gets progressively whiter, and secondly in a metaphor, since *the window square* is presented as actively responsible for the disappearance of the stars.

In the opening line of the poem, it is an abstract noun that occurs as subject of a dynamic verb that typically requires an animate agent:

Love set you going like a fat gold watch,

Here the beginning of the baby's life inside the womb is figuratively described as a watch starting to tick, and love is presented as the initiator of this process. This, on the one hand, gives a positive view of the origin of the baby's existence, while, on the other hand, it plays down the role of the parents as individuals in the conception of the baby, and presents the whole process as a mechanical one.

As I mentioned earlier, the subjects of dynamic verbs in the text are often features of the baby or parts of her body. This does not necessarily result in personification, but highlights the limited space granted to animate and conscious agency in the world of the poem. In a few cases, however, such subjects are described in figurative terms. This applies particularly to *your bald cry/ Took its place among the elements* in lines 2–3 and to *your moth-breath/ Flickers* in lines 10–11. In the former case, the unusual choice of the adjective *bald* to modify *cry* could be regarded as a reference to the fact that babies are often bald, as well as a dead metaphor alongside expressions such as *a bald question* or *the bald truth*, where the adjective stands for 'plain, unmitigated, totally honest'. In the latter example, it is the choice of verb that can be seen as metaphorical, since *flickers* usually applies to light or movement rather than sound.

Overall, the figurative expressions in the poem reflect the complex and partly contradictory nature of the speaker's attitudes towards her child and her own role as mother. The tendency to dehumanize both parents and baby, and the largely negative implications of the two extended metaphors signal a difficulty on the speaker's part in establishing a relationship with her child, and in defining her own function and position as mother. On the other hand, the opening personification of love and the positive associations of some of the similes and metaphors betray feelings of joy

and tenderness that coexist alongside the speaker's apparent sense
of disorientation.

7.3.2 A schema-theory approach

'Morning Song' obviously depends for its basic understanding
on the activation of knowledge to do with birth and young babies.
The interpretation of the poem's similes and metaphors, however,
also requires the application of schemata to do with other areas of
experience, which are related in a variety of ways with the people
and events presented in the poem. In my analysis I will argue that
the poem evokes a novel and partly disharmonious configuration
of schemata, and therefore projects a complex and problematic
view of reality.

The main schema

The people and events described in the poem can be meaning-
fully related to one another on the basis of widely shared knowledge
about birth and the behaviour of parents and small children. The
activation of such knowledge enables the reader to establish the
identity and mutual relationships of the characters in the world
of the text, and to identify the temporal and causal connections
between the scenes described in the poem: the conception of a
new life (line 1), the birth of the baby (lines 2–3), the parents'
reaction to the presence of the child (lines 4–6), the mother's
perception of her own role (lines 7–9), and her wakeful nights
looking after the new baby (lines 10–18).

How can such knowledge best be accounted for in terms of
existing typologies of schemata? The first issue is whether we can
say that the text triggers the activation of a single schema (e.g. a
NEW BABY schema) or whether we need to talk about a variety
of different but related schemata (e.g. a CONCEPTION schema,
a BIRTH schema, and so on). This apparent problem is instruct-
ive because it relates to some of the weaknesses of schema theory
that I discussed in 6.5 above, and particularly to the issue of what
constitutes a separate schema and of where one schema ends and
another begins. In the case of 'Morning Song', on the one hand
it seems rather awkward to postulate a single schema that includes
such relatively distant events as conception and the baby's crying
at night; on the other hand, if the text is interpretable in the light
of several separate schemata, we still need to account for the
connections that exist between them.

Schank and Abelson's (1977) version of schema theory does not directly address problems such as this. Clearly, the experiences described in the poem are too disparate to be part of the same script. The poem, therefore, would presumably be interpretable in the light of several different scripts (such as conception, birth, etc.) and a number of general goals (such as the production and preservation of offspring) and themes (such as being a mother) (see Schank and Abelson (1977) and 6.4.2 above). Within Rumelhart's version of schema theory (see 6.4.1 above), on the other hand, one could account for the interpretability of the poem in terms of a hierarchy of embedded schemata: a NEW BABY schema, for example, could contain CONCEPTION, BIRTH and NIGHT CRYING as sub-schemata. This does not however address the issue of the plausibility of such a schema as a separate structure in memory.

Schank's *Dynamic Memory* (1982) proposes a more promising approach to the solution of these problems. Schank's central claim is that memory contains two types of entities: structures (i.e. scenes and scripts) that contain information about different types of settings and about the sequences of events that take place in them, and organizers of structures (i.e. MOPs, meta-MOPs and TOPs) that provide information about relationships and connections between scenes (see 6.4.3 above and Schank 1982: 15 and throughout). While scenes and scripts are relatively fixed and well-defined entities, MOPs, meta-MOPs and TOPs are sequences or collections of scenes that are assembled and reassembled according to processing needs. This ties in with the claim made within Parallel Distributed Processing models of comprehension that schemata correspond to frequent patterns of activation in networks of low-level units of knowledge (see McClelland *et al.* 1986 and 5.4.1 above), and provides a more satisfactory account of the schemata involved in the comprehension of 'Morning Song'.

The different settings and events described in the poem are comprehended on the basis of a number of knowledge structures that can be captured by Schank's notion of scene. Table 7.4 (overleaf) provides a list of such scenes, specifying the lines of the poem to which they correspond. This accounts for the whole text except for the second and third stanzas. Stanza 2 focuses on the parents' (and perhaps other people's) reaction to the birth of the baby. Depending on its interpretation, it could be included within the BIRTH scene, or it could be seen as instantiating a separate BABY ROOM scene, or a VISIT TO BABY scene. Stanza 3 elaborates on

Table 7.4

CONCEPTION (line 1)
BIRTH (lines 2–3)
NIGHT WITH A SMALL BABY (lines 10–18)

the relationship between the two main participants in all the other scenes, namely the mother and the baby. Both stanzas contain extended metaphors, and therefore also activate other schemata, which I will discuss below.

How can we account for the connection of the various scenes into a coherent sequence? Clearly, the scenes are temporally and causally connected by an organizing structure of the type proposed by Schank, linking different areas of knowledge to do with the birth and care of babies. Such a structure could be described as a NEW BABY MOP, organizing a series of scenes including the ones instantiated by the poem, or alternatively as a NEW BABY meta-MOP organizing a series of MOPs (such as M-CHILDBIRTH, M-BABY CARE, etc.), which in their turn include the scenes that I have identified. The possibility of two different descriptions of the main overarching schema derives from two separate factors. Firstly, the scenes instantiated by the poem do not form such a close sequence as, for example, those identified in 'A Pillowed Head', which leads to the conclusion that they might be held together by a more general structure – such as a meta-MOP – rather than a MOP. Secondly, this ambiguity highlights once again the difficulties involved in the description and categorization of schemata, and the underspecified nature of existing typologies, including that proposed in Schank's *Dynamic Memory* (1982).

In any case, Schank's claim that high-level knowledge structures do not necessarily exist as stable and fixed entities, but are formed in the interaction with the input, provides a possible solution to the problem of the nature of the main schema involved in the comprehension of 'Morning Song'. Making the text coherent depends on the activation of a high-level structure – whether a MOP or a meta-MOP – that brings together knowledge to do with birth, parents and babies. This schema leads to inferences about the connections between different settings and events and about the identities and relationships of different people. It is on the basis of schematic knowledge that we conclude, for example, that the *you* of the poem is a baby, that the moment described in lines 2–3 is the baby's birth, and that this event was preceded and caused by the event described in line 1. More importantly, the activation of appropriate areas of knowledge enables readers to establish the tenors of the many figurative expressions contained in the poem. It is on the basis of the active schema, for example, that we decide that the expression *cow-heavy* in line 13 indicates that the mother's movements are partially affected by the consequences of the recently concluded pregnancy, or, possibly, by the fact that her breasts are, like a cow's udders, heavy with milk. Here, however, as with all figurative expressions, readers need to establish connections between different areas of knowledge – in this case, to do with new (human) mothers and cows – in order to reach a satisfactory interpretation. More importantly, the relationships between tenors and vehicles will inevitably affect the view of the world projected by the text.

Other schemata

The two extended metaphors discussed earlier invite the readers to perceive a series of parallels between the people and events described in the poem and other areas of experience. In other words, the interpretation of the two metaphors involves the establishment of multiple connections between separate schemata. In both cases such connections are not as conventional and immediately obvious as was the case with the association between dawn and birth in 'A Pillowed Head'.

In the second stanza a MUSEUM scene is activated by the references to a *new statue* in line 4 and to a *drafty museum* in line 5. This scene is superimposed, so to speak, on the scene involving the birth of a new baby: as I said earlier, the statue stands for the baby, and the museum stands for the room where the baby is the focus of people's attention. The effect of the metaphor relies on the novelty of the association and on the combination of similarities and contrasts that it brings out between the two schemata. The similarities are mostly to do with the fact that both situations involve a room where people admire an entity that is human in shape (and also with the detail that statues sometimes represent naked human beings, as is the case with the baby described in the poem). The contrasts relate to a number of different factors, of which the following seem particularly central: the tenor is a private event that is usually regarded as highly emotional for the people involved; the vehicle relates to a public situation with more neutral emotional associations; the object of people's attention is a living human being in one case and an inanimate representation of a human being in the other. The largely negative implications of the metaphor result from these contrasts: as I pointed out earlier, the association between the two scenes highlights the value attributed to the child, but also plays down the personal and emotional dimensions of the relationship between the adults, and particularly the parents, and the baby. The comment on the effect of the baby's nakedness and the comparison between the adults and walls in lines 5 and 6 also suggest that the referents of *we* play a passive and rather awkward role in relation to the baby.

An attempt to represent the link between the two schemata by means of Schank's notion of TOP highlights the difference between a metaphor such as this and the connection between birth and dawn evoked in 'A Pillowed Head'. In the latter case, a TOP brings out a number of conventional associations between the schemata involved (see Table 7.3). With the museum metaphor, on the other hand, the relationship between tenor and vehicle is less straightforward and more open-ended, and is therefore less easily accounted for in terms of a TOP.

Table 7.5

Schemata	Goal	Conditions	Features	Emotional Associations
New baby's room/ Museum	Admiring attractive entity	Object of attention in human shape	People in room, naked object of attention, etc.	Wonder, admiration, embarrassment

(Based on Schank 1982: 113ff.)

Table 7.5 clearly does not do justice to the richness and complexity of the effects of the metaphor that I have tried to outline. It does, however, provide some indication of the relatively impersonal and distant view of the relationship between adults and baby that the metaphor evokes: there is no suggestion of physical contact or of any type of interaction, and no emphasis on feelings of love and affection. The metaphor, in other words, establishes novel connections between different schemata and thereby provides an unconventional and potentially disturbing view of a familiar situation.

Similar considerations apply to the extended metaphor in stanza 3, where the relationship between mother and child is compared to that between a cloud and the puddle it forms as it turns into rain. Here the connection established by the metaphor between what I will call a MOTHERHOOD schema and a CLOUD schema is clearly aimed at questioning conventional assumptions to do with the former. Both schemata involve an entity that goes through a process of transformation and produces another entity in which it can somehow see a reflection of itself. In the case of the cloud, however, this process involves the destruction of the original entity, and this is the most disturbing feature that the metaphor projects onto the concept of motherhood. Equally important is the fact that the two schemata are again very different in terms of emotional associations, which are high and usually positive for MOTHERHOOD but low and neutral for CLOUD (see 6.6 above). The reference to the cloud's *slow effacement* in lines 8–9, however, conveys negative emotional associations to both vehicle and tenor. Other significant differences between the schemata are the contrast between the human and the inanimate spheres, and between a personal relationship on the one hand and a purely physical one on the other.

As with the museum metaphor, a TOP representation gives a rather limited account of the connection between the schemata, but it does help to highlight the defamiliarizing effect of the metaphor.

Table 7.6

Schemata	Goal	Conditions	Features	Emotional Associations
Motherhood/ Cloud	Creating reflection of oneself	Physical change, decay	?	Negative

(Based on Schank 1982: 113ff.)

Table 7.6 suggests that the association between the MOTHERHOOD and the CLOUD schemata does not rely on conventionally perceived similarities between two different areas of experience, but rather conveys a defamiliarizing and potentially disturbing view of motherhood. As I mentioned earlier, stanzas 2 and 3 express a sense of disorientation on the part of the speaker, an inability to assume a conventional role of parent, and a tendency to present such a role in negative and problematic terms.

Insofar as metaphors such as these bring together different and normally separate areas of knowledge in novel and challenging combinations, their effect could be described as schema refreshing in Cook's sense (1994). This does not, however, necessarily imply that the reader's store of background knowledge is dramatically or permanently changed as a result of interpreting the poem. Most readers will be aware of the mixture of positive and negative feelings often experienced by new mothers, and will therefore 'learn' nothing new from the way in which such feelings are expressed in 'Morning Song'. On the other hand, it is nevertheless possible that the readers' awareness and understanding of postnatal emotional problems may be sharpened and extended in the processing of Plath's metaphors. In this sense, I would argue, 'Morning Song' has a greater potential for schema refreshment than 'A Pillowed Head'.[13] The applicability and implications of the notion of schema refreshment clearly need to be spelt out in more detail. I will return to this issue in 8.7 and 9.3.

The many other similes and metaphors contained in Plath's poem evoke a constellation of fleeting schemata, which, although unlikely to be instantiated in full, are essential to the comprehension of the various figurative expressions, and contribute to the overall effect of the text. Examples of schemata that seem to be involved include a WATCH schema (line 1), a MOTH schema (line 10), a SEA schema (line 12), a COW schema (line 13), a CAT schema (line 15), and a BALLOONS schema (line 18). In order to interpret each simile and metaphor readers need to establish which element of the schema relating to the vehicle is shared by, or attributed to, the entity that functions as tenor. Such connections tend to involve similarities in what Schank calls low-level features: the beating of the heart and the ticking of the clock in the watch simile; the noise of the baby's breath and, respectively, the sound of a moth and of the distant roar of the sea in the fourth stanza; the role of mother and the possession of a heavy body in the cow metaphor; and the perception of a pleasing upward movement in the balloons simile.

In each case, the establishment of a connection between different areas of experience also leads to the attribution of further features, qualities and emotional associations to the tenor. These are, as is always the case with figurative expressions, too rich and varied to be captured in full, but they do seem to show, as I suggested in 7.3.1 above, some shared tendencies in their effects. Firstly, the focus on fairly evident low-level similarities between the schemata leads to the creation of images that are less striking and interpretatively demanding than the ones conveyed by the two main metaphors, and generally unlikely to challenge the reader's existing schemata. Secondly and more importantly, most of the schemata related to the vehicles have positive emotional associations, either by default or as a result of specific lexical choices: the watch in line 1, for example, is premodified by *gold*, which evokes images of valued heirlooms, while balloons tend to be associated with festive occasions, such as children's parties. These positive associations exist in spite of the fact that, as I mentioned earlier, the schemata that constitute the vehicles of metaphors and similes invariably involve inanimate or non-human entities.

Overall, therefore, the figurative expressions in the poem evoke a number of schemata that pertain to very different areas of experience and relate in different ways to the main basic schema instantiated by the text: in some cases the association is striking and potentially disturbing, in other cases it is more obvious and reassuring.

7.3.3 Final considerations

'Morning Song' clearly evokes a rather different configuration of schemata from 'A Pillowed Head'. Plath's use of figurative language establishes multiple connections among the component elements of the main NEW BABY schema and a variety of other schemata, relating to such disparate areas of experience as museums, clouds, moths and so on. In the case of the two central extended metaphors in stanzas 2 and 3, the association between different schemata is potentially schema refreshing, insofar as it leads readers to make new connections that may challenge or sharpen their perception of familiar experiences (whether or not this results in permanent changes to the schemata involved). In the majority of the other cases, the establishment of a link between different portions of knowledge has more conventional and comforting implications. As a consequence, the view of motherhood that Plath projects in 'Morning Song' is one that combines a sense of ineffectuality, rejection and disorientation, with more positive feelings of tenderness and excitement: the same voice that adopts the unsettling metaphor of stanza 3 confesses, a few lines later, that one cry on the part of the baby is enough to get her out of bed.

Clearly, the text world projected by 'Morning Song' is just as possible as that of 'A Pillowed Head'. If we accept the autobiographic origin of the poem, its text world does not break any of Ryan's accessibility relations; if, on the other hand, the people involved are considered to be imaginary, the text world still fulfils all criteria from chronological compatibility onwards and qualifies as realistic fiction (Ryan 1991a: 34). As I said earlier, exactly the same considerations apply to 'A Pillowed Head'. In fact, Plath's poetic speaker gives voice to a mixture of contradictory feelings that are experienced by many women (and may indeed lead to the pathologic condition of postnatal depression). On the other hand, the world of 'Morning Song' involves a mixture of original insights and internal contradictions that make it less conventional and more complex than that of Heaney's poem, and that are more likely to create the conditions for schema refreshment.

By seeing text worlds as configurations of instantiated schemata, it is possible to describe them not just in terms of their deviations from what is regarded as actual, but also as different types of representations of reality. This opens up the opportunity to consider dimensions that are beyond the reach of possible-world models, such as familiarity, conventionality, internal coherence, schema refreshment and so on. My analyses have also shown how a schema-theory approach can be combined with a linguistic analysis of a text. Equally important is the possibility of accounting for the variability of readers' responses: different interpretations of the poems I have discussed, for example, could be traced back to differences in the background knowledge, beliefs and emotional associations that different readers bring to the same text. Schema theory, in other words, can account for the fact that different people may have different views of the world of reality, and therefore may construct different worlds from the same text.

NOTES
[1] In Ryan's terms, the two poems could be classified either as non-fiction, if they faithfully represent autobiographical experiences, or as realistic fiction, if they deal with imaginary people and events in a world that is fully compatible with the actual world (Ryan 1991: 32–5). I will discuss this point in more detail in 7.3 below.
[2] Readers who fail to activate (or do not possess) schemata to do with childbirth will have difficulties recognizing what the poem is about, and may not be able to form a coherent and satisfactory picture of the world of the poem. This was in fact the case with some of my students, who initially thought that the poem was to do with weddings and marriage: they had difficulties constructing a world that made sense of the whole poem and were acutely aware of the inadequacy of their interpretation.
[3] It is important to bear in mind that schemata do not necessarily arise from direct real-life experience, but can be constructed on the basis of information derived from conversations, written texts, films, and so on.

In other words, you do not need to have experienced or witnessed the birth of a child to possess the background knowledge needed to make sense of this poem.

[4] This does not apply to *all* definite references in the poem. *The first time* (line 12) is an example of the logical use of the definite article (see 2.2 above). *The dawn chorus* refers to a natural phenomenon that is presumably expected to be part of the readers' culturally shared knowledge of the world.

[5] Leech uses the term 'deviation' to include both the breaking of linguistic norms and the establishment of linguistic patterns, or parallelism (Leech 1969, 1985).

[6] In formulating their theory of communication, Sperber and Wilson (1986, 1995) do not espouse any particular model of the organization of background knowledge, but generally relate their notion of 'encyclopaedic entry' to notions such as 'schema', 'frame', 'script', 'prototype' and 'scenario' (Sperber and Wilson 1986, 1995: 88, 138). That Relevance theory is compatible with schema theory is clear from comments such as the following:

> it is generally agreed that encyclopaedic information in long-term memory is organised into chunks of some kind. Such chunks have been discussed in the literature under such names as 'schema', 'frame', 'scenario' and 'prototype'. The encyclopaedic entries we have mentioned are also chunks of a certain size, which may themselves be grouped into larger chunks, and contain smaller chunks. (Sperber and Wilson 1986, 1995: 138)

Sperber and Wilson themselves also occasionally use the term 'schema' or 'encyclopaedic schema' (Sperber and Wilson 1986, 1995: 190, 236).

[7] On the whole, it would be unrealistic to claim that I can provide an exhaustive account of *all* the schemata that participate in my own or anybody else's reading of the poem. This is not only due to the variety and unpredictability of the memories and connections that a text may trigger in different readers, but also to the limits of introspection, which can only provide a rough approximation to what actually happens during text processing.

[8] Although it is possible to explain the connotations mentioned here with reference to default elements of schemata, it would be unreasonable to claim that such associations can always be accounted for in terms of schema theory. Connotation may arise from a wide variety of factors, including not only schematic knowledge, but also episodic memory, phonetic similarities, knowledge of other texts, and so on.

[9] For a similar interpretation of a metaphorical connection between birth and dawn, see Bradford (1993: 2) and Leech (1969: 156).

[10] As I explained in 6.4.3, Schank claims that TOPs operate on the basis of a shared 'goal type, some planning or other condition, and one or more low-level identical features.' (Schank 1982: 113)

[11] As I mentioned earlier, I do not agree with the evaluative implications of Weber's terminology. A schema-reinforcing poem may be less

challenging than a schema-refreshing one, but it does not have to be a 'bad' or 'unsuccessful' poem (as 'A Pillowed Head' demonstrates).

[12] The festive and joyous associations that balloons have for Plath are expressed in the poem 'Balloons', which concludes the series of poems in *Ariel*.

[13] This does not imply, however, that 'A Pillowed Head' could not have a schema-refreshing effect for some readers. Schema refreshment, as I have already pointed out, is a reader-dependent phenomenon.

Metaphor, schema refreshment and text worlds

8.1 Introduction

The method of analysis demonstrated in the previous chapter has highlighted the contribution of figurative language to the projection of particular worlds or world views by means of texts. In the present chapter I focus on metaphor in particular and build on the previous discussion in order to propose a more explicit and systematic account of the way in which metaphorical uses of language affect the process of text-world creation in the reading of poetry.

Possible-world models are rather limited in their treatment of figurative language. Their main contribution is to highlight the fact that literal and figurative language have opposite ontological implications. Literal expressions introduce referents that exist within the text world; figurative expressions have no such power, and therefore tend to be regarded as subsidiary and marginal. Possible-world theorists, in other words, stress the fact that metaphor does not, strictly speaking, contribute to world-projection: a different domain is evoked by the text, but such a domain has no place in the world that the text projects (Eco 1989: 346, 1990: 68; Levin 1989; Ryan 1991: 82–3; see also Hrushovski 1984).[1]

Although theoretically accurate, this argument only deals with metaphor in a negative sense: it simply spells out what metaphor *does not* do. It is undeniable, however, that the use of metaphorical language is part of the way in which states of affairs are presented, and consequently affects the way in which such states of affairs are imagined and perceived by readers: although the museum mentioned in the second stanza of 'Morning Song' does not, strictly speaking, 'exist' in the world of the poem, the choice of the MUSEUM metaphor – and of all the other figurative expressions in the poem – plays an important role in the view of reality projected by the text (see 7.3.1 and 7.3.2). Consider also the first three stanzas of Craig Raine's 'A Martian Sends a Postcard Home', which was briefly mentioned in 5.4.1 above:

> Caxtons are mechanical birds with many wings
> and some are treasured for their markings—
>
> they cause the eyes to melt
> or the body to shriek without pain.
>
> I have seen one fly, but
> sometimes they perch on the hand.

Apart from the identity of the speaker, the world projected by this section of the poem (and indeed by the poem as a whole) is the same as our actual world: it contains books that emotionally affect their readers and that may occasionally be thrown around rather than read; it does *not* contain mechanical birds that have the power to melt people's eyes. Such an account, however, does not adequately capture the text's significance. What is interesting about Raine's poem is that it gives an unusual (and tongue-in-cheek) perspective on a familiar and rather mundane reality. The way in which this is achieved is by referring to everyday objects and actions by means of expressions that are figurative for the readers, but presumably literal for the poem's Martian speaker: books are *Caxtons* and *mechanical birds with many wings*; eyes *melt*, and so on.[2] An approach that treats text worlds as cognitive constructs resulting from the activation of different portions of the reader's background knowledge gives a more adequate account of the peculiar world view projected by the poem. I will return to 'A Martian Sends a Postcard Home' in 8.7.1 below.

8.2 Some preliminaries on metaphor

Broadly speaking, metaphor can be defined as the phenomenon whereby we think and talk about one thing in terms of another, whether or not we are consciously aware of doing so. As such, metaphor is a powerful resource for making sense of our experience of ourselves and of the world we live in, and for expressing such understanding verbally or by other media. Metaphor is therefore a matter of both thought and, for my present purposes, language (for visual metaphors see Forceville 1995).

In its most basic form, metaphor highlights an underlying similarity between two separate entities. Consider the following examples:

(1) Babies have velvet cheeks.
(2) Sailors have leather cheeks.

Here the metaphorical connections that are established between the two types of cheeks and, respectively, velvet and leather, primarily depend on shared physical properties: smoothness, softness, etc., in (1) and toughness, thickness, etc., in (2). In cases such as these, the identification of the connection between the referents of the expressions that are interpreted as figurative (*velvet, leather*) and the entities directly under discussion (*cheeks*) follows from fairly conventional knowledge about the relevant people and materials, and is unlikely to challenge or stretch in a significant way the interpreters' existing notions of any of the entities involved.

Not all metaphors, however, work in an equally straightforward fashion. In my analysis of Plath's 'Morning Song' in the previous chapter (7.3.1 and 7.3.2), I pointed out how the MUSEUM and CLOUD metaphors do not exploit obvious or commonly perceived similarities between the literal and figurative domains, but rather establish unconventional and challenging connections between different areas of experience. As Lakoff and Turner put it, poets may create novel metaphors in order to lead readers 'to explore afresh the ways we see and think' (Lakoff and Turner 1989: 93) and 'create new ways of understanding the world' (Lakoff and Turner 1989: 203).

In this chapter I will show how the diversity of effects that may be achieved by different metaphors can be accounted for within the approach to the analysis of text worlds proposed in the previous chapter. This, in a nutshell, is my central claim: insofar as metaphorical connections exploit obvious or conventionally accepted similarities between two different domains, they will reinforce the readers' existing knowledge and contribute to the creation of a text world that readers recognize as conventional and familiar; on the other hand, insofar as metaphorical connections lead to the attribution of new properties to the tenor domain, they will challenge and potentially refresh the readers' existing sets of beliefs and assumptions, and contribute to the creation of a text world that readers will perceive as unconventional and novel. In other words, I will argue that metaphors vary in their potential for schema refreshment, and that such variability can be captured in terms of a scale, from schema reinforcement at one end to schema refreshment at the other end. The degree of potential for schema refreshment carried by individual metaphors will depend on the nature of the similarity that they establish between the tenor and the vehicle domains.

The role played by similarity across domains in the production and reception of metaphor is one of the most central and controversial issues in the literature on metaphor. The traditional view that metaphors reflect pre-existing similarities that are objectively given in an autonomous reality has been increasingly challenged by more recent theories that attribute to metaphor a much more powerful cognitive function. According to such theories, the existence of a relationship of resemblance between two separate domains only acts as a springboard for the conceptual structuring of one domain in terms of another. As a consequence, metaphor is seen as an essential cognitive tool by means of which we actively construct what we take to be the world of reality (e.g. Lakoff and Johnson 1980; Kittay 1987). In the first half of this chapter I will give an overview of the main trends in the study of metaphor, focusing particularly on the notions of similarity and on the cognitive power attributed to metaphor. In the second half of the chapter I will show how different competing theories of metaphor can be seen as privileging different extremes of a scale of schema refreshment, and can therefore be partially reconciled within an approach that accounts for the different ways in which metaphorical connections can be constructed. The analyses in the second half of the chapter will also demonstrate that the way in which individual metaphors affect the readers' perception of the world projected by the text partly depends on their position on such a scale. The insights into the organization of knowledge provided by schema theory, especially in the version of Schank (1982), will provide the main framework for the description of metaphorical connections and the explanation of their effects.

8.3 Metaphor and the expression of similarity: the comparison and similarity views

As with many central concepts in Western thought, the study of metaphor can be traced back to Aristotle, whose influence has played a major role in shaping subsequent theories and approaches up to the present day. Aristotle claimed that the mastery of metaphor requires the intuitive ability to perceive similarities, and that the main function of metaphor lies in making things clear through resemblance (see Richards 1936; Kittay 1987: 1ff.; Wales 1989: 295). As pointed out by Kittay (1987: 4), Aristotle was by no means unaware of the cognitive role played by metaphor in making salient normally unnoticed properties and in contributing to the reorganization of conceptual structures to accommodate as well as to shape experience. The tradition that developed from Aristotle's influence, however, contributed to the dominance of a view of metaphor as a rhetorical device that simply highlights the existence of some kind of resemblance between separate objects, concepts or situations (Kittay 1987: 4).

The metaphorical expressions in (1) and (2) above provide support for this view of metaphor, since in both cases two different entities (babies' cheeks and velvet in (1), sailors' cheeks and leather in (2)) are brought together on the basis of existing similarities (the possession of a soft/tough surface), which are highlighted by the metaphors and need to be correctly identified by interpreters. Following Leech (1969: 150–1), these metaphors can therefore be attributed a common underlying form, 'A is like B in respect of C', which would yield something like:

(1a) Babies' cheeks are like velvet in respect of their softness/ smoothness, etc.
(2a) Sailors' cheeks are like leather in respect of their toughness/thickness/roughness, etc.

Such a view of metaphor as an implicit comparison follows directly from the idea that the essence of metaphor is the expression of similarity, and leads to the establishment of a strong connection with similes, of which metaphors would be reduced, elliptical variants. The metaphorical expressions discussed above can therefore be seen as compressed versions of similes like:

(1b) Babies' cheeks are as soft as velvet.
(2b) Sailors' cheeks are as tough as leather.

although such a transformation is generally acknowledged as resulting in an inevitable loss of impact and effectiveness (Nowottny 1965: 54–6; Leech 1969: 156–7).

This view of metaphor, which is often referred to by its critics as the **Similarity** or **Comparison View** (Black 1962, 1979; Searle 1979; Levinson 1983: 148ff.), tends to see metaphor primarily as a linguistic phenomenon, whereby a perceived resemblance is expressed by means of a deviant linguistic realization. Metaphors do indeed, by and large, involve some form of linguistic deviation. The metaphorical expressions discussed above, for example, both involve a violation of selection restrictions in the choice of premodifier for the noun *cheeks*. There is, however, almost no limit to the form that metaphors can take, or to the types of words that can be used in deviant ways in the expression of metaphorical connections (Nash 1989: 121; Wales 1989: 296). Insofar as it has been seen as a deviant linguistic realization of a straightforward thought, metaphor has mostly been regarded as a trope or figure of speech, belonging to the realm of rhetoric. This has led to the by now outdated misconception that metaphors are typical of highly specialized types of discourse such as poetry and political oratory, and that they are mostly motivated by a desire to use decorative, ornamental expressions in the place of more common, ordinary ones (see, for example, Nash 1989: 117–18, 121–3).

The whole idea that metaphor should be seen as a way of expressing existing similarities has in recent years come under increasing attack and has been largely replaced by approaches that attribute to metaphor a crucial cognitive function. It is undeniable, however, that the more traditional view does explain some types of metaphorical connections, such as the ones analysed in this section. Indeed I will want to argue that this view accounts for one end of the schema-refreshment scale that I propose for metaphorical relationships.

8.4 Metaphor and the creation of similarity: the interaction view

In two seminal chapters included in *The Philosophy of Rhetoric*, I.A. Richards (1936) laid the foundations for a different approach to the structure and function of metaphor. He questioned the assumption that metaphor is a special and exceptional use of language, and paved the way for a deeper understanding of the cognitive dimension of metaphor:

> In the simplest formulation, when we use a metaphor we have two thoughts of different things active together and supported by a single word, or phrase, whose meaning is a resultant of their interaction.
>
> (Richards 1936: 94)

Richards's labels for the two elements involved in metaphorical connections, **tenor** and **vehicle** (Richards 1936: 97), have been widely adopted in the literature on the subject (e.g. Leech 1969), while his view of metaphor as an interaction between two separate thoughts was developed by Black into what has come to be known as the **Interaction View** of metaphor (Black 1962, 1979; Searle 1979; Levinson 1983; Lakoff and Turner 1989: 131–3).

Richards points out that tenor and vehicle can enter into a wide variety of relationships, which cannot simply be reduced to the previous existence of some similarity between them. Rather, he argued that the meaning that results from the interaction of the two different thoughts evoked by a metaphor depends at least as much on the disparities between them as on their similarities (Richards 1936: 96ff.). Following on the same line of reasoning, Black arrived at a very different view of the role of resemblance in metaphorical connections from the one that results from the Comparison or Similarity views:

> It would be more illuminating in some of these cases to say that the metaphor *creates* the similarity than to say that it *formulates* some similarity antecedently existing. (Black 1962: 37, my italics)

In the theory developed by Black, the interaction triggered by metaphor involves, on the one hand, the tenor (or, in Black's terms, the principal or primary subject) and, on the other, the 'system of related commonplaces' (Black 1962: 41) or 'implicative complex' (Black 1979: 28) associated with the vehicle (or the secondary subject). This is the 'conventional, culturally shared knowledge' (Black 1962: 41) that interpreters possess about the vehicle, or, in some cases, a particular set of assumptions that have been associated with the vehicle in the course of the discourse itself (Black 1962: 44–5). The interpretation of metaphors involves the selection from the system of implications associated with the vehicle of a set that can also be applied to the tenor, and results in the construction of a parallel implicative complex for the tenor.

In his discussion of 'Man is a Wolf', Black points out how the metaphor involves the projection of a selected set of assertions from the 'wolf-system' to the concept of man, so that those properties of man that can be seen in wolf-terms will be highlighted (being fierce, treacherous, constantly involved in struggle, etc.), while others will be suppressed. Black sees metaphor, metaphorically, as a filter, which, by emphasizing certain features and backgrounding others, organizes our view of the tenor (Black 1962: 39–41). This process usually relies on some structural correspondences between the two concepts, but may lead to the attribution of new properties to one or both elements, i.e. to the *creation* rather than simply the *expression* of similarity. Metaphor is therefore attributed a very powerful cognitive function, since it can produce new knowledge by establishing new connections and attributing new properties to concepts (Black 1979: 37–41).

As I mentioned earlier, Richards emphasizes the possibility of different *types* of relationships between tenor and vehicle: from straightforward likeness, in which case the metaphor operates as an implicit comparison, to a combination of resemblance and disparity, in which case a tension will be created and the interpretation of the metaphor may lead to some modification to the assumptions associated with the tenor (Richards 1936: 121–7). Black goes so far as proposing a classification of metaphors, distinguishing between 'substitution-metaphors' and 'comparison-metaphors' on the one hand, and 'interaction-metaphors' on the other. Metaphors falling within the first two categories can be paraphrased into literal equivalents with no serious loss of 'cognitive content' (rather like examples (1) and (2) above), while interaction-metaphors produce complex meanings that are irreducible to the stating of an explicit comparison between the two elements (Black 1962: 45–6).

Both Richards and Black, therefore, hint at the fact that some metaphors seem to fulfil the requirements of the more traditional views, while others need a more complex explanatory apparatus. My suggestion that metaphors can be ordered along a scale of schema refreshment depending on whether the similarity between tenor and vehicle can be said to be mostly *reflected* or rather *established* by the metaphor, elaborates on similar intuitions about the nature of metaphor and the potentialities of different approaches to its definition. Richards and Black also refer to the importance of 'attitudes' towards entities and concepts in the creation and interpretation of metaphor (Richards 1936: 118; Black 1962: 42), which is an implicit recognition of the centrality of what I would call emotional reactions or associations both in the perception and in the creation of similarity.

8.5 Metaphor and the construction of reality: the cognitive view

In his criticism of the Similarity view, Searle points out how metaphors such as 'Sally is a block of ice' and 'Time flies' seem to work on something other than resemblance between the two elements involved (Searle 1979). Building on Searle's criticisms, Levinson highlights the lack of flexibility of the Interaction theory insofar as it tends to view the transferral of features from the vehicle to the tenor in terms of a rigid semantic model based on componential analysis (Levinson 1983: 148–50). Levinson advocates the development of an approach that accounts for the fact that metaphors seem to involve 'the mapping of one whole cognitive domain into another, allowing the tracing of multiple correspondences', and for the fact that they tend to present complex, abstract notions in terms of simpler, concrete ones (Levinson 1983: 159–60).

Writing at the beginning of the 1980s, Levinson recognized the potential of the work that was being done in the United States by George Lakoff and others (especially in Lakoff and Johnson 1980), which has since developed into a very influential theory known as the **Cognitive View** of metaphor (see, for example, Freeman 1993 and Weber 1995). The basic tenet of this view is that metaphor is a pervasive cognitive tool that plays a central role in the way in which we structure our experience and conceptualize the reality we live in. The main function of metaphor is to enable us to use our understanding of familiar domains of experience, such as movement in space or the properties of physical objects, to make sense of more abstract and complex domains, such as life, death, love, and so on. Metaphorical connections do, by and large, arise from the perception of correlations between different types of experiences, but they can also make us see new correspondences or indeed attribute new structure or properties to objects, concepts and situations. This is achieved by means of the mapping of a **source cognitive domain** (Richards's vehicle) onto a **target cognitive domain** (Richards's tenor), which does not simply affect the way in which the latter is talked about, but also the way in which it is viewed, structured and experienced (Lakoff and Johnson 1980; Johnson 1987; Lakoff and Turner 1989; Weber 1992).

8.5.1 The projection of patterns of bodily experience: orientational and ontological metaphors

One of the main concerns within the Cognitive view has been to highlight the centrality of metaphor to our ordinary conceptual system by focusing on those metaphors that we use, largely unconsciously, to think and talk about the most fundamental concepts and emotions. Most of these metaphors are grounded in a number of basic 'image-schemas', i.e. in the patterns that emerge from our experience of our own bodies, our spatial orientation and movements, and our physical perceptions (Johnson 1987).

For example, we know from our experience with physical entities that, if we add to the quantity of a substance in a container or a pile, the level rises. By projecting this image onto the domain of quantity in general, we generate the metaphor MORE IS UP, which is normally extended to non-physical domains, as is the case in 'Unemployment is rising' or 'My income fell last year' (Johnson 1987: 121–4). The UP–DOWN opposition is in fact used to indicate a positive–negative polarity in a large number of metaphors, including, for example, HAPPY IS UP, HEALTHY IS UP, and so on (consider, for instance, expressions such as 'I am feeling down today' and 'She has fallen ill'). These are examples of **Orientational metaphors**, which arise from the projection of our experience of spatial orientation on a variety of abstract domains (Lakoff and Johnson 1980: 14ff.). Another major source of metaphorical projections is the tendency to conceive of abstract notions in terms of our experience with physical concrete objects. This tendency results in what Lakoff and Johnson call **Ontological metaphors** (Lakoff and Johnson 1980: 25ff.), whereby emotions, events, activities etc. are turned into physical entities (e.g. THE MIND IS A MACHINE in 'My mind just isn't operating today' or LIFE IS A CONTAINER in 'She's had a full life').

A rather complex example of this is the structure of the metaphor that dominates the way we conceive of language, or, more precisely, of verbal communication. Expressions like 'I couldn't put my feelings into words' or 'I eventually managed to get the bulk of my argument across to her' share the following underlying metaphors: THOUGHTS/IDEAS ARE OBJECTS and LINGUISTIC EXPRESSIONS ARE CONTAINERS (Lakoff and Johnson 1980: 127; Johnson 1987: 58–9). These two ontological metaphors underlie the more general CONDUIT metaphor, according to which communication involves:

> finding the right word-container for your idea-object, sending this filled container along a conduit or through space to the hearer, who must then take the idea-object out of the word-container.
>
> (Johnson 1987: 59)

Such a view of metaphor as a resource for making sense of the unfamiliar in terms of the familiar, and, in many cases, the abstract in terms of the concrete, can indeed account for the metaphors that troubled Searle in his 1979 paper. Adopting Lakoff and Turner's explanation, 'Time flies' can be seen as resulting from

> ...a combination of the EVENTS ARE ACTIONS metaphor, where time is the actor, with a metaphorical way of understanding temporal

change in terms of motion – the metaphor that TIME MOVES.

(Lakoff and Turner 1989: 44)

Similarly, we are able to explain our interpretation of 'Sally is a block of ice' as indicating that Sally is unemotional, on the basis of the following ontological metaphors: EMOTIONAL ATTITUDES ARE PHYSICAL SENSATIONS (whereby EMOTIONAL IS HOT and UNEMOTIONAL IS COLD) and PEOPLE ARE OBJECTS. It is obvious how metaphors such as these have less to do with the perception of similarity than with a natural tendency to structure abstract and ill-defined domains in terms of concrete, well-defined ones.

8.5.2 Structural metaphors and the construction of reality

Not all metaphors, of course, are grounded exclusively in our bodily or physical experiences. Our knowledge of socially and culturally defined entities and situations also provides a wide variety of source domains for metaphorical projections. Lakoff and Johnson (1980) and Lakoff and Turner (1989) show how whole 'families' of metaphorical expressions arise from the projection of one concept onto another, as is the case, for example, with ARGUMENT IS WAR:

> Your claims are indefensible.
> I demolished his argument. (Lakoff and Johnson 1980: 4)

or LIFE IS A JOURNEY:

> I work hard, but I never get anywhere.
> You need some direction in your life.

Metaphors of this kind are referred to as **Structural metaphors** (Lakoff and Johnson 1980: 61ff.), since they

> . . . allow us to do more than just orient concepts, refer to them, quantify them, etc. as we do with simple orientational and ontological metaphors; they allow us, in addition, to use one highly structured and clearly delineated concept to structure another.

(Lakoff and Johnson 1980: 61)

The way in which different source and target domains are matched with one another is, of course, not random: structural metaphors always tend to capture some kind of correlation or resemblance between different concepts as perceived by a certain individual or by the members of a certain culture. The mapping of features from the source to the target domain, however, is not restricted to the initially perceived similarities, but may lead to a structuring of the target domain that is heavily dependent on the chosen metaphorical connection (Lakoff and Johnson 1980: 61–8, 147–55; Lakoff and Turner 1989: 154–5 and throughout; Kittay 1987: 258ff.).

The ARGUMENT IS WAR metaphor, for example, is grounded in the perception of a correlation between verbal and physical fights (Lakoff and Johnson 1980: 61–5), but the existence of a conventional metaphorical connection (in some languages at least) results in the establishment of systematic correspondences between wars and conversations, which affect the way in which we talk and think about the mutual positions of participants (adversaries, enemies), the stages of the activity (planning of strategies, attacks and counterattacks), its purpose (victory) and possible outcomes (truce, victory, defeat) (Lakoff and Johnson 1980: 78–82). Similarly, the LIFE IS A JOURNEY metaphor captures our perception of life as a series of stages from a starting point to an end point, but leads to a number of more specific correlations, whereby, for example, life involves the choice between different routes and is measured out on the basis of the reaching of intermediate destinations (e.g. 'I am at a crossroads in my life', 'You've certainly made strides, but you haven't quite got there yet') (cf. Lakoff and Turner 1989: 61–5).

Like most of the examples discussed by Lakoff, Johnson and Turner, the ones given above involve highly conventional metaphorical connections, whose linguistic realizations mostly fall under the traditional category of 'dead' metaphors. Contrary to what such a label may indicate, however, these metaphors are particularly powerful precisely because we are not consciously aware of the way in which they affect our perception of reality. Lakoff and Turner indeed question the validity of the traditional label and suggest that such conventionalized metaphors are the most 'alive' since they are part of the way in which the members of a certain culture conceptualize the world they live in (Lakoff and Turner 1989: 128–31). The creation of new metaphors (which, by and large, tend to be of the structural type (Lakoff and Johnson 1980: 152)) is, therefore, one of the means by which new ways of understanding and representing reality can be conceived of and conveyed (Lakoff and Johnson 1980: 139–46; Kittay 1987: 37 and throughout).

8.5.3 Clines of metaphorical connections

Lakoff and Turner suggest that metaphors differ along a variety of dimensions, and that such variability, being mostly a question of degree, is best handled in scalar terms. In particular, they propose a cline of 'conventionalization' and a cline of 'basicness' of metaphorical connections. The former is to do with the degree to which a certain connection is 'automatic, effortless, and generally established as a mode of thought among members of a linguistic community' (Lakoff and Turner 1989: 55); in traditional terms, one would talk about the extent to which a metaphor is 'dead' in a certain language. The latter cline is to do with the extent to which a metaphor is conceptually indispensable for the members of a certain culture: Lakoff and Turner argue, for example, that the metaphor TIME MOVES is fundamental to the conceptual system of Anglophone cultures, and therefore lies at the 'indispensable' end of the scale (consider, for example, expressions such as 'The deadline is coming up'); on the other hand, the connection between the evening and a 'patient etherised upon a table' in Eliot's 'The Love Song of J. Alfred Prufrock' is not a basic component of the way in which speakers of English conceptualize the end of the day, and therefore lies at the 'dispensable' end of the scale (Lakoff and Turner 1989: 54–6).

The schema-refreshment scale that I am proposing is, as I will show, related to Lakoff and Turner's conventionalization cline. Its specific function, however, is to capture the different cognitive effects that metaphors can have, and, more specifically, the varying amounts of potential for cognitive change associated with different metaphors. As such, the schema-refreshment scale brings attention to the way in which metaphors relate to the world-view of a certain culture (the 'actual world' of possible-world models), i.e. to the set of schemata that are likely to be shared by the members of that culture (cf. Arbib *et al.* 1987: 7; Weber 1992: 12–14; see 7.1 above). Conventional metaphors will, by definition, cluster at the schema-reinforcing end of the scale, since they rely on associations that are generally accepted and possibly internalized by the speakers of a certain language. Novel metaphors, on the other hand, carry more potential for schema refreshment, since they establish new connections between domains. However, I will argue that novel metaphors do not necessarily fall at the schema-refreshing end of the scale, but may in fact occupy a range of different positions, from relatively low to high potential for schema

refreshment. This will depend on the extent to which new metaphors mostly work by highlighting similarities that are generally
regarded as properties of the relevant domains independently of
the metaphor, or, conversely, by attributing new properties to the
target domain. As I mentioned earlier, I will show that the position of different metaphors on the schema refreshment scale has
implications for the nature of the text worlds that different metaphors contribute to project.

The schema refreshment scale also accounts for Richards's
and Black's attempts at classification mentioned in 8.4 above, and
captures some of the observations made by Lakoff and Turner
concerning different types of novel metaphors in poetry:

> The image-mappings we have considered so far lead us to map con-
> ventional knowledge about the source-domain image onto the target
> domain in ways that extend but do not disturb what we know of the
> target domain. A poet may, however, wish to break our expectations
> about the image correspondence and disturb what we think we know
> about the target domain. (Lakoff and Turner 1989: 92)

Kittay (1987) describes the difference between different metaphors
along similar lines, and uses such differences as the basis for value-
judgements on the success and necessity of different metaphors:

> If the match (between tenor (topic) and vehicle) is too easy, the
> metaphor is banal, and its effect is decorative rather than cognitive:
> since the use of the vehicle field does little to restructure the topic
> field, the use of a mediating semantic field is relatively gratuitous. . . .
> The degree to which a metaphor is enlightening depends rather on
> the degree to which the vehicle field is going to be productive of new
> meaning and new insight into the topic domain. (Kittay 1987: 287–8)

Ortony (1979b) proposes a distinction between 'predicate promotion' metaphors and 'predicate introduction' metaphors.[3] A
metaphor involves predicate promotion if the interpreter

> . . . already knows that the predicates in question are true of the A
> term (the tenor), so that the information extractable from the meta-
> phor is old information and it is recognized as such by the speaker
> and the hearer. Consequently, all that the hearer does in comprehen-
> sion is to promote the salience of relevant predicates from the A term.
> (Ortony 1979b: 199)

A predicate introduction metaphor, on the other hand, is

> . . . one in which the salience of an existing predicate (or set of predic-
> ates) cannot be increased, because they are not yet predicates of the

A term at all; they are introduced as new predicates as a result of the comprehension process. (...) In predicate promotion metaphors, the predicates are already there, and they get promoted or emphasized. In predicate introduction metaphors, they are not already there and they get introduced. (Ortony 1979b: 199–200)

Ortony suggests that predicate introduction metaphors are 'one of the cornerstones of insight', since they 'help us to see things in different ways' (Ortony 1979b: 200). The schema-refreshment scale captures the distinction identified by Ortony but characterizes it as a matter of degree rather than in terms of an opposition.

8.6 Metaphor as schema connection

In the previous chapter I treated metaphor in terms of a connection between different schemata. This approach is compatible with the ways in which metaphors have been described by different theorists. Whereas Richards talked about 'two thoughts of different things' being simultaneously present in metaphor (Richards 1936: 94), Black developed the notion of 'implicative complex' or 'system of related commonplaces' in an attempt to account for the clusters of conventional, culturally shared knowledge that he felt make up our conceptual representations of situations and entities (Black 1962, 1979; see also 8.4 above). In her discussion of the metaphor 'Afternoon burns upon the wires of the sea', Nowottny similarly refers to the concepts involved as 'our knowledge of the sea-structure' and 'our knowledge of the harp-structure' (Nowottny 1965: 59). More recently, Hrushovski has proposed a view of metaphor as the juxtaposition of two separate 'frames of reference' (Hrushovski 1984), while Kittay has described metaphorical projections as a move across different 'semantic fields', that she defines as the conjunction between a 'lexical set' and a 'content domain' (Kittay 1987: 33). I would argue that the notion of schema as developed within the theories discussed in Chapter 6 can subsume all such attempts to describe the knowledge structures that are involved in metaphorical connections (cf. Ortony 1979b).

Within the cognitive approach to metaphor discussed in 8.5, the notion of 'image-schemas' is introduced to refer to the patterns of knowledge that derive directly from our bodily experiences, such as our notion of balance or force (Johnson 1987: 29, 41ff., 74ff.). The term 'schema', on the other hand, is used in the same sense in which I have used it so far:

a cluster of knowledge representing a particular generic procedure, object, percept, event, sequence of events, or social situation.

(Johnson 1987: 19)

cognitive models of some aspect of the world, that we use in comprehending our experience and in reasoning about it.

(Lakoff and Turner 1989: 65)

Lakoff and Turner (1989: 63–4) use the LIFE IS A JOURNEY metaphor to show how metaphorical mappings may involve different kinds of elements that they identify as making up the internal structure of schemata, namely:

- slots (e.g. traveller mapped onto living person, path producing a new slot in LIFE domain)
- relations (e.g. relationship obtaining between traveller and destination mapped onto relationship between person and purpose)
- properties (e.g. qualities of travellers mapped onto qualities of living people in general)
- knowledge (e.g. inference patterns from the JOURNEY domain mapped onto the LIFE domain).

In my analyses in Chapter 7, I have largely drawn from the versions of schema theory proposed in Schank and Abelson (1977) and Schank (1982). More specifically, I have shown how Schank's notion of TOP can be useful in representing and explaining metaphors, since it provides a framework in which to discuss in detail the connections between schemata that underlie metaphorical relationships, as well as describe the different ways in which such connections may be established. The relevance of Schank's model of comprehension to the study of metaphor is supported by an observation made by Searle (1979):

The question 'How do metaphors work?' is a bit like the question 'How does one thing remind us of another thing?'. There is no single answer to either question, though similarity obviously plays a major role in answering both. (Searle 1979: 113)

The version of schema theory that Schank proposed in *Dynamic Memory* (Schank 1982) was largely motivated by the need to provide an answer for the second of these questions (see 6.4.3 above).

According to Schank, reminding is central to comprehension, since it basically involves 'finding the correct memory structure to process an input' (Schank 1982: 79). At its simplest, therefore, reminding occurs when a present experience, such as being in a restaurant, *reminds* us of one or more similar previous experiences, which, if they have occurred frequently enough, will be stored within a generic memory structure that we call a schema. It is in this sense that reminding can be regarded as essential to comprehension: if we were unable to relate new experiences to old ones, our ability to interact effectively and efficiently with our environment would be greatly impaired. As I explained in 6.4.3, Schank was also interested in exploring the implications that more complex instances of reminding have for a model of the organization of human memory. More specifically, he was interested in accounting for those instances of reminding that occur across different domains. This is the case, for example, in an episode where, on seeing a naked sunbather who had inadvertently placed himself in a visible position despite taking great pains to avoid it, somebody was reminded of an ostrich (Schank 1982: 114; see 6.4.3 above). Schank's notion of TOP (Thematic Organization Point) was meant to account for this kind of phenomenon: TOPs are high-level structures that organize memories on the basis of the existence of similar goals, conditions and low-level features (Schank 1982: 113).

The similarity pointed out by Searle between reminding experiences and metaphor should by now have become clearer. There is a sense in which metaphors can be described as the result of reminding experiences across different domains, which interpreters of metaphorical expressions are somehow forced to reconstruct. Not surprisingly, the cognitive role that recent theories have attributed to metaphor is very similar to the role that Schank attributes to reminding: the tendency, or indeed the need, to make sense of one type of experience in terms of another.

8.6.1 Relevance theory, schema activation and metaphor

I have already pointed out (see 7.2.2 above) that the theory of relevance proposed by Sperber and Wilson (1986, 1995) can provide a solution to the problem of schema activation, which is not adequately dealt with by schema theory itself. Similar considerations apply to the issue of the recognition and the interpretation of metaphors.

The growing belief in the pervasiveness of metaphor as a linguistic and cognitive resource contrasts with the complexity of the debate about the mechanisms that are supposed to explain how metaphors are recognized in the first place (see Kittay 1987: 40–95). Another arduous problem is to do with the way in which certain connections and not others are established in the mapping of the source onto the target domain. Such issues are persuasively dealt with by Sperber and Wilson's (1986, 1995) model of cognition. According to Relevance theory, we interpret all instances of intentional communication by placing the new input against a set of previously held assumptions so that it will achieve the most efficient balance between amount of processing effort and richness of cognitive results. This, according to Sperber and Wilson, applies in the same way to literal and figurative utterances. In order to interpret a metaphor, we do not need to perform any special cognitive operations, but simply search our existing knowledge for the context in which the metaphorical expression will achieve maximum relevance (Sperber and Wilson 1986, 1995: 235–7). The attractiveness of this approach lies in the fact that the same principle accounts both for the way in which we activate appropriate portions of background knowledge, and for the way in which we interpret metaphors by bringing together two different schemata (or 'encyclopaedic entries' in Sperber and Wilson's terms) and by deriving from such conjunction an appropriate set of conclusions.

The specific view of metaphor proposed within Relevance theory, however, is not totally convincing. Sperber and Wilson see figurative language as resulting from the need to give an optimally relevant linguistic realization to a complex thought, which, if expressed literally, would cause excessive processing difficulties (Sperber and Wilson 1986, 1995: 231–7; Pilkington 1990). This seems to assume that thought is fundamentally literal, and that the essence of metaphorical language lies in the relationships between some thoughts and their linguistic realizations. Such a view does not, in other words, allow for metaphorical thought, which, as the cognitive approach has convincingly shown, plays a central role in our basic conceptual system. The possibility for thought to be metaphorical, therefore, seriously undermines Sperber and Wilson's definition of metaphor as a non-literal linguistic realization of a complex thought.

8.7 Similarity, schema refreshment and the role of metaphors in text-world construction

Within the approach developed in the previous chapter, text worlds are seen as resulting from the activation of sets of schemata in the reader's mind, and from the instantiation of such schemata on the basis of the constraints imposed by the text. The reader's perception of individual text worlds depends on the mutual relationships between the activated schemata, and on the extent to which the reader's existing schemata are reinforced or challenged by the textual input. Because metaphor involves the projection of a source domain onto a target domain, and the possibility of establishing multiple mappings between the two schemata, the role of metaphor in the process of text-world construction can be explained by considering the relationship between the schemata involved. The establishment of a metaphorical connection presupposes the existence of some form of similarity between the two domains. However, as I said above, metaphors occupy different positions on what I have called the schema refreshment scale, i.e. they may either reflect pre-existing similarities or force interpreters to find new ones, thereby creating the conditions for at least a temporary reconceptualization of the target domain.[4]

Novel

In what follows I will continue to talk about the *potential* for schema refreshment carried by different metaphors. This is not only because different readers bring different knowledge to the text (so that what is schema refreshing for one reader may not be for another) but also, and crucially, because it is not necessarily the case that the reader's schematic knowledge will be affected by the challenges posed by a new connection between domains. Readers may ignore such challenges (as we often do when experience does not correspond to our expectations), they may resist the implications of a particular metaphorical connection, or they may accept them for the sake of the processing of a certain text without incorporating them within their permanent knowledge store. In the terms used by Kittay, the cognitive reordering induced by some metaphors may have a 'transient' or a 'permanent' effect on our conception of reality, although even the most transient of effects enables us to contemplate, at least momentarily, a new way of conceiving the world (Kittay 1987: 37, 288–9). It is only when a metaphor begins to determine our normal way of understanding some aspect of the world, i.e. when it becomes conventionalized, that its potential for cognitive reorganization is fully realized (cf. Lakoff and Johnson 1980: 145–6). I will return to the problems posed by the notion of schema refreshment in 9.3 below.

In the rest of this chapter I will consider examples of metaphors that fall at different points on the schema-refreshment scale, and discuss their implications for the worlds projected by the poems in which they occur. I will focus in particular on 'realistic' text worlds, i.e. on poems that fall at the top end of Ryan's typology (see 5.4.1 above). This is because I am interested in how metaphors contribute to project particular views of what readers are meant to see as their own reality.

8.7.1 The schema-reinforcing end of the scale

In my discussion of Heaney's 'A Pillowed Head', I claimed that the metaphorical connection that it establishes between birth and dawn does not require any significant reorganization of the schemata involved, but rather builds on a frequent association between the two domains. The BIRTH IS DAWN metaphor is in fact part of a wider conventional metaphor in English whereby A LIFETIME IS A DAY (see Lakoff and Turner 1989: 6, 11–12 and throughout). As Lakoff and Turner put it,

> In this metaphor, birth is dawn, maturity is noon, old age is twilight, the moment of death is sunset, and the state of death is night.
>
> (Lakoff and Turner 1989: 6)

The LIFETIME IS A DAY metaphor is realized in a wide range of everyday expressions (such as 'the dawn of a new life', 'being in one's twilight years', 'going to sleep forever'), and is often exploited by poets (think, for example, of Dylan Thomas's 'Do Not Go Gentle into that Good Night', where night stands for death). According to Lakoff, Johnson and Turner, conventional metaphors are part of the normal conceptual system of the users of a certain language, and associations between domains such as LIFETIME and DAY are therefore stored as units in the mind. As Steen (1994: 17ff.) has pointed out, however, there are problems with this claim, since the presence in a certain language of expressions where life is described in terms of the daily cycle does not necessarily imply that a mapping between the two domains is permanently stored in the mind of each speaker of the language. An additional problem is posed by the fact that some linguistic realizations of conventional metaphors may themselves be conventional, while others may be highly original, as is often the case in poetry (Steen 1994: 7ff.). It is therefore more accurate to say that some metaphorical connections are conventional within a particular culture, and may therefore be stored within the conceptual system of some, but not necessarily all, members of that culture.

In interpreting the association between dawn and birth in Heaney's poem, in other words, some readers may rely on a connection already stored in their background knowledge, while other readers may create the connection during the processing of the text. In Schank's terms, some readers may already possess a TOP linking their BIRTH schema and their DAWN schema, while others may construct the TOP on line while reading the text.[5] Even in the latter case, however, the TOP is unlikely to be new, since it would have been needed in the past to process or produce expressions involving the same metaphor. As I said in Chapter 7, the connection between birth and dawn relies on a set of conventional correspondences involving a shared goal (beginning), shared conditions (new life cycle), and some stereotypical emotional associations (hope, joy, optimism). In addition, Heaney's poem sets up some further correspondences among what Schank calls low-level features (similar noises, similar colours, etc.). A TOP representation of the DAWN–BIRTH association has been given in 7.2.2.[6]

Clearly, conventional metaphors occupy the bottom end of the schema-refreshment scale. In particular, their effect will be totally schema reinforcing if the connection is already part of the permanent knowledge store of the interpreter. Even if this is not the case, however, the creation of the relevant TOP will highlight similarities that are conventionally perceived to exist between the two domains, and will not therefore result in a refreshment of the target domain. Where the *linguistic* realization of the metaphor is creative rather than conventional, additional correspondences may be produced, which may vary in their potential for schema refreshment. In Heaney's poem, for example, the original linguistic realization of the BIRTH IS DAWN metaphor triggers some novel low-level correspondences (e.g. between the baby's crying and birds' song, and between the colours involved in dawn and birth), but, in Ortony's terms, their effect is to promote features that are already part of the target domain, rather than to introduce new ones (Ortony 1979b). As a consequence, I have argued, the BIRTH IS DAWN metaphor reinforces the overall effect of 'A Pillowed Head', which is that of projecting a familiar and harmonious text world by activating a configuration of mutually connected and mutually reinforcing schemata.

While it is not surprising that conventional metaphors should be primarily schema reinforcing, novel metaphors may be expected to be invariably schema refreshing. I want to argue, however, that some novel metaphors may also occupy a relatively low position on the schema-refreshment scale. In my analysis of Plath's 'Morning Song' in the previous chapter, for example, I argued that the metaphors occurring in the second half of the poem, although novel, are unlikely to have a schema refreshing effect. Consider, for example,

Table 8.1

Schemata	Goal	Conditions	Features	Emotional Associations
Baby/moth	–	smallness, vulnerability	soft, intermittent noise	–

(Based on Schank 1982: 113ff.)

the expression *moth-breath* in line 10, where the baby's breathing is metaphorically related to the buzzing sound of a moth. Here the association relies on relatively low-level features (soft, intermittent noise) and conditions (small size, flimsiness, vulnerability, etc.; see 7.3.2 above). A possible TOP representation of this connection is given in Table 8.1.

In this case, I would argue, no correspondences at the level of goals and emotional associations are strongly suggested by the metaphor. Rather, the metaphorical connection involves perceptual similarities that Schank would define as low-level features, and the conditions in which those features apply. This shows, firstly, that Schank's claim that some similarity between patterns of goals is essential for cross-contextual reminding does not constitute a constraining factor for metaphorical connections. Secondly, and more importantly, this metaphor provides an example of a novel metaphor with a relatively low potential for schema refreshment. It is true, on the one hand, that the association between the baby's breathing and a moth is potentially more schema refreshing than a conventional metaphor, since it triggers the establishment of a new connection between schemata: in a case such as this, it is highly unlikely that the relevant TOP already exists in the reader's background knowledge. On the other hand, insofar as the metaphor highlights for individual readers pre-existing properties of the target domain, its overall effect is largely schema reinforcing.[7] In Ortony's (1979b) terms, this is another example of a predicate promotion metaphor.

Similar considerations apply to the metaphors in 'A Martian Sends a Postcard Home', where the connection between tenors (e.g. books) and vehicles (e.g. *mechanical birds with many wings*) is often to do with a similarity in shape or some other perceptual property. Again, these metaphors do establish new connections between domains, but they largely rely on shared low-level features, and are therefore unlikely to lead to a new conceptualization of the target domains. It is because of the relatively low potential for schema refreshment of its metaphors, I would argue, that Raine's

poem reads more as a list of clever and suggestive riddles than as
a serious examination of the customs of a particular society. I will
now turn to a more complex example of an extended metaphor
that also involves a similarity at the level of goals.

Tony Curtis's 'Sick Child (*After Munch*)'

Curtis's poem 'Sick Child (*After Munch*)' provides a verbal counterpart, as it were, to a painting by Edvard Munch ('The Sick Child'),
in which a bed-ridden little girl is assisted by her distraught mother.

SICK CHILD (*AFTER MUNCH*)

Red-haired Sophie
Pillowed in bed, wrecked
Against the headboard.
Caught in the undertow of a treacherous tide,
Her blood swirls in a wash of the sea.   5
Tuberculosis has scoured her out like a shell.

At the bedside her mother sits doubled
With the ache of certain loss,
Her face bleared into her chest.

She holds to Sophie, fingers curled so firmly, so long   10
Around fingers that the knuckles are flushed red
Like rocks poised for the sky's spilling of dawn.

Frail anemone the child against the coral pillow,
Weed-green the bedcover,
Driftwood the table and cupboard.   15

The mother's tight, black hair is tied and twisted back,
Her body curled and falling in a slow
Black wave over a deep rock.

The poem involves a long extended metaphor whereby the scene
involving the sick girl and her mother is described in terms of a
shipwreck. The force and effects of the disease are conveyed by
means of references to rough and stormy waters: tuberculosis is
said to have *scoured* Sophie *out* (line 6), while her blood *swirls in
a wash of the sea* (line 5) as a result of being *Caught in the undertow
of a treacherous tide* (line 4). The little girl's vulnerability is encap-
sulated in a series of figurative expressions where she is described
in terms of entities that could be destroyed by the force of the sea:
in the first stanza she is described as being *wrecked/ Against the
headboard* (lines 2–3), in the second stanza a simile compares her

to a shell (line 6), while in the fifth stanza she is referred to as a *frail anemone*. Sophie's mother and the objects furnishing the room are also metaphorically presented as elements of a storm scene: the table and the cupboard are *driftwood* (line 15), the woman's fingers are as red as *rocks poised for the sky's spilling of dawn* (line 12) and her body is *falling in a slow/ Black wave over a deep rock* (lines 17–18). Within this context, the choice of *coral* as premodifier for *pillow* (line 13) and of *weed-green* as complement for *the bedcover* (line 14) do not simply express nuances of colour, but contribute to a further extension of the metaphor, whereby the objects surrounding the child are also elements of the sea-scene in which the shipwreck takes place. More specifically, the coral mentioned in line 13 and the rock mentioned in line 18 contribute to the effect of the extended metaphor, since their presence in combination with a storm typically creates the conditions for shipwreck.

Overall, the majority of figurative expressions in the poem can therefore be seen as instantiations of the metaphor TERMINAL DISEASE IS SHIPWRECK. The projection of the source onto the target domain clearly involves, first and foremost, a general similarity between the two situations: in both, people are powerless to avoid an adverse outcome involving the loss of life; both, therefore, have negative emotional associations. A number of further, more specific, mappings are induced, as I mentioned above, by the extension of the metaphor: between the child and a ship (line 2), between the effects and strength of the disease and those of the currents (lines 4–6), between the furniture in the room and driftwood (line 15), between the colours of the bedding and the vegetation of the sea (lines 13–14), between the mother and something that is about to crash against a rock (lines 17–18), and so on.

The correspondences between source and target domains that are highlighted by the metaphor are obviously more numerous and complex than in the examples discussed so far, but their overall effect is similar: they point out and reinforce some of the properties that are normally associated with the target domain, such as, in this case, the vulnerability of the sick person and her family, the overwhelming power of the forces they are trying to fight against, and the general feeling of loss and despair.

As shown in Table 8.2, the metaphorical connection is, in this case, a perfect example of the type of reminding that Schank aimed to account for by means of the notion of TOP: the central correspondences between the two schemata involve the main goals that are associated with them (i.e. a frustrated survival goal) and

Table 8.2

Schemata	Goal	Conditions	Features	Emotional Associations
Terminal disease/ Shipwreck	Survival goal blocked	Overpowering natural force	Wooden objects (e.g. headboard/ ship)	Negative: fear, despair, etc.

(Based on Schank 1982: 113ff.)

the conditions affecting such goals (i.e. the overwhelming power of natural forces). Such correspondences are accompanied by less crucial correlations in some of the 'low-level' features involved (e.g. the presence of wooden objects). My revised version of Schank's representation of TOPs also shows the similarity in the affective component of the two schemata, which clearly plays an important role in the effect of the metaphor.

In all of the metaphors analysed in this section, the projection of the source domain onto the target domain mostly exploits conventional and/or pre-existing similarities between the relevant schemata. As a consequence, metaphors such as these can be adequately accounted for by the approaches that have been discussed in 8.3 under the labels of Similarity and Comparison views. In schema-theory terms, these metaphors carry a relatively low potential for schema refreshment, since their interpretation does not involve the attribution of new properties to the target domain, but rather a reinforcement of some aspects that are likely to be already part of the relevant schema within the readers' background knowledge. I have also shown, however, some variation within the bottom part of the schema-refreshment scale. While conventional metaphors lie at the most schema-reinforcing end of the scale, novel metaphors such as Plath's *moth-breath* occupy a higher position, insofar as they trigger new connections between schemata. Moreover, extended metaphors like the one in 'Sick Child' highlight more correspondences than metaphors such as *moth-breath*, and therefore represent a further movement away from the schema-reinforcing end of the scale. In spite of these differences, such metaphors do not pose any considerable challenges to conventional conceptualizations of the target domains, and project world views that are likely to overlap to a large extent with the model of reality shared by the majority of the readers. As a consequence, metaphors such as these tend to play a major role in poems that project fairly conventional views of reality, as is the case with the BIRTH IS DAWN metaphor in Heaney's 'A Pillowed Head'.[8]

8.7.2 The schema-refreshing end of the scale

In my discussion of Plath's 'Morning Song' in the previous chapter I showed how the two extended metaphors (the MUSEUM metaphor and the CLOUD metaphor) do not rely on obvious or conventional similarities between the source and target domains. Rather, they establish novel and striking connections between different areas of background knowledge and lead to the attribution of new properties to the target domains. As such, these metaphors fall within Ortony's (1979b) predicate introduction category and carry a high potential for schema refreshment. I will now discuss in detail a further example.

Robert Graves's 'The Cool Web'

The following poem presents language as essential to human life, but also attributes to it some negative effects.

THE COOL WEB

Children are dumb to say how hot the day is,
How hot the scent is of the summer rose,
How dreadful the black wastes of evening sky,
How dreadful the tall soldiers drumming by.

But we have speech, to chill the angry day,   5
And speech, to dull the rose's cruel scent.
We spell away the overhanging night,
We spell away the soldiers and the fright.

There's a cool web of language winds us in,
Retreat from too much joy or too much fear: 10
We grow sea-green at last and coldly die
In brininess and volubility.

But if we let our tongues lose self-possession,
Throwing off language and its watery clasp
Before our death instead of when death comes,   15
Facing the wide glare of the children's day,
Facing the rose, the dark sky and the drums,
We shall go mad no doubt and die that way.

On the one hand, language is described as a necessary form of protection against the overwhelming power of sensory and affective experiences: words are an essential resource for human beings to come to terms with reality and to keep the most powerful sensations under control; without language we would regress to the inarticulate vulnerability of childhood, and face insanity and pre-mature death. By the same token, however, language exercises a constraining and limiting force on the scope and intensity of our experiences, as expressed by the metaphorical connection between language and a web.

The threats posed by a direct exposure to perceptual reality without the mediation of language are epitomized by means of repeated references to hot days (lines 1, 5, 16), powerfully scented roses (lines 2, 6, 17), dark nights (lines 3, 7, 17) and the noise and sight of soldiers (lines 4, 8, 17). A network of similarity relation-ships between this varied sample of experiences is established by means of closely-knit patterns of deviation and parallelism (for a detailed linguistic analysis of this poem, see Semino 1990b). It is against this background that the central metaphor LANGUAGE IS A WEB needs to be interpreted. On the one hand, the metaphor may be seen as emphasizing the protective power of language, whereby human beings are defended from potentially overwhelm-ing experiences:

There's a cool web of language winds us in,
Retreat from too much joy or too much fear:

On the other hand, by identifying the condition of articulate human beings with that of insects wrapped up in webs, the meta-phor constructs language as an instrument of imprisonment. Our linguistic abilities may protect our sanity, but also constrain the range of our thoughts, feelings and perceptions. After all, some of the experiences that language is supposed to help us keep at bay are in fact pleasurable ones (hot days, scent of summer roses), while the prospect of death under the protection of language is rather unappealing: *We grow sea-green at last and coldly die/ In brini-ness and volubility* (lines 11–12).

It is clear that, in this case, it is not very helpful to try to ground the metaphor in a series of pre-existing correspondences between source and target domains. The similarity between the two partly originates from the world-view that is projected by the poem as a whole and is partly triggered by the metaphor itself. In other words, the projection of the WEB domain onto the LANGUAGE domain forces interpreters to construct the latter in ways that may not have been conceived of independently of the metaphor: we are encouraged to see language as something that envelops its users in some kind of necessary, but not therefore pleasurable, captivity.

Table 8.3

Schemata	Goal	Conditions	Features	Emotional Associations
Language/web	Limitation of freedom, imprisonment	?	?	Negative

(Based on Schank 1982: 113ff.)

A TOP representation of the metaphorical connection (Table 8.3) predictably poses a number of problems. The reminding experience that could be said to underlie the metaphor involves primarily a correspondence at the level of goals – namely, those of imprisoning and of limiting the freedom of the participants involved. As a consequence, the two domains also share negative emotional associations. No other correspondences are suggested by the poem, so that it is difficult to fill in the CONDITIONS and FEATURES boxes in Table 8.3. This highlights the absence of straightforward similarities between source and target domains, which different readers may perceive as a weakness in the conceptual grounding of the text, or, conversely, as an essential part of the poem's significance and appeal.

How can the WEB metaphor be related to the overall world view projected by the poem on the one hand, and to the knowledge and assumptions that are likely to be shared by the readers on the other? As far as the first question is concerned, the metaphor contributes to the duality of the view of language presented in the poem: language is said to provide a necessary screen from the effects of a variety of experiences, but is simultaneously constructed as a constraining force and is associated with rather unpleasant sensory perceptions (coldness, wetness). The second question is more complex. The way in which the domain of language is constructed by the text as a whole and by the WEB metaphor in particular clashes with the view of language reflected by the CONDUIT metaphor, which, if cognitive theorists of metaphor are right, is likely to be part of the basic conceptual system of English-speaking readers (see 8.5.1 above). According to the CONDUIT metaphor, language tends to be conceived of as a transparent medium for the transferral of information, rather than as a (necessary) source of constraint on our cognitive, perceptual and emotional experiences. The WEB metaphor, therefore, challenges some aspects of what can be regarded as a widely shared view of reality, and proposes a less common alternative.[9]

Like the MUSEUM and CLOUD metaphors in 'Morning Song', the WEB metaphor has a high potential for schema refreshment. The effect of these metaphors is not so much to highlight existing similarities between domains, but rather to impose less obvious or novel ones, thereby creating the conditions for a partial reconceptualization of the target domain. As a consequence, metaphors such as the one discussed in this section do not easily fit into the Similarity and Comparison views, but are more successfully accounted for within the Interaction view and within the Cognitive approach to metaphor. More importantly, my analyses of realistic text worlds in the last two chapters have shown how metaphors that are high on the schema-refreshment scale tend to play a major role in texts that project unconventional and challenging views of reality. This is the case, I have argued, both with the central metaphors in 'The Cool Web', and with the two extended metaphor in Plath's 'Morning Song' (see 7.3.1 and 7.3.2 above).

The method for the analysis of text worlds developed in Part III of this book represents a useful alternative to possible-world frameworks. While it is necessary to recognize the different ontological implications of literal and figurative language, it is also important to be able to account for the way in which figurative expressions affect the process of text-world creation. This applies particularly to the realistic text worlds considered in the previous and present chapters, since they are likely to be perceived as representations of the readers' own 'actual' world. It is now time to explore the possibility of adopting an eclectic approach to the analysis of text worlds, that combines the different frameworks exemplified in the course of this book. This is the aim of the final chapter.

NOTES

[1] In his work on text worlds, Werth (1994 and forthcoming) has proposed an elegant solution to the issue of the ontological status of the referents of metaphorical expressions. Werth draws a distinction between 'discourse world' and 'text world'. The discourse world is the situation in which a text is produced and received, which involves speakers/writers and hearers/readers as 'participants'. The text world is the situation projected by the text, which is inhabited by characters. Within this framework, metaphors outline subworlds that are accessible to the participants of the discourse world, but not to the characters of the text world.

[2] Notice that the conclusion that the poem describes a realistic world depends on the decision to interpret expressions such as these in figurative terms. If they were read literally, they would outline a physically and taxonomically impossible world (see 4.6.3 and 5.4.1 above). Levin (1989)

highlights the fact that a literal reading of metaphorical expressions often results in the construction of an impossible world. I will return to this point in 9.2.2. below.

[3] In Ortony's terms, predicates are parts of schemata which are highlighted by metaphors: 'A predicate . . . can represent knowledge, a belief, or an attitude about or toward something' (Ortony 1979b: 191).

[4] Some empirical evidence that metaphors do not necessarily reflect similarities but create new associations between domains is given in Camac and Glucksberg (1984).

[5] Schank does state that TOPs are assembled *ad hoc* in cognitive processing, but will also be stored in memory on a more permanent basis depending on their usefulness (Schank 1982: 114–15). The idea that metaphors trigger the online construction of appropriate cognitive structures is central to a recently developed theory, according to which the comprehension of metaphor involves a process of *ad hoc* category formation (see Keysar and Glucksberg 1992; Shen 1992).

[6] A further advantage of describing metaphors in terms of TOPs (particularly with the addition of a slot for emotional associations) is the possibility of accounting systematically for different kinds of similarities across domains. McCabe (1983) shows how different studies of metaphor have highlighted different types of similarities that may be involved in metaphorical connections (e.g. similarity of perceptual properties, functions, attitudes, etc.).

[7] As I argued in Chapter 7, the overall effect of 'Morning Song' is schema refreshing, but this results from the two extended metaphors in the second and third stanzes, rather than from metaphors such as *moth-breath* in the second half of the poem.

[8] This does not, however, detract from the poetic qualities or artistic value of poems such as 'A Pillowed Head' and 'Sick Child'. As I have repeatedly pointed out, schema refreshment does not straightforwardly correlate with literary value.

[9] A similar view of language to that suggested by the WEB metaphor is held by many linguists, from Sapir (1970) and Whorf (1956) to contemporary practioners of critical discourse analysis (e.g. Fairclough 1992). Indeed, Graves's metaphor has been borrowed as the title of several linguistics publications, such as *The Web of Words* by Carter and Long (1987).

Part III: Suggestions for further analysis

1. Poetic text worlds as configurations of instantiated schemata

(a) Consider Seamus Heaney's poem 'Mid-Term Break'. What main schemata need to be activated in order to interpret the text? To what extent does the poem assume culture-specific versions of these schemata? How can the various schemata be described in terms of the three different versions of schema theory discussed in Chapter 6? What features of the text act as headers for the activation of each schema? How does the use of definite reference in the poem relate to schema activation (see 2.2, 6.4.2 and 7.2.1)? How does the activation of relevant schemata enable us to infer 'missing' bits of information (e.g. the relationship between the first-person speaker and the referent of *him* in the sixth stanza)? How does the activation of relevant schemata enable us to establish connections between different scenes and events? Are there any peculiarities in the instantiation of the different schemata during the processing of this particular text? If you had any difficulties in your initial approach to the text, can you account for them in terms of schema theory? How can you explain, for example, the fact that readers may be surprised by the content of the poem after reading its title? How would you describe the world projected by the text in terms of the approach proposed in Chapters 6 and 7? More specifically, how would you rate it in terms of Cook's notion of schema refreshment (see 6.7.2) and Weber's notion of positive manipulation (see 6.7.3)? Do your reactions to the poem lead you to agree or disagree with the claims made by Cook and Weber on the definition of literariness and (in Weber's case) on aesthetic value?

(b) Philip Larkin's poem 'Nothing to be Said' focuses on the idea that no matter who you are, where you live and what you do *Life is slow dying*. In order to emphasize the universality of this condition, a series of parallels are set up between different types of people and activities. Look in detail at the way in which parallelism is used in the poem to suggest a fundamental similarity across geographical, cultural and social boundaries. What schemata are activated and brought together by the lists which make up most of the poem? To what extent can the connections between the various schemata be captured in terms of Schank's notion of TOP (including the addition of a slot for Emotional Associations as suggested in Chapter 7)? I would argue that much of the effect of the poem depends on the perception of differences rather than similarities between different schemata (e.g. between a HUNTING schema and a GARDEN PARTY schema). Do you agree with this? What contrasts across schemata play a role in your interpretation of the poem? To what extent can these contrasts be captured in terms of schema theory? How would you describe the world view projected by the poem as a whole? To what extent do you think it could have a schema-refreshing effect? How does it compare in this respect with the poems analysed in Chapter 7?

2. Metaphor and schema refreshment in poetry

In Chapter 8 I argued that some metaphors bring together different areas of knowledge in a way that may trigger some degree of schema refreshment. Consider W.H. Auden's poem 'Schoolchildren' from this point of view. The text centres around an extended metaphor whereby SCHOOLCHILDREN ARE PRISONERS, or, more generally, SCHOOLS ARE PRISONS. Look carefully at the text and note the multiple mappings that are established from the PRISON source domain to the SCHOOL target domain. How can this metaphorical connection be captured in terms of Schank's notion of TOP, or indeed in terms of the extension of Schank's framework suggested in Chapters 7 and 8? What types of features are projected from source to target domain? In other words, what connections are established in terms of goals, conditions, low-level features and emotional associations? What are the possible effects of this metaphor on the readers' existing knowledge about schools and schoolchildren? To what extent can these effects be described in terms of the notion of schema refreshment? How does this metaphor compare with the ones discussed in Chapters 7 and 8? Where would you place it on the schema-refreshment scale that I proposed in Chapter 8? How does the main metaphor affect the world view projected by the poem as a whole? How does 'School-children' compare with the poems discussed in Chapter 7 in terms of the type of world it projects?

3. Schema theory and deviant world views in novels

In Chapters 7 and 8 I have argued that the nature of the config-uration of schemata evoked by a text leads to the projection of a more or less conventional or schema-refreshing view of reality. Here I want you to focus on the effect that is produced when a reality that is familiar to the reader is described from the point of view of someone who lacks the relevant background knowledge. Look up the opening of William Faulkner's *The Sound and the Fury*, focusing particularly on the first six paragraphs.

If you have never come across this passage before, you may experience some difficulty recognizing that it is a description of a game of golf. The first-person narrator in this part of the novel is Benjy, who is thirty-three years old and mentally disabled. Benjy clearly does not understand golf: he only watches the game in order to hear the players utter the word 'caddie', which is also the name of his beloved sister. How does Faulkner make it difficult for readers to recognize a type of activity they are likely to be familiar with? In other words, how does the text delay or impede the activation of our GOLF schema? What lexical items that would normally function as headers for the activation of a GOLF schema are avoided in the text? What lexical items are used instead? How does our perception of the passage change before and after the activation of the relevant schema? (You may want to compare this passage with the 'Washing Clothes' text discussed in 6.2.) What conclusions can you eventually draw about Benjy's world view (in Ryan's term, his epistemic or knowledge world)?

Benjy's defamiliarizing description of a golf game has been discussed by Leech and Short (1981: 202–7) and Fowler (1986: 133–4) as an example of a highly deviant 'mind style' – an idio-syncratic way of perceiving and making sense of reality (see also Bockting 1994). See these analyses for a detailed account of the linguistic features of the text and their role in creating Benjy's particular view of reality.

4. Schema clashes in absurdist drama

Absurdist drama is a genre which can often be usefully analysed in terms of schema theory, possible-world theory, or a combination of the two. Here I want you to focus on Harold Pinter's sketch 'Applicant'.

In 'Applicant' we are presented with an interview scene which soon takes a rather surprising course. Schema theory can go a long way in explaining how this leads to an absurdist and humorous effect. How is our INTERVIEW schema activated by the opening of the text? What expectations does this schema give rise to? To what extent are these expectations fulfilled by the rest of the sketch? What aspects of the conversation clash with the expectations created by the activation of the INTERVIEW schema? What other schemata may be activated in the course of the sketch? What features of the conversation act as headers for their activation? How do these schema relate to the INTERVIEW schema? In other words, what are the differences and the similarities between these schemata? How do the clashes between different active schemata lead to absurdity? Why is the very end of the sketch likely to have a humorous effect? In considering these questions, you may also want to bear in mind the possible effects of the availability of formal schemata to do with absurdist drama in general and Pinter's plays in particular (see 6.4.1). Another interesting aspect for consideration is the way in which Pinter plays with stereotypes and conventional expectations about gender differences and relations between men and women, particularly as regards power and sexual matters (do not forget that this sketch was first broadcast on BBC television in 1964). A further issue is to do with the text's potential for schema refreshment. To what extent do you think Pinter's sketch might refresh the schemata that the audience applies to its interpretation?

Some of the oddities that you are likely to have noticed in reading the sketch can also be captured in terms of possible-world theory. This applies particularly to some of the presuppositions carried by Miss Piffs's utterances, which suggest that her view of the world (in Ryan's terms, her epistemic or knowledge world) clashes with ours. Consider particularly the point where she asks Mr Lamb whether he suffers from falling coat, as well as the following sequence of utterances:

PIFFS: Are you virgo intacta?
LAMB: Yes, I am, actually. I'll make no secret of it.
PIFFS: Have you always been virgo intacta?
LAMB: Oh yes, always. Always.
PIFFS: From the word go?
LAMB: Go? Oh yes, from the word go.

What presuppositions are carried by the question to do with falling coat and by the question *Have you always been virgo intacta?* What do these presuppositions suggest about Miss Piffs's knowledge world? How can the relationship between her view of reality and your own actual world be described in terms of Ryan's typology of accessibility relations (see 4.6.3)?

The possibility of combining schema theory and possible world theory in the analysis of a single text will be demonstrated in detail in the next chapter. In fact, the parallels between Pinter's sketch and Sylvia Plath's 'The Applicant' analysed in the next chapter go well beyond the fact that they have almost identical titles. You may want to come back to this sketch after reading my analysis of Plath's poem, in order to consider differences and similarities between the ways in which the two texts achieve their effects.

For an analysis of 'Applicant' that makes use of schema theory, see Short (1996: 243ff.).

5. Switches between schemata and humour

(a) In 6.4.2 I gave an example of a joke that works by tricking interpreters into activating a portion of background knowledge which then turns out to be inadequate to the interpretation of the punchline. Here are two more examples, both taken from Chiaro (1992):

> 'Mummy, Mummy, can I play with Grandma?'
> 'No dear, you've dug her up twice this week already!'
> (Chiaro1992: 61)

> 'Mummy, Mummy, I don't want to go to France!'
> 'Shut up and keep swimming!' (Chiaro 1992: 87, 96)

How can schema theory be used to explain the way in which these jokes achieve their effects? Note that, although in 6.4.2 I discussed the 'Daddy' joke in terms of Schank and Abelson's notion of script, you may want to adopt the more general notion of schema, or refer to any of the versions of the theory discussed in Chapter 6. Which areas of background knowledge are involved in the interpretation of each joke? What interpretative adjustments are forced upon the adressees by each of the two punchlines? What is the contrast between the worlds projected by the first and second parts of each joke? How can schema theory be used to explain the oddity of the world projected by each punchline?

(b) A different type of schematic clash is involved in the following sketch by British comedians Stephen Fry and Hugh Laurie:

> *Hugh is a bank teller. Stephen approaches the counter wearing some sort of mask and carrying a sawn-off shotgun.*

STEPHEN Be clever.

HUGH I beg your pardon?

STEPHEN Be clever. If you even breathe too loud, I'll blow you in half. Now, slowly and carefully, open the till and take out all the notes.

HUGH All the notes?

STEPHEN All the notes.

HUGH Yes. Is your account actually with this branch?

STEPHEN What?

HUGH If not, I'll have to make a phone call. Shouldn't take long.

STEPHEN If you even look at a telephone, I'll spread your brains all over the wall. I'm robbing the bank.

HUGH Robbing the . . . oh God.

STEPHEN Now just take it easy.

HUGH Oh God.

STEPHEN Mouth shut. Nice and relaxed. Put all the notes into this bag.

HUGH Don't kill me.

STEPHEN Just do it, alright?

HUGH Yes, yes. All the notes . . .

STEPHEN That's it. nice and easy.

> *Hugh nervously takes out all the cash, then suddenly stops.*

HUGH Oh oh. Wait a minute.

STEPHEN What?

HUGH Oh I don't believe it. I don't believe it.

STEPHEN Come on, I haven't got all day.

HUGH Who put you up to this?

STEPHEN Put me up . . . ?

HUGH It was Carol, wasn't it? I knew it! She's crazy. Tscch! Where's the camera then?

STEPHEN What are you talking about?

HUGH You're that Jeremy Beadle, aren't you?

STEPHEN What!?

HUGH I didn't recognise you at first. I'll kill her! She's a right minx. Oh I feel such an idiot!

STEPHEN Listen, you twerp, put all the money . . .

HUGH I must say this is brilliant. You people are so clever. So when's it going to be on television?

STEPHEN Look, I am not Jeremy bleeding Beadle! Now put the notes in the bag.

HUGH 'Course you'll have to bleep that out, won't you?

STEPHEN What?

HUGH Jeremy bleeding Beadle. You can't really say Jeremy bleeding Beadle on family television. Unless of course 'Bleeding' is actually your middle name.

STEPHEN Look, I am not Jeremy Beadle. I don't look anything like Jeremy Beadle.

HUGH Well, not with that mask on, obviously.

Stephen removes the mask.

STEPHEN Satisfied?

HUGH That's brilliant.

STEPHEN What is?

HUGH You've got a false head on, have you? That's incredible.

STEPHEN If you don't fill that bag and pass it over in ten seconds, I'll kill you.

HUGH I can't wait to see this.

STEPHEN One, two . . .

HUGH Actually, to tell you the truth, I used to prefer 'Candid Camera' . . .

STEPHEN Five, six . . .

HUGH You just stole their idea, really, didn't you?

STEPHEN Nine . . .

HUGH Oh I just wish I'd put that other shirt on this morning. Still . . .

Stephen fires into Hugh's chest. Lots of blood.

(Dying) You will send me a tape, won't you?

(Fry and Laurie 1990: 188–90)

Clearly, the effect of the sketch revolves around Hugh's failure to accept that he is in fact involved in a bank robbery. Instead, he interprets the situation in terms of different schemata, which the audience also needs to activate in order to make sense of what he says, and perceive the humour. What schema does Hugh operate with in the first eight turns? Given the context, why is his misunderstanding a source of humour? What schema does he operate with from the point when he says *Oh oh. Wait a minute?* How does the final utterance in particular result in a humorous effect? (NB: Jeremy Beadle is the well-known presenter of a 'candid camera' programme on British television called 'Beadle's About'. Beadle himself is usually involved in the practical jokes played at the expense of unknowing victims. A bleeping sound is used in the programme to erase any swearing.)

As in the case of Pinter's 'Applicant', possible-world theory can provide further insights into the analysis of this text. How can Hugh's inappropriate schema activation be captured in terms of Ryan's framework for the description of the internal structure of fictional worlds (see 4.5.1)? As in the case of some of Miss Piffs's utterances, it is possible to interpret Hugh's comment about Stephen wearing a false head as indicating that his view of the world is incompatible with ours. How can such a clash be accounted for in terms of Ryan's typology of accessibility relations (see 4.6.3)?

6. Schema refreshment in advertising

In 6.7.2 I mentioned Cook's claim that advertisements tend to have a schema-reinforcing effect, even when they are innovative and creative in terms of their formal features. Indeed, it is easy to find examples of advertisements that rely on and confirm stereo-typical assumptions about people, gender differences, society, and so on. Some advertisements, however, may be deliberately aimed at disrupting our conventional expectations about people, the world, and/or advertisements themselves. Think, for example, of the advertising campaigns produced for Benetton by Oliviero Toscani over the last few years. Some of the most controversial advertisements (which were even banned in some countries) included pictures of a blood-streaked newborn baby, a young man dying of AIDS, a priest and a nun kissing, a black woman breast-feeding a white baby, and a colourful array of condoms. Consider the ways in which advertisements such as these may refresh the public's world schemata and formal schemata (see 6.4.1 for this distinction). A statement made in Benetton's *Colours* magazine in 1991 explicitly suggests that one of the aims of the company's advertising campaigns is to induce what may be described as schema refreshment:

> We believe that advertising can do more than sell products. It can broaden minds. (*Colours* 1991: 61)

Of course, one could cynically point out that the shocking effect produced by schema-refreshing advertising can itself become a very effective selling strategy. Can you think of any other examples of advertisements that have a high potential for schema refreshment? How is this effect achieved? To what extent are linguistic devices involved? What areas of background knowledge are involved? What are the consequences of your findings for the claims made by Cook concerning the distinction between literary and non-literary texts (see 6.7.1)?

9

Conclusion: The world of Sylvia Plath's 'The Applicant'

9.1 Introduction

In the course of this book I have explored three approaches to the study of text worlds in poetry. In Part I, I considered poetic text worlds as discourse situations and I highlighted the role of definite and indefinite articles and deictics in the projection of different types of contexts. In Part II, I considered poetic text worlds as possible worlds and I showed how possible-world theory can be applied to the description and classification of the worlds of poetry. In Part III, I considered poetic text worlds as cognitive constructs and I demonstrated how schema theory can be applied to text analysis, particularly in order to account for differences between text worlds that would broadly be defined as 'realistic'. I also showed how schema theory can provide an account of metaphor's role in text-world creation. In this final chapter I bring together all these different approaches in the analysis of a single poem. The text I have selected is the poem I used in Chapter 1 in order to begin to introduce the possibility of defining text worlds in different ways, namely 'The Applicant' by Sylvia Plath (the full text is quoted in 1.1). My discussion of this poem will shed further light on the strengths and weaknesses of different approaches, and, more importantly, demonstrate that linguistic analysis, possible-world theory and schema theory can productively complement one another in the study of texts.

9.2 Sylvia Plath's 'The Applicant'

'The Applicant' appeared in the *London Magazine* in January 1963, and was subsequently included in the collection *Ariel*, which was published posthumously in 1965. In the poem Plath makes a bitter satirical attack against the social practice of marriage by presenting what seems to be a marriage arrangement scene as a combination of a social benefit interview and a sales pitch. The text world projected by the poem is puzzling, challenging and disturbing. On the one hand, we recognize in it attitudes and beliefs that we may have encountered in our experience of the actual world, such as the tendency to see women as primarily providers of care, or worse, as objects. On the other hand, we are likely to perceive it as improbable, deviant or absurdist because of the way in which these attitudes to women and marriage are taken to extremes. The poem was composed on 11 October 1962, a few days after Plath's decision to get a divorce from Ted Hughes and exactly four months before her suicide (Bassnett 1987: 96; Stevenson 1989).

I will begin by discussing the complexities of the discourse situation projected by the text. I will then move on to consider how the world of the poem can be described respectively in possible-worlds and schema-theory terms.

9.2.1 The discourse situation of the poem

Like John Donne's 'The Flea' (see 3.3.1), 'The Applicant' projects a situation of direct address, involving a first-person speaker and a silent addressee located within a shared deictic environment.[1] This is brought about by the cumulative effect of a number of linguistic features: the presence of first-person pronouns (*I/me*, *we/our*) referring to the speaker; the presence of second-person pronouns (*you/your*) referring to the addressee; the use of direct questions (e.g. line 1) and commands (e.g. line 7) signalling the presence of another participant within the communicative context in which the speaker's utterance takes place; the use of the present tense (e.g. line 26) suggesting the simultaneity of content and coding time; and the use of proximal space deixis (*here* in line 10, *this* in line 20) in reference to various elements of a situational context that includes both the addresser and the addressee.

As in 'The Flea', the projected discourse situation is a canonical situation of utterance in which no interaction actually occurs: the *you* of the poem remains silent throughout. Here, however, the roles, identities and mutual relationship of the two (or possibly more) participants are problematic. The marriage arrangement scene projected by the text is initially conducted as some kind of probing interview and gradually develops into what seems to be the speech of a salesperson. Because of the differences between these three types of interactions, the roles and identities of the poetic addresser and addressee seem to shift from one part of the poem to the other. As I will show in more detail below, this can be related to the different default values of participant roles in the various schemata evoked by the text.

In the first half of the poem, the speaker repeatedly uses the first-person plural pronoun *we* (lines 1, 7, 18). This can be interpreted either as signalling the presence of a single speaker talking on behalf of a group or an institution, or of more than one speaker alternating in the role of spokesperson. The former interpretation is more likely, since there are no clear indications of shifts between different speakers. More importantly, the speaking voice seems to belong to a *persona* that is quite separate from the poet herself. This impression results from a number of factors: firstly, the dramatic nature of the discourse situation, which, as I pointed out in 3.3.1, often tends to highlight the fictionality of addresser and addressee; secondly, the fact that the speaker is likely to be constructed as male (among other things, he addresses the woman introduced in line 28 as *sweetie*); and thirdly, and most importantly, the fact that the speaker expresses a set of attitudes and beliefs concerning marriage and women that the author clearly aims to expose and satirize.

In the first four stanzas of the poem, the pronoun *we* is employed in its exclusive sense: its reference includes the speaker and the people or body he represents, but excludes the hearer, who is referred to solely by means of the second-person pronoun *you*.[2] This coincides with a rather aggressive and authoritative tone on the part of the speaker. The poem opens with a series of very direct and rather brutal questions, apparently aimed at ascertaining the addressee's suitability for whatever it is that the speaker has the power to provide:

> First, are you our sort of a person?
> Do you wear
> A glass eye, false teeth or a crutch,
> A brace or a hook,
> Rubber breasts or a rubber crotch,
>
> Stitches to show something's missing? No, no? Then
> How can we give you a thing?

In lines 8–9, the speaking *persona* also addresses to the hearer two bald-on-record commands (Brown and Levinson 1987), that is to say, two orders expressed as direct imperatives, without any attempt to tone down the force of the speaker's authority:

> Stop crying.
> Open your hand.

Although both utterances show the speaker's concern for the addressee's well-being, their directness reinforces the impression that at this point the balance of power is heavily on the addresser's side.

In line 19 there is a shift from the plural *we* to the use of the singular form of the first-person pronoun *I* (*I notice you are stark naked . . .*). This marks the onset of a more personal, one-to-one relationship between addresser and addressee, and coincides with a reversal in the apparent distribution of power between the two. The speaker does not issue any more orders in the form of direct imperatives; rather, he asks questions that have the force of offers, which the addressee has the power to accept or refuse.

> Will you marry it? (lines 14, 22)
> How about this suit— (line 20)
> Well, what do you think of that? (line 29)
> Will you marry it, marry it, marry it. (line 40)

The social distance between speaker and hearer also decreases as a result of the changes in person deixis and in the implied power relationship: the speaker's words now suggest a much closer personal relationship than was the case in the first half of the poem. It is significant that the last reference to the addressee is not made deictically, but by means of a vocative implying closeness and familiarity: *My boy* in line 39. The final vocative is also relevant to the question of the sex of the silent addressee, who is unmistakably male at the end of the poem, but who had been previously asked to produce any *rubber breasts* (line 5).

The discourse situation projected by the text is therefore complex and deviant: the roles and identities of the communicative participants are rather elusive since they seem to change as the poem progresses, with corresponding shifts in the distribution of power and in the social distance between them. I will argue that this can be related to the different schemata that are evoked by the text and to the oddity of their conflation in the world of the poem.

9.2.2 Possible worlds and 'The Applicant'

The absurdist nature of the world projected by the speaking voice of 'The Applicant' can be captured to some extent by the notions and categories developed within possible-world theories.

As I mentioned earlier, the poem seems to involve an internal contradiction concerning the gender of the poetic addressee. The list of physical aids that the speaker suggests the hearer might possess includes any *rubber breasts* (line 5), which may imply that the hearer is at this point (perceived as) female. This is inconsistent with the fact that in the rest of the poem the hearer is constructed as male: he is offered a woman in marriage and he is addressed as *My boy* in the final stanza. This apparent inconsistency can be interpreted in a number of ways, which I will consider in increasing order of 'strength' as to the implications for the nature of the world projected by the poem.

The reference to rubber breasts could be seen as merely an error (deliberate or otherwise) on the part of the speaker, who may initially fail to adapt his speech to the actual identity of the addressee, possibly as a result of absent-mindedness, lack of interest, humour, and so on. In this case, the inconsistency would have implications for the characterization of the speaker, but it would not affect the essence of the text world. On the other hand, the contradiction could be seen as reflecting a feature of the world projected by the poem: in this case, the text world would include human males who possess breasts, and who may therefore have their breasts replaced by artificial ones.[3] In Ryan's terms, the existence of such androgynous beings breaks the rule of taxonomic compatibility, which she describes as follows (in the quotation below TAW stands for Textual Actual World and AW for Actual World):

> (F) *Taxonomic compatibility* (F/taxonomy): TAW is accessible from AW if both worlds contain the same species, and the species are characterized by the same properties. Within F, it may be useful to distinguish a narrower version F' stipulating that TAW must contain not only the same inventory of natural species, but also the same type of manufactured objects as found in AW up to the present.
>
> (Ryan 1991a: 33; see 4.6.3)

The existence of male human beings endowed with breasts contradicts the properties of the human species in the real world, and would therefore result in the projection of a taxonomically impossible world.[4]

An even stronger reading could suggest that the world of the poem includes a human being (X) such that the propositions 'X is male' and 'X is not male' are both true. This violates the logical rule of non-contradiction, which, as I explained in 4.2, states that two contradictory propositions cannot be simultaneously true in an individual world. In Ryan's scale of accessibility relations, the rule of logical compatibility immediately follows taxonomic compatibility:

> (G) *Logical compatibility* (G/logic): TAW is accessible from AW if both worlds respect the principles of non-contradiction and of excluded middle. (Ryan 1991a: 33; see also 4.6.3)

In this case 'The Applicant' would project a logically impossible world similar to those that possible-world theorists regard as being typical of fiction, and particularly of postmodernist fiction (Wolterstoff 1980: 155–7; Doležel 1989: 238–40; Eco 1990: 75–9; Pavel 1989: 259). In Eco's terms, this is the type of world that can be *mentioned* but not *constructed* (Eco 1990: 76): we can, in other words, say that the world of 'The Applicant' contains an individual who is both truly male and truly female, but we cannot fully construct and explore such a world in our minds. In 5.4.1 I made a similar point about the puzzling worlds of the rhyme 'Ladies and Jellispoons' and of Graves's poem 'Welsh Incident'.

Having gone this far, I am prepared to accept the charge of overinterpreting a feature of the text that might, after all, be dismissed as an oversight on Plath's part. There is, however, an important point behind all this: the overall oddity of the world of the poem (which I have only begun to describe) lends some measure of plausibility even to such relatively far-fetched claims as to the impossible nature of its component elements. This relates to a point often made by possible-world theorists: the greater the distance between a fictional world and the actual world, the smaller the scope for straightforwardly importing our expectations about the actual world into the fictional world (Maitre 1983: 81; Pavel 1986: 101; Ryan 1991a: 57–8). In the case of 'The Applicant', the presence of a number of deviant features legitimizes, to some extent at least, readings that clearly challenge what Ryan calls the Principle of Minimal Departure, namely the notion that we expect fictional worlds to resemble the actual world unless we are told otherwise. As I mentioned in 4.6.2, Ryan herself points out that the authority of her principle decreases as the distance between fictional worlds and the actual world increases.

What other 'impossible' elements are included within the world of 'The Applicant'? The list of physical aids that the speaker presupposes the hearer might possess (lines 3–6) includes a *rubber crotch* that can presumably be worn as a replacement for a real one. This type of object, as far as I know, is not part of the range of physical aids that are manufactured in the current state of technological development of the actual world. Similarly, in stanza 5 the speaker attributes to the suit he is describing some properties that cannot apply to real world suits:

> It is waterproof, shatterproof, proof
> Against fire and bombs through the roof.

Suits can be waterproof and, to some extent, fireproof (although not normally), but they cannot be shatterproof or bombproof.

Both the reference to the rubber crotch and the boastful praise of the properties of the suit could be regarded as hyperboles, which, if taken literally, outline a world that is impossible according to the narrower version of Ryan's rule of taxonomic compatibility (in bold in the quotation below):

> (F) *Taxonomic compatibility* (F/taxonomy): TAW is accessible from AW if both worlds contain the same species, and the species are characterized by the same properties. **Within F, it may be useful to distinguish a narrower version F' stipulating that TAW must contain not only the same inventory of natural species, but also the same type of manufactured objects as found in AW up to the present.** (Ryan 1991a: 33)

In fact, the description of the suit could also be regarded as leading to an analytical impossibility. Ryan states her rule of analytical compatibility thus:

> (H) *Analytical compatibility* (H/analytical): TAW is accessible from AW if they share analytical truths, i.e. if objects designated by the same words share the same essential properties. (Ryan 1991a: 33; see 4.6.3)

This rule would be broken by the existence in the world of the poem of an object which is designated by the word 'suit' but which possesses properties that real-world 'suits' cannot possess, such as being shatterproof.

Whatever the interpretation, it is clear that possible-world theories, and Ryan's framework in particular, go some way towards explaining the oddity of the world of 'The Applicant'. It is also clear that the degree of impossibility of the text world largely depends on whether readers opt for literal or non-literal interpretations of potentially impossible features: the reference to the rubber crotch could be a joke on the part of the speaker (as could the reference to rubber breasts); the description of the rubber suit may be read as a deliberate exaggeration. This, I would argue, is precisely the point. In my reading of the poem, Plath is trying to expose the ludicrousness and absurdity of treating the arrangement of marriage simply as a series of transactions to do with services and commodities. Giving the readers glimpses of a highly impossible world is one of the strategies that she adopts in order to achieve this effect.

In fact, a number of examples can be found in the poem where the text seems to legitimize, to some extent at least, the contemplation of the literal meaning of figurative expressions. The hand described in lines 10–14, for example, clearly functions as a synecdoche for wife (as is the case when the somewhat outdated idiom 'asking for someone's hand' is used as an alternative to 'asking for permission to marry someone'). However, the use of the inanimate pronoun *it* in *do whatever you tell it* (line 13) and in the repeated question *Will you marry it?* seems to privilege the literal reference to the part (the hand) over the figurative reference to the whole (the person). As before, a literal reading results in an impossible world, where it is possible to marry inanimate entities. Similar considerations apply to the alleged emptiness of the addressee's head in line 26 (*Now, your head, excuse me, is empty*). Here the temptation to contemplate the literal meaning of the metaphor is partly due to the parallelism with lines 9–10 (*Open your hand./ Empty? Empty*), where the emptiness of the addressee's hand can be interpreted literally (although this does not detract from the oddity of the situation, to which I will return below). As possible-world theorists point out, the literal interpretation of metaphors (and, I would argue, of other types of figurative expressions, such as synecdoche) often leads to the construction of impossible worlds (Levin 1989; Eco 1990: 68).

The impossible features discussed so far only partly justify my claim that the poem's text world is outlandish enough to reduce the applicability of the Principle of Minimal Departure. Clearly, there are crucial peculiarities in the world of 'The Applicant' that a possible-world approach does not account for. One cannot, for example, easily account for the strangeness of the addressee's nakedness (line 19), or of the inclusion of *false teeth* in the list of physical aids in lines 3–6. More importantly, one cannot account for the fact that, apart from the presence of counterfactual or impossible details, the poem is effective precisely because of the oddly 'mixed' situation it projects. It is at this point that schema theory can take the analysis a step further.

9.2.3 Schema theory and 'The Applicant'

A more exhaustive account of the nature of the world of 'The Applicant' can be provided by considering the configuration of schemata that the text is likely to evoke. I will suggest that the interpretation of the poem does not simply require the straightforward instantiation of a schema or a set of interconnected schemata, but rather involves a clash between several partially incompatible schemata. This, as I will show, can be related to the nature of the language of the text. In my discussion of the poem's discourse situation I highlighted the shifts in the implied roles and mutual relationship of the poetic speaker and the person he appears to address. Here I will focus in more detail on how the speech of the poem's *persona* mixes together different styles, that are reminiscent of different types of situations. More specifically, I will show that the language of the poem displays a mixture of stylistic features that can be captured by Bakhtin's notion of heteroglossia (Bakhtin 1981), and that such heteroglossia results in the evocation of a partially conflicting configuration of schemata on the part of the reader.

Bakhtin coined the notion of heteroglossia to describe the mixture of voices, styles and registers that he regarded as the essence of the novel as a genre (Bakhtin 1981: 262–3 and throughout). However, while he stressed the pervasiveness of heteroglossia in language in general, he went to great lengths to argue that poetry is uniquely immune from it:

> But – we repeat – in the majority of poetic genres, the unity of the language system and the unity (and uniqueness) of the poet's individuality as reflected in his language and speech, which is directly realized in this unity, are indispensable prerequisites of poetic style.
>
> (Bakhtin 1981: 264)

> In genres that are poetic in the narrow sense, the natural dialogization of the word is not put to artistic use, the word is sufficient unto itself and does not presume alien utterances beyond its own boundaries. Poetic style is by convention suspended from any mutual interaction with alien discourse, any allusion to alien discourse.
>
> (Bakhtin 1981: 285)

> The language of the poetic genre is a unitary and singular Ptolemaic world outside of which nothing else exists and nothing is needed. The concept of many worlds of language, all equal in their ability to conceptualize and be expressive, is organically denied to poetic style.
>
> (Bakhtin 1981: 286)

Not surprisingly, this argument has been repeatedly challenged. In particular, Wales (1988, 1993) and Geyer-Ryan (1988) have shown how heteroglossia is not only widely present, but also aesthetically central in poetry as much as it is in novelistic prose.

In 'The Applicant' heteroglossia results from the fact that an offer of marriage is made in a combination of sales-talk and what sounds like a parody of welfare interviews. Hence the poem is likely to evoke three main schemata, to do, respectively, with marriage arrangements, interviews, and sales pitches. I will consider each of these in turn, focusing on the linguistic features of the text that function as triggers for their activation.[5]

The INTERVIEW schema

The title of the poem 'The Applicant' seems to indicate that the text will require the activation of the readers' knowledge concerning the conventions and procedures that lead to the allocation of jobs, benefits, university places, and so on, which normally start with an individual's formal request (application) to the relevant body or institution. The opening of the poem partly confirms these expectations, but also shows that the applicant referred to by the title is being handled in a rather unconventional way.

The content of the opening questions suggests that the speaker is trying to determine whether the addressee qualifies for the help that is reserved for people with physical disabilities:

> First, are you our sort of a person?
> Do you wear
> A glass eye, false teeth or a crutch,
> A brace or a hook,
> Rubber breasts or a rubber crotch,
>
> Stitches to show something's missing? No, no? Then
> How can we give you a thing?

In lines 10–13 the speaker provides a description of what appears to be the service that he has the power to allocate:

> ... Here is a hand
>
> To fill it and willing
> To bring teacups and roll away headaches
> And do whatever you tell it.

At a first reading of the poem, the referent of *a hand* could be interpreted as the metaphorical caring hand of an institution or the physical hand of a nurse or a social worker. The functions that are attributed to it are strongly reminiscent of welfare benefits: the 'hand' is supposed to 'fill' the addressee's empty hands (presumably with money or food), and to provide teacups and assistance with medical conditions. The metaphorical reference to headaches being 'rolled away' is likely to conjure up images of institutions such as hospitals and homes for the elderly and disabled, where trolleys are used to distribute food and medicines to patients.

The reading of the first 13 lines of the poem, therefore, is likely to trigger the activation of the readers' knowledge about welfare interviews. Such knowledge can be described as an INTERVIEW schema, containing information about the typical setting of interviews (a room with, minimally, tables and chairs), the participants (interviewer(s) and interviewee), the format of the interaction (questions and answers), the power relationship between participants (interviewer in control of topic, turn-taking, etc.), the goal of the activity (the establishment of the addressee's suitability to receive what the institution represented by the interviewer has to offer), and so on. Such a schema can be captured by Schank's notion of scene, or, more precisely, by his definition of *societal* scene (see 6.4.3). Its setting can be defined not so much in physical terms as in societal terms: an activity taking place within the domain of an institution and whose main goal is the establishment of the interviewee's suitability to receive what the institution has to offer. Within Schank's framework, the INTERVIEW scene will include different scripts for different types of interviews. In the case of 'The Applicant', readers might have specific expectations about welfare interviews (as opposed to job or university interviews): the WELFARE INTERVIEW scene of British readers may include, for example, a glass window separating the interviewer from the interviewee, since this is standard practice within the British National Health and Social Security System.

As I said earlier, the power distribution implied by the first 13 lines of the poem corresponds to conventional expectations about the relationship between interviewers and interviewees: various linguistic choices in the opening part of the text suggest that the speaker is more powerful than the addressee. On the other hand, the speaker's openly aggressive tone (e.g. *Then/ How can we give you a thing?... Open your hand.*) and the absence of any response on the part of the addressee are rather odd for an interview, where we would expect a formal, polite interaction, and a substantial amount of talk from the interviewee. More importantly, the list of physical aids in lines 3–6 has a surreal flavour, since it juxtaposes fairly conventional aids (e.g. *a glass eye*) with non-actual objects (*the rubber crotch* discussed above), and fairly ordinary items not normally regarded as remedies for a serious disability (e.g. *false teeth*). Similarly absurdist is the speaker's concern for the fact that the addressee's hands are, literally, empty (lines 9–10), where what we expect to be relevant is a metaphorical empty-handedness corresponding to lack of money or resources. The contrast between such aspects of the text and the knowledge that is required for its interpretation accounts for much of the bitter irony in the poem. In other words, it is only against the background of our expectations about welfare interviews that we can perceive the oddities of the poetic voice's speech and appreciate the parodic effect that the poet appears to want to achieve.

The SALES PITCH schema

The shift in personal deixis and in the implied power distribution that occurs across the third and the fourth stanzas corresponds to a change in the content and style of the poetic *persona*'s discourse. The speaker is now extolling the qualities of various entities (the 'hand', the suit, the 'living doll') in order to get the addressee interested in them. More importantly, the use of phrases such as *It is guaranteed to* (lines 15–16), *How about* (line 20), *I have the ticket for that* (line 27), *It works, there is nothing wrong with it* (line 36), is part of the jargon used by sellers to convince potential customers of the product's excellence and of their own reliability. The enthusiastic claims about the virtues of the suit in lines 23–5 and of the woman in lines 31–9 are also reminiscent of the style of hard selling, while the use of hyperbole leads to the absurdist effects that I discussed earlier.

A large part of the poem, therefore, seems to rely upon the activation of a SALES PITCH schema, which, like the INTERVIEW schema, can be captured by Schank's (1982) definition of societal scene: the schema relates not so much to a particular physical setting as to the relationship between seller and potential customer, and to the seller's goal of making a sale. The SALES PITCH scene is, however, a rather different type of scene from the INTERVIEW scene discussed in the previous section. Not only does it occur within a different range of MOPs, but it makes very different constraints about setting (e.g. shop, market, advertising event), participants (salesperson and potential customer) and goals (e.g. making a sale for the seller, making a bargain for the customer). Such differences will be discussed in more detail below. What is relevant here is that, as with the INTERVIEW scene, the activation of a SALES PITCH scene contributes both to the reader's understanding of the text and to the perception of the oddities of the projected text world. Such oddities are to do with the nature of the entities that the speaker seems to be making a pitch for (particularly the 'hand' described in stanzas 2–3 and the woman introduced in stanza 6) and to the way in which sales-talk is applied to what we have to conclude is an offer of marriage.

The MARRIAGE schema

The first reference to marriage in the poem occurs in line 14, where the speaker asks for the first time the question *Will you marry it?*. As I said earlier, the pronoun *it* refers back to the *hand* introduced in line 10, which can be interpreted as a fairly conventional synecdoche for wife. At a first reading of the poem, however, the speaker's question might produce a surprise effect, since up to this point the poem may read as a satire of social benefits interviews, within which *a hand* would count as a figurative reference to the assistance provided by the welfare system. The question *Will you marry it?* is reiterated again in line 22 and in the final line of the poem, where the repetition of *marry it, marry it, marry it* lends additional force to the speaker's utterance (and might in fact sound like a return to the authoritative and coercive tone adopted at the opening of the poem). The oddity of the use of the inanimate pronoun *it* as object of the verb *marry* is enhanced by the fact that its referent seems to shift from the hand to the suit in line 22 (which leads to absurdity), and then to the woman introduced in the second half of the poem (who should normally be referred to by means of the feminine personal pronoun *her*).

The repetition of the question *Will you marry it?* clearly signals that some kind of offer of marriage constitutes the speaker's central concern. In schema-theory terms, the question functions as a header for the activation of the readers' knowledge to do with marriage, which is crucial for the comprehension of the text as a coherent whole. I have already mentioned how the first reference to marriage in line 13 leads to a particular figurative interpretation of the reference to *a hand* in line 10. In the same way, the lines

. . . Here is a hand

To fill it and willing
To bring teacups and roll away headaches

can be interpreted retrospectively as a reference to the stereotypical function of the wife within the family.

A number of other elements in the text can only be interpreted and related to one another in the light of the reader's knowledge about the conventions and assumptions to do with marriage: the black suit introduced in line 20 is described as a typical wedding suit (*Black and stiff, but not a bad fit*); the woman introduced as a prospective bride in line 28 is attributed the skills that are associated with the traditional role of the wife (*It can sew, it can cook*), as well as the loquaciousness that characterizes the stereotype of the wife (*It can talk, talk, talk*); the description of the woman in lines 31–2 (*in twenty-five years she'll be silver,/ In fifty gold*) puns on the traditional description of twenty-fifth and fiftieth wedding anniversaries ('silver' and 'gold' anniversaries).

To sum up, in addition to the other schemata already discussed, the text crucially relies for its interpretation on the activation of various elements of a MARRIAGE schema. Such a schema, I would argue, is best accounted for in terms of Schank's notion of meta-MOP. This is because the MARRIAGE schema includes a number of sub-schemata that can be described as MOPs, such as M-MARRIAGE PREPARATIONS, M-WEDDING, M-WEDDING ANNIVERSARY, and so on. My previous discussion has shown how different parts of the text relate to information contained in different MOPs included within a MARRIAGE meta-MOP. More specifically, the comprehension of the particular situation evoked by the text seems to require the instantiation of a MARRIAGE ARRANGEMENT scene, where a woman is offered in marriage to a prospective husband. Such a scene, however, is instantiated in an odd and defamiliarizing manner, largely because of the conflict with the other two main schemata that I have suggested are also activated in the processing of the text. I will now explore this contrast in more detail.

Schema conflict and the world of 'The Applicant'

What I have argued so far is that the shifts in the topic and style of the poetic voice's speech lead to the activation of three main schemata, which, following Schank, I have described as a WELFARE INTERVIEW scene, a SALES PITCH scene and a MARRIAGE

ARRANGEMENT scene. Although the latter is clearly dominant in the construction of the world of 'The Applicant', its instantiation in the reading of this particular text includes elements that belong to the other two schemata, such as the list of questions about physical aids and the use of sales-talk. It is the peculiar nature of this conflation of different schemata in the processing of the text that results in the construction of a particular text world.

The combination of the INTERVIEW and MARKET SALE scenes with the MARRIAGE REQUEST scene in the world projected by 'The Applicant' relies upon some basic similarities in the content of the three schemata. All three involve a one-to-one or one-to-many verbal interaction aimed at reaching a decision or agreement concerning some form of control over a particular entity. In all three cases the goal of one communicative party is to persuade the other(s). It is also significant that at least one of the objects that are included within the fictional world, namely, the suit, is relevant to all three scenes: it is a standard requirement of formal interviews, a necessary component of weddings (and, consequently, of wedding preparations) and a possible object for sale (although, admittedly, practically anything could qualify as the latter). On the other hand, some features of the evoked situation, such as the nakedness of the addressee (*I notice you are stark naked*) and of the woman (*naked as paper to start*), conflict with the expectations induced by all three scenes.

A certain amount of overlap between activated schemata is necessary to the intelligibility of the projected world. An attempt to combine totally incompatible schemata into a single situation would probably result in a largely incomprehensible text world. The impact of the text and the nature of the projected text world, however, are mostly dependent on the *differences* between the main activated schemata. Such differences concern, above all, the roles and relationships of participants, the outcome of the interaction and the likely emotional associations of each type of event.

As I mentioned earlier, the situation evoked by the poem includes two main communicative participants, namely a speaker and a silent addressee. Within an INTERVIEW schema, they would occupy the roles of interviewer and interviewee, with the former being the more powerful participant for the purposes of the interaction. Within a SALES PITCH schema, the addresser occupies the role of salesperson, whereas the addressee is a potential customer. Here it is the addressee who ultimately has the power to determine the outcome of the interaction, by deciding whether or not to buy the product(s) on sale. Within a MARRIAGE ARRANGEMENT schema, the addressee is a potential husband, while the speaker is someone who has some kind of power or interest over the prospective wife's future, such as a parent, a guardian, or, possibly, a dating agency employee. These differences in roles and relationships between the different types of situations are highlighted by the heterogeneous nature of the language of the text and by the shifts in the implied power distribution between speaker and hearer. As a result of the interference of other schemata in the instantiation of a MARRIAGE ARRANGEMENT scene, the speaker comes across as a rather aggressive welfare system interviewer in the first half of the text and as an eager seller in the second; similarly, the prospective husband is initially treated as a potential invalid and then as a prospective customer.

As for the goal of the interaction, both the INTERVIEW schema and the SALES PITCH schema involve the transfer of some kind of entity from the addresser to the addressee. In an interview context this may be a job, or, in this particular case, some form of help or benefit; in a seller–customer interaction, it is an object for sale. By making allusions to these different types of situations, Plath satirizes the idea of marriage as a transfer of benefits or property. As I mentioned earlier, in the first stanzas the 'hand' that the hearer is invited to marry is described as a provider of help. In the second part of the poem, the woman who is summoned to the speaker's and hearer's presence in stanza 6 is presented as if she was an object for sale, rather than a direct participant in the interaction and a person in control of her own future. She is addressed directly only once, by means of the command in line 28 (*Come here, sweetie*); she appears to be kept in a closet as if she was an inanimate object; she is repeatedly referred to by the inanimate pronoun *it*; and she is described by means of dehumanizing similes and metaphors (Leech 1969: 158), which also tend to highlight how she can be of benefit to the addressee: *Naked as paper* (line 30), *she'll be silver,/ . . . gold* (lines 31–2), *A living doll* (line 33), *It works, there is nothing wrong with it* (line 36), *it's a poultice* (line 37), *it's an image* (line 38).

Finally, the emotional states that are likely to be associated with the situations captured by the three main schemata are also very different. Marriage is normally imbued with a high level of affective involvement for all concerned, which, as I pointed out in 6.6, may involve both positive and negative feelings, such as a mixture of sadness and happiness (see Isen 1984: 202). On the other hand, interviews and sales pitches are likely to be associated with less intense emotional states, particularly from the perspective of the interviewer and the customer respectively.

In sum, by mixing different styles, 'The Applicant' evokes a configuration of partly incompatible schemata, that are combined together in the processing of the text to produce a rather disturbing and deviant text world. I have suggested that the creation of such a world can be interpreted as a critique on Plath's part of those aspects of her own reality that the poem presents in a distorted but nevertheless recognizable manner. The oddity of the world of the poem and its relevance to the 'real' world, therefore, go beyond the distinctions and categories of possible-world models, and can only be adequately captured by considering the way in which the reader's knowledge and expectations interact with the language of the text.

9.3 Schema refreshment revisited

To what extent can Cook's (1994) notion of schema refreshment be applied to the effect of the deviant schematic configuration that makes up the world of 'The Applicant'?

On the one hand, I would not want to argue that presenting a view of marriage as a contract or as some kind of financial deal is so new and original as to cause a dramatic change in the readers' schemata (within the realm of literature, one only needs to think of Shakespeare's *The Taming of the Shrew* or of Jane Austen's novels). More importantly, one needs to be extremely careful in making claims about schema change. Empirical evidence suggests that we tend to ignore, distort or forget aspects of experience that go against our expectations, which clearly amounts to a tendency to preserve rather than alter existing schemata (e.g. Spiro 1980).

On the other hand, 'The Applicant' does appear to require readers to at least 'stretch' their schemata, in order to contemplate a situation where what they know about the actual world or other fictional worlds is taken to rather disturbing extremes. As I have argued in my analysis, the scene evoked by the poem does not straightforwardly correspond to a schema that readers are likely to possess, but involves the combination of elements from different areas of knowledge. The contrast between the content of the different schemata involved, and the oddity of a situation that brings them together, may remind readers of some aspects of non-transparent social organization, and thereby lead them to become newly aware of their assumptions and beliefs concerning marriage, and perhaps to reconsider their validity. From this point of view, 'The Applicant' is more challenging as a text than Heaney's 'A Pillowed Head', for example, or many other poems that project more conventional and less problematic views of reality.

In this respect it is useful to be able to distinguish between different degrees of potential for schema refreshment, and to be able to characterize 'The Applicant' as a schema-refreshing text. Two caveats are needed, however. Firstly, it seems appropriate to talk about the 'potential' or the 'conditions' for schema refreshment (as I have done in the last two chapters), since actual schema change is not only rare but also hard to verify. Secondly, I would want to partially redefine the notion of schema refreshment in order to include not only schema change, but also less dramatic and less permanent experiences, such as connecting normally separate schemata in unusual ways in the processing of a particular text, becoming aware of one's own schematic assumptions, questioning the validity of one's schemata in the light of new experiences and so on. In this sense the notion of schema refreshment can be usefully applied to poems such as 'The Applicant' and 'Morning Song' without making unreasonable claims about the impact of such texts on the readers' views of the world.

9.4 Conclusions

My analysis of 'The Applicant' has demonstrated the possibility of adopting an eclectic approach to the study of text worlds. The different perspectives explored in the course of this book clearly have complementary strengths and weaknesses as far as textual analysis is concerned.

The analysis of the poetic use of deixis and of the contrast between definite and indefinite reference has highlighted the way in which these linguistic features contribute to the construction of contexts from texts. In Chapter 2 I explored the function of definite reference in 'furnishing' text worlds, and I argued that the alternation between definite and indefinite articles can be exploited to foreground some elements of the world of a poem and to background others. In Chapter 3 I showed how different combinations of deictic expressions result in the projection of different types of poetic *personae* and speech situations. In discussing poems such as Larkin's 'Talking in Bed' and Plath's 'The Applicant', I have demonstrated how a detailed study of deictic choices can capture shifts in modes and contexts of discourse that play a crucial role in the overall effect of the texts. In the course of the book I have also explicitly related the analysis of choices in reference and deixis to possible-world and schema-theory approaches to the study of text worlds. In Chapter 5 I showed how possible-world frameworks can provide elegant and comprehensive categorizations of different types of poetic speakers and discourse situations. In Chapters 3, 7 and 9 I explored the role of definite reference in schema activation, and highlighted the way in which the roles and identities of poetic speakers are inferred on the basis of the default components of the schemata that are applied to the interpretation of the text.

By applying possible-world frameworks to the analysis of poetry, I have been able to account for different types of impossible features in poetic text worlds. In this chapter a possible-world approach has enabled me to describe and categorize the most obviously counterfactual elements of the world of 'The Applicant', such as the contradictory information about the gender of the addressee and the presence of non-actual objects. More specifically, the use of Ryan's typology of accessibility relations can lead to fairly precise judgements as to the distance between text worlds and the actual world: as I pointed out in Chapters 4 and 5, Ryan lists her rules of inter-world compatibility 'in decreasing order of stringency' (Ryan 1991b: 32). According to my analysis, 'The Applicant' involves breaches of the rule of taxonomic compatibility, and possibly also of the rules of logical and analytical compatibility. This places the world of the poem towards the 'highly incompatible' end of Ryan's scale. The main advantage of this type of approach is that it allows fairly clear descriptions and categorizations, which can lead to detailed comparisons between different texts. One could, for example, compare 'The Applicant' with other poems by Sylvia Plath, or with some of the poems that I discussed in Chapter 5. Ryan's scale can also be used, as I mentioned earlier, to explain the conditions under which the Principle of Minimal Departure may be relaxed in the interpretation of texts: if breaches of accessibility relations occur at the top end of the list, the Principle of Minimal Departure has a considerable weight in interpretation. Conversely, when rules are broken at the bottom end of the scale (as is the case with 'The Applicant'), the Principle is likely to be applied less extensively.

Chapters 4 and 5 have, I hope, demonstrated the usefulness of possible-worlds approaches in dealing with the notion of fictionality, describing the internal structure of text worlds and drawing distinctions between different genres on the basis of the kind of worlds they tend to project. The limitations of possible-world models have also been repeatedly pointed out: they operate on the basis of very abstract and rigid distinctions; they treat the concept of 'actual world' as a largely unproblematic notion; they are hard to relate to the cognitive processes of comprehension and to the linguistic properties of texts. In the case of 'The Applicant', a possible-world approach clearly stops short of accounting for what I regard as the main feature of the world of the poem, i.e. the 'mixed' nature of the situation projected by the text, and its interpretative significance. The possible-world analyses of a wide range of poetic texts have also highlighted the difficulties that inevitably arise when a framework is extended beyond its original scope: some of Ryan's accessibility relations (notably identity of inventory and compatibility of inventory) do not seem as relevant and applicable to poetry as they are to prose fiction; others, such as physical compatibility, cover an excessively diverse range of phenomena and therefore need to be defined in more detail. The extension of possible-world typologies to include drama and non-literary fictional texts (such as jokes), as well as poetry, would lead to the production of more powerful models, and to a better understanding of fiction-making as a cultural phenomenon.

A schema-theory approach captures the cognitive dimension of text-world construction, and is also easily related, as I have shown, to a linguistic analysis of texts. This is a considerable advantage, since text worlds are ultimately cognitive products of the interplay between readers and language. My analyses have shown how a combination of schema theory and linguistic analysis accounts for the drawing of inferences and the establishment of coherence in interpretation, and can also include the affective dimension of cognitive processing. More importantly, the application of notions such as schema reinforcement and schema refreshment has enabled me to relate different text worlds to their interpretative and cognitive effects, as well as to make comparisons that are not solely based on different types of counterfactuality. This, I have argued, is particularly useful when one wishes to consider text worlds as views of reality, rather than as alternatives to the actual world. In the case of 'The Applicant', I have shown that an exhaustive description of the poem's world needs to account for its inclusion of elements that are normally associated with very different types of situations. In fact, I would argue that the activation of a deviant configuration of schemata in the processing of the text plays a major role in reducing the scope of Ryan's Principle of Minimal Departure, since it contributes to the absurdist and surreal flavour of the world of the poem. This is an example of how the two approaches can usefully complement one another.

More generally, schema theory goes beyond possible-world models in dealing with more elusive socio-cultural norms and expectations, and in accounting for the fact that different readers may have different assumptions about the real world, and may therefore differ in their perception of the world of a particular text. Chapter 8 has shown how schema theory is compatible with recent cognitive theories of metaphor, and can therefore effectively account for the role of figurative language in text-world construction. The weaknesses of a schema-theory approach have also become apparent. When it comes to comparing texts, schema theory leads to vaguer and more subjective judgements than possible-world models: a criterion such as 'more or less schema refreshing' compares unfavourably with a list of graded criteria such as Ryan's typology of accessibility relations. Schema theory also poses much more fundamental questions. The difficulty of empirical verification casts doubts on any analysis based on the existence and activation of specific schemata. It is also generally problematic to decide what constitutes a schema and where the boundaries between different schemata are. More generally, it is difficult to account for knowledge that is not easily described as belonging to a schema (e.g. knowledge about other texts and the knowledge captured by logical rules). One can only hope that developments in cognitive science will provide more reliable but equally applicable models of knowledge and comprehension.

In conclusion, this book has, I hope, demonstrated that there is much to be gained by exploring the relationship between theories from different fields, and by developing interdisciplinary approaches to text analysis. In my discussion of 'The Applicant' possible-world theory and schema theory have shed light on different but equally crucial aspects of the defamiliarizing world projected by the poem. In this and other chapters the conjunction of linguistic analysis and schema theory has proved to be particularly productive, and advantageous to both approaches: on the one hand, I have made reference to schemata in order to account for the interpretation of linguistic features and patterns that I identified in the texts; on the other hand, I have made reference to grammatical, lexical and pragmatic choices in order to support my claims about the configuration of schemata that make up a particular text world. I have also used my detailed text analyses as a test-bed for different theories and as the basis for suggesting possible developments and improvements. Further interdisciplinary research on the connections between philosophy, psychology, artificial intelligence and language study will lead to considerable advances in our understanding of texts and text processing.

NOTES

[1] In the course of the discussion the term 'addressee' will be used to indicate the referent of the second-person pronoun *you*, which occurs throughout the poem (e.g. lines 1, 7, 14, 25, 40). The woman introduced in line 28 (*Come here, sweetie, out of the closet*) could be regarded as a second addressee, but her role is somewhat subsidiary: after the command in line 28, she is never again addressed directly, but only referred to in the third person (e.g. line 31).

[2] The inclusive use of *we*, on the other hand, includes both the speaker and the hearer. A poetic example of *we* in its inclusive sense is in Larkin's 'Days' (see 3.3.1), where the pronoun is likely to be interpreted as referring to the readers as well as the poetic *persona*.

[3] An additional oddity is due to the fact that in the actual world artificial breasts are not normally made of rubber.

[4] I would claim that the existence of transsexual people does not invalidate my general point here.

[5] By and large, schema theorists tend to explain the activation of background knowledge on the basis of textual references to one or more component elements of a particular schema (see 6.4.2). In my analysis of 'The Applicant', on the other hand, I will partly trace schema activation to the reader's response to a certain type of register or conversational strategy. People's perceptions of linguistic choices at the levels of vocabulary, grammar, speech acts, etc. (which we can subsume under a general notion of style) undoubtedly play a major role in the way in which they recognize and interpret situations, people and texts. This leads to the conclusion that schemata must include information about the type of language that is normally associated with a particular type of person or situation. The activation of schemata in comprehension, therefore, does not simply result from textual references to their component elements, but also from the occurrence of stylistic choices that are recognized as normal or default within a particular schema.

References

Abbott, V., Black, J.B. and Smith, E.E. (1985) 'The representation of scripts in memory', *Journal of Memory and Language*, 24, 179–99

Abelson, R.P. (1987) 'Artificial intelligence and literary appreciation: how big is the gap?', in Halász, L. (ed.), 1–37

Aird, M. (1973) *Sylvia Plath*, Edinburgh: Oliver & Boyd

Alderson, J.C. and Urquhart, A.H. (eds) (1984) *Reading in a Foreign Language*, London: Longman

Allén, S. (ed.) (1989) *Possible Worlds in Humanities, Arts and Sciences: Proceedings of Nobel Symposium 65*, New York and Berlin: de Gruyter

Anderson, J.R. (ed.) (1981) *Cognitive Skills and their Acquisition*, Hillsdale, NJ: Lawrence Erlbaum Associates

Anderson, R.C. and Pichert, J.W. (1978) 'Recall of previously unrecallable information following a shift in perspective', *Journal of Verbal Learning and Verbal Behaviour*, 17, 1–12

Anderson, R.C. and Pearson, P.D. (1988) 'A schema-theoretic view of basic processes in reading comprehension', in Carrel, P.L. *et al.* (eds), 37–55

Anderson, R.C., Spiro, R.J. and Montague, W.E. (eds) (1977) *Schooling and the Acquisition of Knowledge*, Hillsdale, NJ: Lawrence Erlbaum Associates

Arbib, M.A., Conklin, E.J. and Hill, J.C. (1987) *From Schema Theory to Language*, New York and Oxford: Oxford University Press

Austin, J.K. (1962) *How to Do Things with Words*, Oxford: Clarendon Press

Austin, T.R. (1994) *Poetic Voices: Discourse Linguistics and the Poetic Text*, Tuscaloosa and London: The University of Alabama Press

Bakhtin, M.M. (1981) *The Dialogic Imagination: Four Essays*, Austin: University of Texas

Ballard, J.G. (1991) *War Fever*, London: Paladin Books

Bar-Hillel, Y. (1954) 'Indexical expressions', *Mind*, LXIII, 359–79

Barber, C. (1976) *Early Modern English*, London: André Deutsch

Barney, T. (1990) 'The forms of enjambment: a study of the different strengths of run-on between lines of poetry and their prosodic correlates', unpublished MA dissertation, Lancaster University

Bartlett, F.C. (1932) *Remembering: A Study in Experimental and Social Psychology*, Cambridge: Cambridge University Press

Bassnett, S. (1987) *Sylvia Plath*, Houndmills and London: Macmillan

de Beaugrande, R. (1980) *Text, Discourse and Process*, London: Longman

de Beaugrande, R. (1987) 'Schemas for literary communication', in Halász, L. (ed.), 49–99

de Beaugrande, R. and Dressler, W. (1981) *Introduction to Text Linguistics*, London: Longman

Benveniste, E. (1971) *Problems in General Linguistics*, Coral Gables, Fla.: University of Miami Press

Betar, G. (1972) 'Stevens' *Earthy Anecdote*' in Ehrenpreis, I. (ed.), 252–3

Black, M. (1962) *Models and Metaphors: Studies in Language and Philosophy*, Ithaca, NY: Cornell University Press

Black, M. (1979) 'More about metaphor', in Ortony, A. (ed.), 19–43

Bobrow, D.G. and Collins, A. (1975) *Representation and Understanding*, New York: Academic Press

Bockting, I. (1994) 'Mind style as an interdisciplinary approach to characterisation', *Language and Literature*, 3, 157–74

Bower, G.H., Black, J.B. and Turner, T.R. (1979) 'Scripts in memory for text' *Cognitive Psychology*, 11, 177–220

Bradford, R. (1993) *A Linguistic History of English Poetry*, London and New York: Routledge

Bradley, R. and Swartz, N. (1979) *Possible Worlds: An Introduction to Logic and its Philosophy*, Oxford: Basil Blackwell

Bransford, J.D. (1979) *Human Cognition: Learning, Understanding and Remembering*, Belmont, California: Wadsworth

Bransford, J.D. and Johnson, M.K. (1972) 'Contextual prerequisites for understanding: some investigations of comprehension and recall', *Journal of Verbal Learning and Verbal Behaviour*, 11, 717–26

Bransford, J.D., Stein, B.S. and Shelton, T. (1984) 'Learning from the perspective of the comprehender', in Alderson, J.C. and Urquhart, A.H. (eds), 28–44

Brewer, W.F. and Nakamura, G.V. (1984) 'The nature and function of schemas', in Wyer, R.S. and Srull, T.K. (eds), 119–60

Brown, G. and Yule, G. (1983) *Discourse Analysis*, Cambridge: Cambridge University Press

Brown, G., Malmkjaer, K., Pollitt, A. and Williams, J. (1994) *Language and Understanding*, Oxford: Oxford University Press

Brown, P. and Levinson, S. (1987) *Politeness*, Cambridge: Cambridge University Press

Burks, A. (1948) 'Icon, index and symbol', *Philosophy and Phenomenological Research*, IX, 673–89

Bühler, K. (1982), 'The deictic field of language and deictic words', in Jarvella, R.J. and Klein, W. (eds), 9–30

Camac, M.K. and Glucksberg, S. (1984) 'Metaphors do not use associations between concepts, they are used to create them', *Journal of Psycholinguistic Research*, 13, 6, 443–55

Carey, J. (1978) 'Reversals transposed', in Patrides, C.A. (ed.), 136–54

Carrel, P.L., Devine, J. and Eskey, D. (eds) (1988) *Interactive Approaches to Second Language Reading*, Cambridge: Cambridge University Press

Carrel, P.L. and Eisterhold, J.C. (1988) 'Schema theory and ESL pedagogy', in Carrel, P.L. *et al.* (eds), 73–92

Carter, R. and Long, M.N. (1987) *The Web of Words: Exploring Literature through Language*, Cambridge: Cambridge University Press

Carter, R. and Simpson, P. (1989) *Language, Discourse and Literature*, London: Unwin Hyman

Chafe, W.L. (ed.) (1980) *The Pear Stories: Cognitive, Cultural and Linguistic Aspects of Narrative Production*, Norwood, NJ: Ablex

Chatman, S. (1971) *Literary Style: A Symposium*, Oxford and London: Oxford University Press

Chiaro, D. (1992) *The Language of Jokes: Analysing Verbal Play*, London: Routledge

Churchill, C. (1982) *Top Girls*, London and New York: Methuen

Conway, M.A. and Bekerian, D.A. (1987) 'Situational knowledge and emotions', *Cognition and Emotions*, 1, 2, 145–91

Cook, G. (1990) 'A theory of discourse deviation: the application of schema theory to the analysis of literary discourse', unpublished PhD thesis, University of Leeds

Cook, G. (1992) *The Discourse of Advertising*, London: Routledge

Cook, G. (1994) *Discourse and Literature*, Oxford: Oxford University Press

Cotton, J.W. and Klatzky, R.L. (eds) (1978) *Semantic Factors in Cognition*, Hillsdale, NJ: Lawrence Erlbaum Associates

Culler, J. (1975) *Structuralist Poetics*, London: Routledge & Kegan Paul

van Dijk, T.A. (ed.) (1976) *Pragmatics of Language and Literature*, Amsterdam: North Holland Publishing Corporation

van Dijk, T.A. (1980) *Macrostructures: An Interdisciplinary Study of Global Structures in Discourse, Interaction and Cognition*, Hillsdale, NJ: Lawrence Erlbaum Associates

van Dijk, T.A. (ed.) (1985) *Discourse and Literature: New Approaches to the Analysis of Literary Genres*, Amsterdam: John Benjamins

Dillon, G.L. (1978) *Language Processing and the Reading of Literature: Towards a Model of Comprehension*, Bloomington, Indiana: Indiana University Press

Doležel, L. (1976a) 'Narrative modalities', *Journal of Literary Semantics*, V, 1, 5–14

Doležel, L. (1976b) 'Narrative semantics', *A Journal for Descriptive Poetics and Theory of Literature (PTL)*, 1, 129–51

Doležel, L. (1979) 'Extensional and intensional narrative worlds', *Poetics*, 8, 193–211

Doležel, L. (1980) 'Truth and authenticity in narrative', *Poetics Today*, 1, 3, 7–25

Doležel, L. (1988) 'Mimesis and possible worlds', *Poetics Today*, 9, 3, 475–97

Doležel, L. (1989) 'Possible worlds and literary fictions' in Allén, S. (ed.), 223–42

Douglas, J.D. (1980) *The Illustrated Bible Dictionary (Part 2)*, Hodder & Stoughton: Inter-Varsity Press

Du Bois, J.W. (1980) 'Beyond definiteness: the trace of identity in discourse', in Chafe, W.L. (ed.), 206–39

Ducrot, O. and Todorov, T. (eds) (1981) *Encyclopedic Dictionary of the Sciences of Language*, tr. C. Porter, Oxford: Basil Blackwell

Easthope, A. (1983) *Poetry as Discourse*, London: Methuen

Eco, U. (1979) *The Role of the Reader*, London: Hutchinson

Eco, U. (1989) 'Report on session 3: literature and the arts', in Allén, S. (ed.), 343–55

Eco, U. (1990) *The Limits of Interpretation*, Bloomington and Indianapolis: Indiana University Press

Ehrenpreis, I. (ed.) (1972) *Wallace Stevens: A Critical Anthology*, Harmondsworth: Penguin

Ellrodt, R. (1978) 'Marvell's mind and mystery', in Patrides, C.A. (ed.), 31–55

Enkvist, N.E. (1989) 'Possible worlds in humanities, arts and sciences', in Allén, S. (ed.), 162–86

Enkvist, N.E. (1991) 'On the interpretability of text in general and of literary texts in particular', in Sell, R. (ed.), 1–25

Enkvist, N.E. and Leppiniemi, G. (1989) 'Anticipation and disappointment: an experiment in protocolled reading of Auden's "Gare du Midi"', in Hickey, L. (ed.), 191–207

Eysenck, M.W. and Keane, M.T. (1990) *Cognitive Psychology: A Student's Handbook*, Hove and London: Lawrence Erlbaum Associates

Fairclough, N. (1992) *Discourse and Social Change*, Cambridge: Polity Press

Fairley, I. (1988) 'The reader's need for conventions: when is a mushroom not a mushroom?', in van Peer, W. (ed.), 292–316

Fillmore, C.J. (1985) 'Frames and the semantics of understanding', *Quaderni di Semantica*, 6, 2, 222–54

Forceville, C. (1995) *Pictorial Metaphor in Advertising*, London: Routledge

Fowler, R. (1986) *Linguistic Criticism*, Oxford and New York: Oxford University Press

Freedle, R.O. (ed.) (1984) *New Directions in Discourse Processing*, Norwood, NJ: Ablex

Freeman, D.C. (1993) '"According to my bond": *King Lear* and recognition', *Language and Literature*, 2, 1, 1–18

Freundlieb, D. (1982) 'Understanding Poe's tales: a schema-theoretic view', *Poetics*, 11, 25–44

Fry, S. and Laurie, H. (1990) *A Bit of Fry and Laurie*, London: Mandarin

Gallaway, C. (1987) 'The emergence of a and the', unpublished PhD thesis, Lancaster University

Geyer-Ryan, H. (1988) 'Heteroglossia in the poetry of Bertolt Brecht and Tony Harrison', in van Peer, W. (ed.), 193–221

Givón, T. (1978) 'Definiteness and referentiality', in Greenberg, J.H. (ed.), 291–330

Gladsky, R.K. (1992) 'Schema theory and literary texts: Anthony Burgess's Nadsat', *Language Quarterly*, 30, 1–2, 39–46

Görlach, M. (1991) *Introduction to Early Modern English*, Cambridge: Cambridge University Press

Green, K. (1992) 'Deixis and the poetic persona', *Language and Literature*, 1, 2, 121–34

Green, K. (ed.) (1995) *New Essays in Deixis: Discourse, Narrative, Literature*, Amsterdam and Atlanta: Rodopi

Greenberg, J.H. (ed.) (1978) *Universals of Human Language*, Vol. 4, Stanford, California: Stanford University Press

Halász, L. (ed.) (1987) *Literary Discourse*, Berlin: de Gruyter

Halliday, M.A.K. (1985) *Introduction to Functional Grammar*, London: Arnold

Halliday, M.A.K. and Hasan, R. (1976) *Cohesion in English*, London: Longman

Hawkins, J.A. (1978) *Definiteness and Indefiniteness*, London: Croom Helm

Hawthorn, J. (1987) *Unlocking the Text: Fundamental Issues in Literary Theory*, London: Edward Arnold

Head, H. (1920) *Studies in Neurology*, Oxford: Oxford University Press

Herman, V. (1989) 'Subject construction as stylistic strategy in Gerard Manley Hopkins', in Carter, R. and Simpson, P. (eds), 213–34

Heydrich, W. (1989) 'Possible worlds and Enkvist's worlds', in Allén, S. (ed.), 187–98

Hickey, L. (ed.) (1989) *The Pragmatics of Style*, London: Routledge

Hodge, R. (1990) *Literature as Discourse*, Cambridge: Polity Press

Hoek, L. (1981) *La Marque du Titre*, Le Hague: Mouton

Hrushovski, B. (1984) 'Poetic metaphor and frames of reference', *Poetics Today*, 5, 1, 5–43

Hughes, T. (1970) 'The chronological order of Sylvia Plath's poems', in Newman, C. (ed.), 187–95

Ingarden, R. (1973) *The Literary Work of Art*, Evanston: Northwestern University Press

Isen, A.M. (1984) 'Toward understanding the role of affect in cognition', in Wyer, R.S. and Srull, T.K. (eds), 179–236

Iser, W. (1978) *The Act of Reading*, Baltimore and London: John Hopkins University Press

Jarvella, R.J. and Klein, W. (eds) (1982) *Speech, Place and Action: Studies in Deixis and Related Topics*, Chichester: John Wiley & Sons

Jefferson, A. and Robey, D. (eds) (1982) *Modern Literary Theory: A Comparative Introduction*, London: Batsford Academic and Educational

Jespersen, O. (1954) *A Modern English Grammar on Historical Principles: Syntax* (3rd volume), London: George Allen & Unwin

Johnson, M. (1987) *The Body in the Mind: The Bodily Basis of Meaning, Imagination and Reason*, Chicago: The University of Chicago Press

Johnson-Laird, P.N. and Garnham A. (1979) 'Descriptions and discourse models', *Linguistics and Philosophy*, 3, 371–93

Jones, P. (1995) 'Philosophical and theoretical issues in the study of deixis: a critique of the standard account', in Green, K. (ed.), 27–48

Kant, E. (1963) *Critique of Pure Reason*, London: Macmillan (original work published in 1787)

Keysar, B. and Glucksberg, S. (1992) 'Metaphor and communication', *Poetics Today*, 13, 4, 633–58

Kittay, E.F. (1987) *Metaphor: Its Cognitive Force and Linguistic Structure*, Oxford: Clarendon Press

Konuk, B.M. (1987) *American Poetry: The Rhetoric of its Forms*, New Haven and London: Yale University Press

Kripke, S. (1971) 'Semantical considerations on modal logic' in Linsky, L. (ed.), 63–72

Lakoff, G. and Johnson, M. (1980) *Metaphors We Live By*, Chicago: The University of Chicago Press

Lakoff, G. and Turner, M. (1989) *More than Cool Reason: A Field Guide to Poetic Metaphor*, Chicago: The University of Chicago Press

Leech, G.N. (1969) *A Linguistic Guide to English Poetry*, London: Longman

Leech, G.N. (1981) *Semantics*, London: Penguin

Leech, G.N. (1983) *The Principles of Pragmatics*, London: Longman

Leech, Geoffrey N. (1985) 'Stylistics', in van Dijk, T.A. (ed.), 39–57

Leech, G.N. and Short, M.H. (1981) *Style in Fiction*, London: Longman

Lehnert, W.G. and Vine, E.W. (1987) 'The role of affect in narrative structure', *Cognition and Emotion*, 1, 3, 299–322

Leibniz, G.W. (1969) *Philosophical Papers and Letters*, 2nd edition, translated and edited by L.E. Loemker, Dodrecht: D. Reidel Publishing Company

Lenders, W. (1989) 'On the perspectives of artificial intelligence research in literary understanding processes', in Meutsch, D. and Viehoff, R. (eds), 226–50

Leventhal, H. and Scherer, K. (1987) 'The relationship of emotion to cognition: a functional approach to a semantic controversy', *Cognition and Emotion*, 1, 1, 3–28

Levin, S.R. (1976) 'Concerning what kind of speech act a poem is', in van Dijk, T.A. (ed.), 141–60

Levin, S.R. (1989) 'Duality and deviance: two semantic modes', in Allén, S. (ed.), 260–6

Levinson, S.C. (1983) *Pragmatics*, Cambridge: Cambridge University Press

Linsky, L. (ed.) (1971) *Reference and Modality*, Oxford: Clarendon Press

Loux, M.J. (ed.) (1979) *The Possible and the Actual*, Ithaca and London: Cornell University Press

Lyons, J. (1977) *Semantics*, Cambridge: Cambridge University Press

Maitre, D. (1983) *Literature and Possible Worlds*, London: Middlesex Polytechnic Press

Malinowski, B. (1935) *Coral Gardens and their Magic*, London: George Allen & Unwin

Mandler, J.M. and Johnson, N.S. (1977) 'Remembrance of things parsed: story structure and recall', *Cognitive Psychology*, 9, 111–15

Martínez-Bonati, F. (1981) *Fictive Discourse and the Structures of Literature*, Ithaca and London: Cornell University Press

McCabe, A. (1983) 'Conceptual similarity and the quality of metaphor in isolated sentences versus extended contexts', *Journal of Psycholinguistic Research*, 12, 1, 41–68

McCawley, J. (1981) *Everything that Linguists have Always Wanted to Know about Logic but were Ashamed to Ask*, Chicago: University of Chicago Press

McClelland, J.L., Rumelhart, D.E. and the PDP Research Group (1986) *Parallel Distributed Processing: Explorations in the Microstructure of Cognition* (Vol. 2: Psychological and Biological Models), Cambridge, Mass.: MIT Press

McCormick, K. and Waller, G.F. (1987) 'Text, reader, ideology: the interactive nature of the reading situation', *Poetics*, 16, 1, 193–208

McHale, B. (1987) *Postmodernist Fiction*, New York and London: Methuen

McHale, B. (1992) 'Making (non)sense of postmodernist poetry', in Toolan, M. (ed.), 6–36

Meneses, P. (1991) 'Poetic worlds: *Martin Codax*', *Style*, 25, 2, 291–309

Meutsch, D. and Viehoff, R. (1989) *Comprehension of Literary Discourse*, Berlin: de Gruyter

Miall, D.S. (1988) 'Affect and narrative: a model of response to stories', *Poetics*, 17, 259–72

Miall, D.S. (1989) 'Beyond the schema given: affective comprehension of literary narratives', *Cognition and Emotion*, 3, 1, 55–78

Minsky, M. (1975) 'A framework for representing knowledge', in Winston, P.E. (ed.), 221–77

Müske, E. (1990) 'Frame and literary discourse', *Poetics*, 19, 433–61

Myers, G. (1994) *Words in Ads*, London, Edward Arnold

Nash, W. (1989) *Rhetoric: The Wit of Persuasion*, Oxford: Basil Blackwell

Nassar, E.P. (1965) *Wallace Stevens: An Anatomy of Configuration*, Philadelphia: University of Pennsylvania Press

Neisser, U. (1976) *Cognition and Reality: Principles and Implications of Cognitive Psychology*, San Francisco: W.H. Freeman.

Newman, C. (ed.) (1970) *The Art of Sylvia Plath: A Symposium*, London: Faber & Faber

Norton Anthology of English Literature, The (1979) London and New York: W.W. Norton & Co.

Nowottny, W. (1965) *The Language Poets Use*, London: The Athlone Press

Ohmann, R. (1971) 'Speech, action and style', in Chatman, S. (ed.), 241–62

Ortony, A. (1979a) *Metaphor and Thought*, Cambridge: Cambridge University Press

Ortony, A. (1979b) 'The role of similarity in similes and metaphors', in Ortony, A. (ed.), (1979a) 186–201

Ortony, A., Clore, G.L. and Collins. A. (1988) *The Cognitive Structure of Emotions*, Cambridge: Cambridge University Press

Pallotti, D. (1990) *Weaving Words*, Bologna: CLUEB

Patrides, C.A. (ed.) (1978) *Approaches to Marvell: The York Tercentenary Lectures*, London: Routledge & Kegan Paul

Pavel, T.G. (1975) '"Possible worlds" in literary semantics', *The Journal of Aesthetics and Art Criticism*, XXXIV, 2, 165–76

Pavel, T.G. (1980) 'Narrative domains', *Poetics Today*, 1, 4, 105–14

Pavel, T. G. (1983a) 'The borders of fiction', *Poetics Today*, 4, 1, 83–8

Pavel, T.G. (1983b) 'Incomplete worlds, ritual emotions', *Philosophy and Literature*, 7, 2, 48–58

Pavel, T.G. (1986) *Fictional Worlds*, Cambridge, Mass. and London: Harvard University Press

Pavel, T.G. (1989) 'Fictional worlds and the economy of the imaginary', in Allén, S. (ed.), 250–9

van Peer, W. (1986) *Stylistics and Psychology: Investigations of Foregrounding*, London: Croom Helm

van Peer, W. (ed.) (1988) *The Taming of the Text: Explorations in Language, Literature and Culture*, London and New York: Routledge

Peirce, C.S. (1932) *Collected Papers of Charles Sanders Peirce* (edited by C. Hartshorne and P. Weiss), Cambridge, Mass.: Harvard University Press

Piaget, J. (1953) *The Origin of Intelligence in the Child*, London: Routledge & Kegan Paul

Piaget, J. and Inhelder, B. (1969) *The Psychology of the Child*, London: Routledge & Kegan Paul

Pilkington, A. (1990) 'A relevance-theoretic view of metaphor', *Parlance*, 2, 2, 102–17

Pratt, M.L. (1977) *Toward a Speech Act Theory of Literature*, Bloomington: Indiana University Press

Quirk, R., Greenbaum, S., Leech, G. and Svartvik, J. (1985) *A Comprehensive Grammar of the English Language*, London: Longman

Rader, R.W. (1984) 'Notes on some structural varieties and variations in dramatic "I" poems and their theoretical implications', *Victorian Poetry*, 22, 103–20

Rader, R.W. (1989) 'Literary constructs: experience and explanation', *Poetics*, 18, 1–2, 342–51

Rajan, B. (1978) 'Andrew Marvell: the aesthetics of inconclusiveness', in Patrides, C.A. (ed.), 155–73

Rauh, G. (ed.) (1983) *Essays on Deixis*, Tübingen: Gunter Narr Verlag

Rescher, N. (1979) 'The ontology of the possible' in Loux, M.J. (ed.), 166–81

Richards, I.A. (1936) *The Philosophy of Rhetoric*, London: Oxford University Press

Ronen, R. (1994) *Possible Worlds in Literary Theory*, Cambridge: Cambridge University Press

Rumelhart, D.E. (1975) 'Notes on a schema for stories', in Bobrow, D.G. and Collins, A. (eds), 211–36

Rumelhart, D.E. (1980) 'Schemata: the building blocks of cognition', in Spiro, R.J. *et al.* (eds), 33–58

Rumelhart, D.E. (1984) 'Schemata and the cognitive system', in Wyer, R.S. and Srull, T.K. (eds), 161–88.

Rumelhart, D.E. and Norman, D.A. (1978) 'Accretion, tuning and restructuring: three modes of learning' in Cotton, J.W. and Klatzky, R.L. (eds), 37–53

Rumelhart, D.E. and Norman, D.A. (1981) 'Analogical processes in learning', in Anderson, R.C. (ed.), 335–59

Rumelhart, D.E. and Ortony, A. (1977) 'The representation of knowledge in memory', in Anderson, R.C. *et al.* (eds), 99–135

Rumelhart, D.E., Smolensky, P., McClelland, J.L. and Hinton, G.E. (1986) 'Schemata and sequential thought processes in PDP models', in McClelland, J.L. *et al.*, 7–57

Ryan, M.L. (1980) 'Fiction, non-factuals, and the Principle of Minimal Departure', *Poetics*, 9, 403–22

Ryan, M.L. (1984) 'Fiction as a logical, ontological and illocutionary issue: review of *Fictive Discourse and the Structures of Literature* by Felix Martínez-Bonati', *Style*, 18, 2, 121–39

Ryan, M.L. (1985) 'The modal structure of narrative universes', *Poetics Today*, 6, 4, 717–55

Ryan, M.L. (1991a) *Possible Worlds, Artificial Intelligence and Narrative Theory*, Bloomington and Indianapolis: Indiana University Press

Ryan, M.L. (1991b) 'Possible worlds and accessibility relations: a semantics typology of fiction', *Poetics Today*, 12, 3, 553–76

Sagar, K. (1975) *The Art of Ted Hughes*, Cambridge: Cambridge University Press

Sanford, A.J. and Garrod, S.C. (1981) *Understanding Written Language*, New York: Wiley

Sapir, E. (1970) *Culture, Language and Personality: Selected Essays*, Berkeley and Los Angeles: University of California Press

Schank, R.C. (1982) *Dynamic Memory: A Theory of Reminding and Learning in Computers and People*, Cambridge: Cambridge University Press

Schank, R.C. and Abelson, R. (1977) *Scripts, Plans, Goals and Understanding*, Hillsdale, NJ: Lawrence Erlbaum Associates

Schmidt, S.J. (1980) 'Fictionality in literary and non-literary discourse', *Poetics*, 9, 525–46

Schmidt S.J. (1982) *Foundations for the Empirical Study of Literature*, Hamburg: Helmut Buske Verlag

Searle, J.R. (1969) *Speech Acts*, London: Cambridge University Press

Searle, J.R. (1975) 'The logical status of fictional discourse', *New Literary History*, VI, 2, 319–32

Searle, J.R. (1979) 'Metaphor', in Ortony, A. (ed.), 92–123

Sell, R. (1991) *Literary Pragmatics*, London: Routledge

Semino, E. (1990a) 'Towards a theory of poetic titles', unpublished MA dissertation, University of Lancaster

Semino, E. (1990b) 'A stylistic analysis of the poem "The Cool Web" by Robert Graves', *Lingua e Stile*, XXV, 2, 305–16

Semino, E. (1993) 'Review of *Possible Worlds, Artificial Intelligence and Narrative Theory* by M.L. Ryan', *Language and Literature*, 2, 2, 146–8

Semino, E. (1995) 'Deixis and the dynamics of poetic voice', in Green, K. (ed.), 145–60

Shen, Y. (1992) 'Metaphors and categories', *Poetics Today*, 13, 4, 771–94

Short, M. (1994) 'Understanding texts: point of view', in Brown, G. *et al.* (eds), 170–90.

Short, M. (1996) *Exploring the Language of Poems, Plays and Prose*, London: Longman

Smith, F. (1982) *Understanding Reading: A Psycholinguistic Analysis of Reading and Learning to Read*, New York: Holt, Rinehart & Winston

Smith, L.E. (1987) *Discourse Across Cultures*, New York: Prentice Hall

Sperber, D. and Wilson, D. (1986) *Relevance: Communication and Cognition*, Oxford: Basil Blackwell

Sperber, D. and Wilson, D. (1995) *Relevance: Communication and Cognition* (2nd edition), Oxford: Basil Blackwell

Spiro, R.J. (1980) 'Prior knowledge and story processing: integration, selection and variation', *Poetics*, 9, 313–27

Spiro, R.J. (1982) 'Long-term comprehension: schema-based versus experiential and evaluative understanding', *Poetics*, 11, 77–86

Spiro, R., Bruce, B. and Brewer, W. (eds) (1980) *Theoretical Issues in Reading Comprehension: Perspectives from Cognitive Psychology, Linguistics, Artificial Intelligence and Education*, Hillsdale, NJ: Lawrence Erlbaum Associates

Steen, G. (1994) *Understanding Metaphor in Literature*, London and New York: Longman

Stevenson, A. (1989) *Bitter Fame: A Life of Sylvia Plath*, London: Viking

Stewart, S. (1978) *Nonsense: Aspects of Intertextuality in Folklore and Literature*, Baltimore and London: The John Hopkins University Press

Tannen, D. (1984) 'What's in a frame? Surface evidence for underlying expectations', in Freedle, R.O. (ed.), 137–81

Tate, A. (1995) 'Deictic markers and the disruption of voice in Modernist poetry', in Green, K. (ed.), 131–43

Teleman, U. (1989) 'The world of words – and pictures', in Allén, S. (ed.), 199–208

Thorndyke, P.W. (1977) 'Cognitive structures in comprehension and memory of narrative discourse', *Cognitive Psychology*, 9, 77–110.

Thorndyke, P.W. and Yekovich, F.R. (1980) 'A critique of schema-based theories of human story memory', *Poetics*, 9, 23–49.

Todorov, T. (1981) 'Enunciation', in Ducrot, O. and Todorov, T. (eds), 323–8

Toolan, M.J. (1988) *Narrative: A Critical Linguistic Introduction*, London: Routledge

Toolan, M. (ed.) (1992) *Language, Text and Context: Essay in Stylistics*, London and New York: Routledge

Tsur, R. (1992) *Towards a Theory of Cognitive Poetics*, Amsterdam: North Holland

den Uyl, M. and van Oostendorp, H. (1980) 'The use of scripts in text-comprehension', *Poetics*, 9, 275–294

Verdonk, P. (1991) 'Poems as text and discourse', in Sell, R. (ed.), 94–109

Verdonk, P. (ed.) (1993) *Twentieth Century Poetry: From Text to Context*, London: Routledge

Verdonk, P. and Weber, J.J. (eds) (1995) *Twentieth Century Fiction: From Text to Context*, London: Routledge

Waggoner, H.H. (1984) *American Poets: From the Puritans to the Present*, Baton Rouge and London: Louisiana State University

Wales, K. (1988) 'Back to the future: Bakhtin, stylistics and discourse', in van Peer, W. (ed.), 176–92

Wales, K. (1989) *A Dictionary of Stylistics*, London: Longman

Wales, K. (1993) 'Teach yourself "rhetoric": an analysis of Philip Larkin's "Church Going"', in Verdonk, P. (ed.), 87–99

Weber, J.J. (1992) *Critical Analysis of Fiction*, Amsterdam and Atlanta: Rodopi

Weber, J.J. (1995) 'How metaphor leads Susan Rawlings to suicide: a cognitive-linguistics analysis of Doris Lessing's "To Room Nineteen"', in Verdonk, P. and Weber, J.J. (eds)

Weinreich, H. (1971) 'The textual function the French article', in Chatman, S. (ed.), 221–40

Werth, P.N. (1994) 'Extended metaphor: a text-world account', *Language and Literature*, 3, 2, 79–103

Werth, P.N. (forthcoming) *Text-worlds: Representing Conceptual Space in Discourse*, London: Longman

West, T. (1985) *Ted Hughes*, London and New York: Methuen

Whorf, B.L. (1956) *Language, Thought and Reality*, Cambridge, Mass.: MIT Press

Widdowson, H.G. (1975) *Stylistics and the Teaching of Literature*, London: Longman

Widdowson, H.G. (1984) *Explorations in Applied Linguistics*, Oxford University Press

Widdowson, H.G. (1987) 'Significance in conventional and literary discourse' in Smith, L.E. (ed.), 9–21

Widdowson, H.G. (1992) *Practical Stylistics*, Oxford: Oxford University Press

Winston, P.E. (ed.) (1975) *The Psychology of Computer Vision*, New York: McGraw-Hill

Wolterstoff, N. (1980) *Works and Worlds of Art*, Oxford: Clarendon Press

Wyer, R.S. and Srull, T.K. (1984) *Handbook of Social Cognition*, Hillsdale, NJ: Lawrence Erlbaum Associates

Index